MOTHER WORKED AT

'AVRO'

MOTHER WORKED AT 'AVRO'

THE STORY OF AVRO (YEADON):

AND ITS CONTRIBUTION TO BRITAIN'S WAR EFFORT

BY

Gerald Myers

Compaid Graphics

1995

First Published
May 1995
To mark the fiftieth anniversaries of
V.E. Day and V.J. Day
In the hope of future peace

Published and printed in the UK by
Compaid Graphics
T'otherside
Drumacre Lane East
Longton
Preston
PR4 4SD

Typeset using Ventura Publisher version 5.0

Copyright Gerald W. Myers
All rights reserved

ISBN 0 9517965 77

Table Of Contents

Dedication

Acknowledgements

Foreword 1

Preface 3

Prologue 5

Beginnings 7

Overture to War 13

War 17

Build Up 25

Conscription 33

Production Begins in Earnest 43

Flight Testing and the A.T.A. 53

The Advent of the Lancaster 59

Visits from the Luftwaffe - and Further Development at the Factory 69

"Lighter Moments" 79

Ad Extremum - Press on Regardless 87

Onto Victory 93

Peace 101

Legacy 113

Postscript 119

Appendix A (a) 121

Appendix A (b) 123

Appendix A (c) 125

Appendix B 131

Appendix C 133

Appendix D 135

Appendix E 139

Bibliography (and secondary reading) 141

Acknowledgements

The formulation of this book, through its research and writing has occupied some six years of my "spare" time. Since I am not a professional writer, the task has often seemed beyond my capabilities and, even now, within sight of its publication, I remain concerned that the subject has not received due justice.

Be that as it may, little of what follows would have been possible without the assistance of a substantial number of people and, irrespective of the size of their contribution, I feel it right that they should receive due recognition here. To those whom, through inadvertance, I have omitted to mention I offer my sincere apologies.

Aireborough and Horsforth Museum Society; A.M. Alderson, for permission to reproduce drawings; Ian Allan Ltd.; E.G. Appleby DFC.; Sqdn Ldr. R.C.B. Ashworth R.A.F. (Ret'd); The B.B.C.; "Bill" Berry; Mrs M. Birkbeck; Miss N. Blezard ; D Boon; Duncan Booth; John Booth, for permission to quote from his book: 'The Day War Broke Out"; Chaz Bowyer; M.J. Bowyer; D. Brown; L. Briggs; Mrs M.G. Bruce, for permission to use some of her late husband's 'heraldic symbols' of the former factory; The Bundesarchiv, Koblenz; The Bundesarchiv, Freiburg; Mrs R. Calloway; D. Charlwood DFC; The late Group Captain Lord Cheshire VC, OM, DSO*, DFC*; K Cluddery; The late Barney Colehan M.B.E.; Mrs A.M. Cooper; Dr A.W. Cooper; "Bill" Cotton C.B.E.; Group Capt. E.W. Cropper RAF (Ret'd); Miss L. Curtis; G.C. Dennison; Ken Ellis; P. England; B. Entwistle F.R.I.C. S.; Mrs L. Evans; M. Evans; J. Fawcett; D.W. Fell; Mrs E. Flesher; Mrs E. Fitzgerald; Mrs J.M.D. Forster M.A., Archive Library,University of Leeds; Mrs D. Foster; K. Freeman; J.W. Gee DFC; Goodalls Publications Ltd.; Good Housekeeping Magazine; A. Goodrum; B. Goulding; P. C. T. Green, for photographic assistance; S. Greaves; The Grimsby Evening Telegraph; D. Gulliver B. A., Leeds City Libraries (H.Q.) and staff of the Guiseley branch for their unfailing assistance over a lengthy period; Bill Gunston; J.M. Hagerty; D. Hanson; S.B. Hanson DFC; Flt. Lt. S.H. Hanson MBE, AE, R.A.F. (Ret'd); B.B. Halpenny; A. Harris; Mrs E. Hardwick, Mrs M.A. Heap M.A., A.L.A. and staff, Local History Department at Leeds City Library; William Heineman Ltd; J. Holroyd; Harry Holmes; T Illingworth; The Imperial War Museum; David Jacobs DL; Sqdn. Ldr. 'Jacko' Jackson DFC.;P Jarrett; B. Jewell; J. A. Kell; D. Kennedy; D. J. Kilvington; The Hon. Gerald Lascelles; G. A. Lee; Leeds City Council (Planning department); Mrs Y. 'Peggy'Lucas; Mrs A. Ludlum; Macmillan Publishers; D. McNeill; Mrs D. Mc Nulty; Russell Margerison, for permission to quote from his book 'Boys at War; Mr and Mrs A. Marland; Ray and Kay Marshall; P. J. Marson; R. Mayhill DFC; Martin Middlebrook; M.O.D. (Air Historical Branch) R.A.F.; G Modley; Dr. P. Morris; Mrs M. Mullinder; Joe and Elsie Munns; Mrs R. Murray, for priceless reminiscences of her involvement in wartime billeting; Ian Myers (my son) for much assistance with the reproduction of the finished manuscipt; Mrs R. Myers; R. Conyers Nesbit; Mrs M. O'Neil; P. Otter; R. Paine; W. Patchett; L. Peacock; A. Pearey AMRAeS; H. Penrose O.B.E., C. Eng, F.R.A.e.S.; R. Pierson; R. Powers; D. Prescott; Dr. Alfred Price; M.K. Proctor; Staff at the Public Record Office, Kew; The Royal Air Force Association, The Royal Air Force Museum; D. Reed B.A; W. Reid V.C., BSc.; Richard Riding; Bruce Robertson; A. Rowley; J. Rowbotham; 'Burt' Rhodes; Ross Anderson Publications; F. Ryner; The Editor 'The Stage'; N. Sherburn; Ron Smith DFM., for permission to quote his poem: 'I will remember'; Mrs L. Spencer; C. Stansfield; Patrick Stephens Ltd; L. Stott; the late J.A. Seamus Stuart; Mrs J.A. Stuart; Miss G. Stuart; R. T. Sturtivant; S. Taylor; J. Telford; J. R. Tetlow; Staff at the National Archives of the U.S.A., Washington D.C.; E.J. Viles M.B.E.; Mrs D. Varley; Ken Wakefield; Miss A. Walker; Wg.Cdr. A.B. Walker R.A.F. (Ret'd); C. Walker; J. Walton; H. Ward; Mrs M. Westropp; Mrs S. Westrup; The proprietors of the Wharfedale and Airedale Observer, its editorial staff and, especially, former editor Bill Pearson; Mrs E. Wilson; D. Williams; Miss E. Wilmot MA, ALA, and staff, Local History Department Bradford City Library; H. Winchester; Mrs M. Windross; Miss G. Winfield; the late Donald Winn; Mrs L.M. Winterbothan; D. Wood; L. Woodgate; F. Wright; Peter Smith; David Smith; Mrs M. Wright; D. Yeadon; Yorkshire Post Newspapers Ltd.; Staff at the Keighley News; Ian Dewhirst; Terry Taylor, publicity department AVRO International Aerospace, Woodford; AVRO International Aerospace, for permission to use the AVRO logo.

In addition to the forenamed there have been a number of individuals without the considerable assistance of whom this book would not have seen the light of day: theirs being an extra special contribution.

Acknowledgements

Firstly, Mrs Cordelia Booth, who has spent many hours deciphering my almost illegible draft and, thereafter, reproducing its contents as perfect transcript; Eric Dean whose substantial and crystal clear memories of the factory have been fundamental to the construction of large sections of the narrative; Terry Carter, similarly gifted with a photographic memory, who supplied significant detail pertaining to the more amusing episodes of factory and aerodrome life; Eric Webster, reseacher extraordinary, whose voluntary visits to the Public Record Office and R.A.F. Museum invariably provided more information than expected; George Jenks of The Avro Research Group and Fl Lt G.R. Sunderland R.A.F. (Ret'd) who, through the provision of specific detail on aircraft built at Yeadon and other material have saved me much embarrassment; the late Roland 'Roly' Scatchard posthumous Honorary Citizen of the town of Otley, whose initial interest, library of pertinent photographs and frequent assistance in the reproduction of others proved the catalyst for what follows; Terry Sykes, for granting unrestricted access to his work; "The Yorkshire Aeroplane Club"; Bernard Hepton for his reminiscences and generous comments in the Foreword and Mike Mansfield - Compaid Graphics- for his expertise and advice.

Finally, very special thanks are due to my wife, Nancy, who according to a third party *"has had to put up with a husband who, for more than six years, has lived with his mind at 20,000 feet"*. Without her understanding and huge forebearance, none of this would have been possible.

If through inability to trace the present copyright owners, any copyright material is included for which permission has not specifically been sought, apologies are offered in advance to individuals, proprietors, and publishers concerned.

Gerald Myers,
Guiseley,
February 1995

Dedication

This book is dedicated to the workforce of AVRO, Yeadon, and to the personnel of the Royal Air Force and their Allies, who utilised the aircraft built there to help extinguish the Axis threat; and in special remembrance of Flying Officer Charles Clifford Smith DFC, a native of Yeadon: one of the 55,539 men of Bomber Command who 'Failed to Return'.

> The time will come, when thou shalt lift thine eyes
> To watch a long-drawn battle in the skies,
> While aged peasants, too amazed for words,
> Stare at the flying fleets of wondrous birds.
> England, so long the mistress of the sea,
> Where winds and waves confess her sovereignty,
> Her ancient triumphs yet on high shall bear,
> and reign, the sovereign of the conquered air.
>
> Thomas Gray. Luna Habitabilis
> (That the moon is inhabitable) 1738

Foreword

My first day working at AVRO, naive, 16, and excited to be amongst aeroplanes, I was given a box of tools by a fitter, told to carry it and follow him. He led me to an Anson on the production line and told me to wait. I was thrilled. Here I was, standing outside an Anson, a real one, already in camouflage paint, at least on the fuselage. The wings and engines were nowhere to be seen! The fitter explained, "Stand here and watch. I'm going in the nose and when I drill a hole, tell me you've seen it; then tap it." I watched. I saw the drill make the hole. I saw it withdraw. I saw the hole it left. I shouted that I saw the hole. Then I got out a hammer and tapped it. The laughter from inside the fuselage was deafening! (To tap a hole means to put a thread in it using a thread cutter called a "tap".) That was my first lesson in Engineering. It was not however to be my first humiliation by engineers, who are - or were - noted for their practical jokes. I was sent to the stores for "The Long Stand" - interminable - and "The Glass Hammer and Rubber Nails" and many other mythical objects, mercifully forgotten. Thus began my apprenticeship. I worked in the Tool Room, Jig and Tool Design, most departments on the factory floor, finishing in the Design Office working on the AVRO 700, never developed. What an experience for a young man straight out of school!

It was during my time at the factory that I developed an intense interest in acting and the Theatre Arts, working at AVRO during the day, travelling to the Bradford Civic Playhouse at night to rehearse, or perform, or attend classes. King George not wanting me in his armed forces, all my concentration went into the building of aircraft and the Theatre, a very pleasant combination. Where the energy came from for such a crowded schedule I'll never know!

For those who, like me, worked at AVRO during the war years, this book will awaken many potent memories. For those people who have no knowledge or recollection of those years it will tell of a time of effort, of achievement, of danger, of laughter and tears, and above all of comradeship. And it will pose the question "Does it take a war to bring people together in mutual dependency and trust?" If so, we are poor creatures indeed.

Gerald Myers has written an outstanding history of one factory during those years. It was the one I worked in. I salute his painstaking research, his sense of humour and his enthusiastic reporting of ordinary people in an extraordinary place during a very dangerous and difficult time.

Bernard Hepton

Foreword

Preface

The Allied Air Forces Memorial and Yorkshire Air Museum, Elvington, York, to which proceeds from this book are to be donated, is a charitable organisation run by a group of very dedicated volunteers.

The primary aim of its Trustees and Members, - the latter now numbered world wide, - has been to create a tangible and permanent reminder of the service and sacrifice made by thousands of young airmen and airwomen, from many nations, who served at, or flew from, more than fifty Yorkshire bases in two wars and, furthermore, through the painstaking reconstruction of a Halifax bomber and the display of other aircraft, artifacts and memorabilia, to promote an ongoing interest in the history of aviation in Yorkshire through peace and war.

It was, after all, a Yorkshireman, Sir George Cayley (1773-1857), who initially identified the principles of heavier than air flight and who, from a hill-top on his estate at Brompton Hall, near Scarborough, first launched a manned glider.

Within the county, in more recent times, the Royal Flying Corps; the Royal Air Force; the Royal Naval Air Service; the Royal Navy; the Royal Canadian Air Force; the Royal Australian Air Force; the French Air Force; and other Allies in war; Airspeed at York; Blackburn Aircraft at Leeds, Filey and Brough (latterly British Aerospace); A.V. Roe & Co. Ltd., at Yeadon; Handley Page at Clifton (York); Slingsby at Kirkby Moorside and countless other manufacturers and individuals have, directly or indirectly, played a part in furthering his ideas.

By purchasing this book you are helping to ensure that such worthy endeavour will not go unnoticed by future generations.

Preface

Prologue

There was a sudden, heavy, rattle of cannon, which could be heard distinctly above the roar of the engines, and vicious, sparkling, white tracer, whipped either side and through the aircraft. The Lancaster appeared to stop dead, as if to gasp for breath, then lurch on like a drunken man. Both port engines were ablaze, and flames spewed back over the port tailplane and fin. The firing from the unseen enemy fighter lasted for no more than two seconds, but it was more than enough. Down went the nose of the stricken aircraft, its engines screaming in agony.

"Pull the bugger out, pull the bugger out", someone shouted over the intercom. "Feather port engines", ordered Max Dowden the Lancaster's pilot then, immediately, "abandon aircraft, abandon aircraft".

Mid-Upper gunner F/Sgt. Russell Margerison watched unbelievingly as curls of metal peeled off the aircraft's tail-fin, shocked at the suddenness at which events were moving. Uncoupling his oxygen supply, and heated suit, he vacated the turret in record time. The whole of the fuselage near his position was an inferno. He grabbed his parachute, which lay on the floor with flames licking around it and, with difficulty, engaged the metal hooks onto his harness. The heat was intense, and ammunition in the racks was exploding as he reached the door of the fuselage where an icy blast whipped him away into the night.

He quickly pulled the ripcord of his parachute which then gradually steadied above him, but he could only watch helplessly as the bomber curled downwards, streaming flame as it went. Lancaster: LM 513, Y-Yorker of No. 625 Squadron, Kelstern, on its thirteenth operational sortie and homeward bound from Duisberg, was doomed. It was 1.30 a.m., 23rd May, 1944.

On more than twenty 'Ops', Russell Margerison had seen many bombers go down; but this was his aircraft, and inside it still were his crew; his mates. As the Lancaster hit the ground leaving a widening circle of fire he turned his head away.

He remained unaware until many months later that four others had also succeeded in escaping from the Lancaster and, similarly, had parachuted safely into the Belgian countryside to become P.O.W.'s. Sadly, this fate was not shared by their pilot, 1st Lt. Max Dowden [1], USAAF, from Santa Cruz, California, nor his flight engineer, nineteen years old Sgt. Frank Moody, from Huddersfield, as both perished with their blazing aircraft.

LM 513, a Mark III Lancaster, fitted with Rolls Royce Merlin Type 38 engines, had joined No. 625 Squadron in early April, 1944, from the Yeadon factory of A.V. Roe & Co. Ltd., being the two hundred and twelfth Lancaster built there.

This massive, extensively camouflaged 'shadow' factory, constructed during the first year and a half of the Second World War, immediately to the north of Yeadon Aerodrome (Leeds/Bradford Municipal Airport) existed, in a specific aviation role, for little more than six years; yet, in that relatively short period, built more than 5,000 aircraft, employing in their construction in excess of 17,000 people: a highly valuable, but largely unsung, contribution to Britain's war effort.

---

[1] 1st Lt. Max Dowden was one of a number of Americans who, before the U.S.A. became involved in the Second World War, volunteered for service with the R.A.F. or Royal Canadian Air Force (R.C.A.F.) to fight the Nazi threat. When their country subsequently entered the conflict they were automatically enlisted in the United States Army Air Force and given the choice of immediately joining one of its units, or doing so after the completion of a 'tour' of Operations with their current R.A.F. or R.C.A.F. Squadron. The majority, not surprisingly, opted to transfer to an American unit, but others decided to carry on with their British or Commonwealth crews knowing full well that even if they were fortunate enough to survive a bombing 'tour' of 30 Ops., (or the equivalent if serving with a Fighter Squadron) they would, thereafter, also be required to undertake a further 25 Missions with an American Squadron. To his eternal credit, 27 years old Max Dowden, chose the latter course. (Photo 1 - centre)

Prologue

What follows is the story of the factory, its workforce and of some of those who flew the aircraft built there. It is also, at least in part, a record of the early development of Leeds/Bradford Airport, for the history of it and that of the factory, are inextricably combined. The book is not, however, a definitive rivet by nut account of day to day production, nor a daily log of flying activities; its content being intended, primarily, as a testimonial to the men and women involved: the majority of them just ordinary folk who, when faced with grim adversity, proved themselves capable of performing extraordinary feats.

The 'Mother' contained in the title of the book is not an allusion to any one individual, but a generic acknowledgement of the many Mothers spoken of as having been involved in this enormous wartime enterprise. The appellation could, equally, have read: Father, Sister, Brother, Aunt, Uncle et al for, in addition to those who had a personal connection with the factory, there are thousands who can (and readily do) claim a similar affinity through one or other of their family.

In the intervening years, public recognition of their achievements has been conspicuous by its absence but, perhaps, the compiling of these reminiscences will, belatedly, go some way to redressing such tardy omission?

For those to whom, hitherto, aviation matters have had little interest it might be of benefit to learn that, by the time AVRO became involved at Yeadon, it had been in the business of building aeroplanes for more than thirty years; and was acknowledged as being one of the best in the world.

Formed, in Manchester, on 1st January 1910 as A.V. Roe & Company Ltd., (the world's first registered aircraft manufacturing company) by Edwin Alliott Verdon Roe and his brother, Humphrey, it very soon developed into an innovative and successful enterprise; albeit that Alliott Roe departed in 1928 (he was Knighted the following year) and the company was sold, firstly, to Crossley Motors then, in 1928, to Armstrong-Siddeley, prior to being incorporated into the Hawker-Siddeley Group seven years later. Under the inspired leadership of Roy (later Sir Roy) Dobson who, during the 'Thirties' became its General Manager (later, Chairman of the H.S. Group) and Roy Chadwick who, since the very early days with Alliott Roe had gradually established himself as one of the very best aeroplane designers, AVRO prospered. During the Second World War it employed at its Manchester based factories alone - Chadderton, Newton Heath, Ringway, Woodford and a number of smaller units, in excess of 40,000 workers.

AVRO's first successful aeroplane was the type 504 bi-plane trainer; the last to bear its illustrious insignia: the 748. In the intervening years came a host of other designs; notable among which were the Tutor, the Anson, the superb Lancaster and the mighty Vulcan. A pedigree of which anyone could be proud.

Beginnings

The name Yeadon, pronounced Yeedon, is derived from the old English words 'geah' meaning steep, and 'don' signifying hill, and in his 'Directory of the West Riding' (of Yorkshire) published in 1838, William White aptly described Yeadon as being 'a large clothing village on a lofty moorland hill on the north side of Airedale', adding that, at the time, it contained 2,761 inhabitants of whom the majority were involved in the woollen manufacturing industry. **(Photo 2 - centre pages)**

Thereafter, local trade prospered and soon Yeadon became a town: the tangible evidence to this being its Town Hall built, at the lower end of High Street, following the laying of the foundation stone on 10th May, 1879, by Colonel W.H. Crompton Stansfield, Lord of the Manor who, with a donation of £500, headed the list of subscribers to its estimated £5,000 construction cost.

Designed by the architect Hill of Leeds, the building was officially opened by William Beckett Denson, also of Leeds, on 21st June, 1880, since when it has stood astride the skyline as a testimony to Victorian civic pride (albeit that £4,000 towards its original cost remained unpaid up to 1914!) and continues to this day in regular use by the local community for a variety of activities.

A mile or so to the north is another of the town's well loved landmarks: the Tarn; so called, that is, by outsiders and cartographers, for Yeadoners know it as the Moor Dam or, in the vernacular, simply as t'Dam, a half mile long shallow depression into which drains the surface water from surrounding hills. It marks the western edge of Yeadon Moor (once a popular venue for the ancient game of Knur and Spell) which runs eastwards at almost seven hundred feet (212 metres) above sea level, to form an undulating plateau, the southern side of which is notoriously wet and marshy. Immediately to the south stands the crest of Plane Tree Hill with that of Rawdon Billing a little way beyond, and the still higher ground of Otley Chevin looming a mile or so away to the north-west.

Not, one would think, the ideal location for the siting of an aerodrome yet, on 3rd July, 1929, an historic meeting, which was to have far reaching consequences, took place between representatives of the then Yeadon Urban District Council and Mr.J. Milner, Chairman of the Leeds Improvement Committee; Mr.J.E. Acfield, Leeds City Surveyor and Mr.F. Marsden, the Bradford City Engineer, to discuss the planning of a municipal aerodrome to be sited on Yeadon Moor, and to be known as Yeadon Aerodrome.

The site was one of several considered by local dignitaries who, at the behest of Sir Alan Cobham during his national Municipal Airports Campaign, were flown around the area by him in his DH Giant Moth:G-AAEV 'Youth of Britain'.

Interestingly, some seventy years previously one James Fox had surveyed the same area on behalf of the Leeds - Thirsk Railway (later incorporated into the North Eastern Railway) and, thereafter, he proposed two new routes: one to Yeadon, the other to neighbouring Guiseley, both directed across the northern edge of the moor, to join up near Horsforth with the existing line between Leeds and Harrogate. Thus if Fox's proposals had been accepted by the Company local history would have been very different!

In the late Nineteen-Twenties, however, it was the Depression which filled the minds of most people and yet, even in those most stringent days, there were some with the perception to foresee the commercial potential offered by the aeroplane. Indeed there was a growing body of local opinion which favoured an airport being located as close as possible to the heavily populated conurbation of the West Riding.

This was a view supported by a majority of members of the Yorkshire Aeroplane Club: an organisation which, with some justification, can claim through its precursor the Yorkshire Light Aeroplane Club, formed in 1909, to be the oldest such body in the country. The Club had, since 10th January, 1926, been using as its Headquarters the aerodrome at Sherburn-in-Elmet, some twenty miles east of Leeds, but as many of its members originated from the Leeds/Bradford area they, not surprisingly, welcomed the prospect of flying facilities being available closer to home.

Subsequent to the meeting of representatives of the three local Authorities in July, 1929, a joint Airport Committee was formed to develop the site, it being agreed that this would, initially, comprise 60 acres (24.28 hectares) of grassland bounded in the south east by parts of Horsforth golf course, and to the west by the A658 Bradford - Harrogate road, with two other minor roads completing the perimeter.

Beginnings

Leeds/Bradford Municipal Airport (Yeadon) located at latitude 53° 52' 10" N. Longitude 01° 39' 40° W, 7 miles N.W. of Leeds, 6 miles N.N.E. of Bradford, elevation 653 ft (199 metres) above sea level, was officially opened on 17th October, 1931, by Councillor H. Jennings, deputy Chairman of Yeadon Urban District Council, it being operated by the Yorkshire Aeroplane Club on behalf of the joint Airport Committee

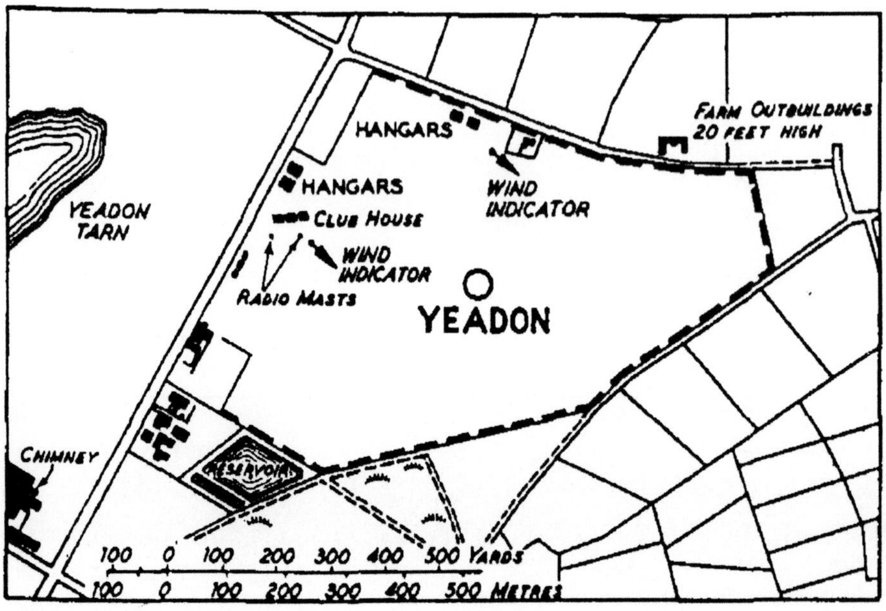

Photo 3. Yeadon (1933).

Two semi-detached houses on the western perimeter were converted into a spacious Clubhouse, and two small hangars (canvas covered) were provided nearby for Club aircraft. These were, initially, de Havilland Gipsy and Cirrus Moths, augmented later by Puss and Leopard Moths: aircraft which soon became a familiar sight resplendent in their Club livery of pale blue fuselage, undercarriage and struts; with silver wings, tailplane, fin and rudder.

A redoubtable Australian, Captain Henry Vernon Worrall, D.S.C and Bar, Croix de Guerre, acted as Chief Flying Instructor (C.F.I.), the third such appointee, having served in this capacity at Sherburn-in-Elmet since 1929. Before joining the Club he had accumulated considerable flying experience, firstly with the R.N.A.S. and R.A.F. in the First World War. During this period, when stationed in the Middle East, he had as his Observer a certain Lt. Wedgewood-Benn (later, Viscount Stansgate DSO, DFC), the father of the current Member of Parliament for Chesterfield.[1] Subsequently, Captain or 'Skipper' Worrall (less frequently 'Digger') as he was known, became a test pilot with Blackburn Aircraft at Brough and, during the Nineteen-Twenties, joined Sir Alan Cobham as his co-pilot on long distance flights of exploration. Henry Worrall was no snob about his flying, however, as is confirmed by the fact that within a year of taking up his duties at Yeadon, he had devised a scheme whereby tram and bus drivers could, if they wished, aim for a pilot's licence for less than 1/-d (5p) per week!

He was a man much respected by Nevil Shute Norway (the author, Nevil Shute) who was in sole charge of the Yorkshire Aeroplane Club at that time and who with Alfred Hessel Tiltman, both former de Havilland employees and, thereafter, colleagues of Dr. Barnes Wallis on the design of the Vickers R100 Airship at Howden, had formed the subsequently famous Airspeed Ltd., in a disused garage in York during April 1931, with the then Lord Grimethorpe as Chairman and Sir Alan Cobham as a Director.

Although this activity is not directly pertinent to what follows it is, nevertheless, fascinating to contemplate the possible alternatives to Yorkshire's aviation history if, in 1934, it had been the cities of York or Leeds/Bradford which had offered Airspeed much needed financial support and flying facilities, rather than Portsmouth. For the sum of only £14,000 and a convenient runway, as provided to the Company by that Authority, the lovely little Envoy and its notable successor, the Oxford, might well have been built within Yorkshire's broad acres.

---

1   In the spring of 1945 Tony Benn qualified as a pilot with the R.A.F.

Disappointed White Rose xenophobes can, however, take comfort in the knowledge that between fifty and seventy personnel from York went with Airspeed to Portsmouth, thus ensuring some measure of Yorkshire grit and resource was embodied in future developments of the Company!

On the departure of N.S. Norway, Captain Worrall assumed the duties of Club Manager/Secretary in addition to continuing as C.F.I.; three offices which, apparently, he maintained until the outbreak of the Second World War.

During the first three and a half years of operations at Yeadon there were no scheduled commercial services from the aerodrome, the period being utilised by the Club to expand its activities.

Pleasures then were, of necessity, simple ones: for decades Yeadoners had spent summer weekends enjoying the amenities available on or around the Dam and, with the advent of an aerodrome almost alongside, it too quickly became part of their itinerary. Many were the picnics enjoyed on its grassy perimeter, - no need for security measures in those days, - watching the tiny silver and blue Moths as they bobbed in and out on their excursions; or enjoying lunch or afternoon tea at the newly established, and white painted, Aerodrome Cafe, situated alongside Victoria Avenue (the A658) opposite the hangars.

In retrospect, it seems highly unlikely that any of those who participated in such simple recreation could have foreseen even in their wildest dreams, that some of the young men then being tutored by the Club's instructors would, in the not too distant future, be called upon to fight for their lives in the skies of Europe and elsewhere. Nor could they have perceived that the very spot where they lazily consumed their summer picnics would, all too soon, reverberate to the sound of engines from a host of aircraft which would emerge pristine, yet malevolent, from a giant factory destined to be built just a few hundred yards away!

On 20th June and, again, on 5th August 1932, 'National Aviation Day' events were organised at Yeadon by Sir Alan Cobham: these attractions becoming commonly, but erroneously, known as 'Cobham's Flying Circus'.

With flights available at 5/-d (25p) or 7/6d (37½p), depending on their duration these, and similar events, introduced flying to a wide and eager public at a time when the wind-up gramophone, and crystal-set wireless were in vogue, and television was unknown!

The importance to Britain and the Free World of those "Thirties" aviation events should not be underestimated, for it was at such gatherings that many of the young men who would, subsequently,

Photo 7.

Gipsy Moths: G-AAJW, G-AALN, G-ABJN, G-AAMR, G-ABVV,

Hornet Moth: G-ADNE and Short Scion: G-ACJI pictured at Yeadon in 1937.

Club house of the Yorkshire Flying Club at bottom right.

Beginnings

play a vital rôle in the air battles of the Second World War, gained their first experience of flight.

The displays attracted a number of irate protestors, however, included among whom was the Rev. F.M. Cooper, who went unheeded, as did twice Prime Minister Stanley Baldwin when, in the same year, he warned: ".... I think it is as well for the man in the street to realize that there is no power on earth that can protect him from being bombed. Whatever people may tell him, the bomber will always get through...... the only defence is offence, which means you will have to kill more women and children more quickly than the enemy if you want to save yourself......."

Also during 1932 permission was granted to Mr. Geo. Ambler (of whom more later) to erect a hangar on site, and 2,056 acres (832.06 hectares) of land at Coldwell Quarry, Yeadon Moor, was acquired by the Joint Authority for further development of the Aerodrome.

More ominously, in Germany, a certain Adolph Hitler, who became its Chancellor on 30th January, 1933, aided by cohorts in the National Sozialistiche Deutsche Arbeiter Partei (Nazi Party) began what was to become a reign of terror and bloodshed the like of which the world had never known.

Concurrently, Yeadon Council, along with other authorities, received from the Government a handbook relating to "Anti Gas Precautions", and the members of the Council, all of whom had lived through the First World War, were prompted to voice their concern as exemplified in this Minute, which was sent to the Government:

"That the U.D.C. of Yeadon, in the interests of Peace, deplores the worldwide armaments race. It realises that another world war conducted on modern, scientific lines by the use of poison gas, and aerial bombs, would be an attack on defenceless populations, and imperial civilisation itself. It believes that the people of the world are far in advance of their governments on the peace question. It, therefore, calls on the people of all countries to abandon the competition in armaments and seek the solution of all international disputes by peaceful means".

Shortly after the Jubilee of King George V (6th May 1935), Yeadon Council was approached by the Leeds Town Planning Advisory Council "To ensure protection of the Aerodrome in your planning", similar entreaties being sent to neighbouring authorities. In the same year, a further thirty-five acres (14.16 hectares) of grassland was added to the aerodrome.

Photo 4. The Hindenburg pictured over Riddlesden, Nr. Keighley.

(photo credit Ian Dewhurst)

Ironically, as the situation worsened in Europe, so began the development of commercial operations at Yeadon. On 8th April 1935, North Eastern Airways commenced a London (Heston) - Leeds/Bradford - Newcastle (Cramlington) - Edinburgh service, using Airspeed Envoy's: G-ADBB 'Wharfedale' and :G-ADAZ 'Tynedale'; joined, some weeks later, by: G-ADBZ 'Swaledale': the first scheduled passenger service to be routed through the airport. Within the year, others to Blackpool (Squires Gate and, later, Stanley Park), Manchester (Barton), Liverpool, The Isle of Man and Perth (Scone-opened in 1936), were inaugurated by either Blackpool and West Coast Air Services; United Airlines and/or Manx Airways (R.A.S.), using DH 84. Dragon or DH 89. Rapide aircraft.

During the evening of Friday, 22nd May 1936, the largest airship ever built: the Hydrogen filled, 840ft (245 metres) 'Hindenburg', greater in length than four Boeing 747 'Jumbos' placed nose to tail, flew sedately over Yeadon, having cruised down Airedale at 60 m.p.h. en route from the U.S.A. to Frankfurt. Mrs. Lena Evans recalled the event: "We were living in Esholt at the time, and the Hindenburg came over without any warning. It was so big it seemed to blot out the sky".

Indeed the pride of Germany, which had a capacity of more than seven million cubic feet (198,240 cubic metres), adorned with the Nazi Swastika and the 1936 Olympic emblem, flew so low that its serial number LZ-129 and the passengers peering from its cabin windows, could be plainly seen by the many hundreds who watched its progress with fascination.

This, and another ostensibly 'goodwill' flying visit made by the giant airship on 16th June, cause such excitement that, in some quarters, it was suggested that, as a reciprocal gesture to Germany, a mooring mast for its accommodation should be erected at Yeadon! Others were somewhat more apprehensive, wondering why it had been necessary for the Hindenburg to fly so low over parts of the industrial heartland of the West Riding? (The Hindenburg journeyed elsewhere over Britain performing a similar function.) In the event the sceptics were proved correct for the visits were, in fact, 'spy' flights, during which aerial photographs were obtained of strategic industrial areas and aerodromes, and that of Leeds which is presented elsewhere in this book - and used by the Luftwaffe in its attacks on the city - was almost certainly so acquired.

Such clandestine activities on board the airship were to be short-lived, however, for on 6th May, 1937, the Hindenburg was destroyed with tragic loss of life when, for reasons never satisfactorily explained, it burst into flames when approaching moorings at Lakehurst, New Jersey, U.S.A.

During 1936 plans were announced for a new £40,000 terminal building at Yeadon, but, in the event, only one wing was completed, in 1938 (which became known as the Clubhouse), along with a new hangar nearby.

On 1st April, 1937, 'All Fools Day', - a fact many locals thought not insignificant! - Yeadon amalgamated with the neighbouring towns of Guiseley and Rawdon, and the village of Hawksworth, to form Aireborough Urban District: an Authority which was to remain in being until the boundary changes of 1974.

Photo 4a. An advertisement for the commencement of services from LBA to the Isle of Man. Apart from the War years, and a short period thereafter, the route has remained a regular summer schedule operated, at different times, by a variety of airlines.

Beginnings

With the situation worsening in Europe, however, developments at Yeadon, as at other commercial aerodromes, were destined to take a dramatically different course from that planned.

Information

Proceeds from the Air Day collection are for the R.A.F. and other charities.

Teas will be provided in the Civil hangar, Harrogate-Bradford Road, by Messrs. Lewis's (Leeds) Ltd.

Spectators are requested to refrain from smoking while visiting the hangars to see R.A.F. and equipment.

Aircraft and equipment will be on view and instructors will be available to answer questions.

Joy riding will be carried out by four aircraft of the Yorkshire Aeroplane Club. Flights 5/- each.

Empire Air Day Yeadon 1939

HEADQUARTERS OF
No. 609 WEST RIDING (FIGHTER) SQUADRON
AUXILIARY AIR FORCE
, AND
THE YORKSHIRE AEROPLANE CLUB

Programme 2d.

PROGRAMME

14.15 Hours. EVENT 1.
Formation Flying and Air Drill by five Hinds of No. 609 (W.R.) (F) Squadron.

14.51 Hours. EVENT 2.
Speed demonstration by a Supermarine Spitfire, Single Seater Fighter, from Royal Air Force Station, CATTERICK.

15.00 Hours. EVENT 3.
Pupil Pilot Peabody receiving flying instruction in an Avro Tutor.
The conversation between the Instructor and Pupil will be relayed by wireless to the loud speakers.

15.30 Hours. EVENT 4.
Arrival of a flight of Whitley heavy bombers to bomb an aerodrome target.

15.50 Hours. EVENT 5.
Individual Aerobatics by a Hind of No. 609 (W.R.) (F) Squadron.

16.14 Hours. EVENT 6
Fly Past by a formation of Battle Aircraft from No. 106 (Bomber) Squadron, THORNABY.

16.30 Hours. EVENT 7.
Front Gun attack on drogue by a Hind of No. 609 (W.R.) (F) Squadron.

17.10 Hours. EVENT 8.
Demonstration of range of speed by a Lysander (Army Co-operation) Aircraft from R.A.F. Station, CATTERICK.

17.40 Hours. EVENT 9.
Formation Flying and Air Drill by five Hinds of No. 609 (W.R.) (F) Squadron.

Photo 4b, 4c. Programme for the Empire Day display, held at Yeadon on Saturday, 20th May 1939. Copyright via D. Yeadon.

Overture to War

During the early Nineteen-Thirties Britain's aircraft industry was small but, from 1936, it was required to expand quite rapidly; a development made no easier by the shortage of capital and capacity. Nevertheless, the Air Ministry was determined to enlarge and modernise the Royal Air Force despite a general mood of appeasement and opposition for funds from the Royal Navy and the Army, which still regarded the R.A.F. as a secondary force!

Fortunately, there were some manufacturing companies (including Rolls Royce and Vickers) which, despite not having obtained specific contracts, were prepared to go it alone in the development of new aircraft and engines.

A vital constituent in the expansion of the R.A.F. was the build up in the number of its Auxiliary Squadrons: one of which No. 609 (West Riding) Squadron formed at Yeadon as a Light Bomber Squadron, on 10th February, 1936, in response to Air Ministry Order, A.M.O. N6/1936; being equipped, initially, with AVRO Tutors and Hawker Harts; the latter, subsequently, being replaced by Hawker Hinds. **(Photo 5 & 5a centre pages)**

The 6th Earl of Harewood became '609's' first Honorary Air Commodore, and Squadron Leader Harold Peake its first Honorary Commanding Officer. He was assisted by a Regular Adjutant; F/Lt. N.C. Odbert aided, as his deputy, by another regular officer F/Lt. A.W.S. Matheson (an Australian who, subsequently, commanded a Squadron in Bomber Command), both of whom arrived at Yeadon during July, 1936, to take up their duties, among which was that of the Squadron's flying instructors. Earlier, on 24th April, F/O. the Earl of Lincoln (later the 9th Duke of Newcastle who subsequently became C.O. of No. 616 South Yorkshire Squadron) became Auxiliary Adjutant, and other appointments included that of F/O. T. McM. Boyle as Medical Officer, F/Lt. R. Burges, Equipment Officer, and W/O. H. Faux as Station Warrant Officer in charge of discipline.

Despite the spartan facilities at Yeadon, the Auxiliary 'weekend' pilots and their ground crews led, firstly by Peake and, from December, 1938, by Squadron Leader Geoffrey H. Ambler (he who, earlier, had erected a hangar at Yeadon) worked hard to knit themselves into a cohesive and highly effective unit. That they did so is borne out by a subsequent record of achievement during the Second World War which was second to non.

In December, 1938, No. 609 (West Riding) Squadron transferred to Fighter Command and, concurrently, the Yorkshire Aeroplane Club volunteered to take part in a national scheme to train pilots for a new body to be known as the Civil Air Guard. The idea for this had developed after the Munich crisis earlier in the year, when it became obvious that there was a desperate shortage of trained pilots. In the scheme the Club, and similar organisations elsewhere, agreed to train would be pilots (civilians) at a subsidised rate of less than 10/-d (50p) per hour up to 'A' licence standard, for which the Club would receive £3 per hour from the Government for the first six hours of training, and £32 when the student gained his licence. This was intended to be a four year contract, with the Club providing all facilities and equipment and, by the Spring of 1939, it had 19 aircraft and 9 instructors involved in the work.

By January, 1939, No. 609 Squadron had two new hangars, and Auxiliary officers commanded A and B flights, each operating six Hinds. T 'Training' flight utilised the Tutors, four Hinds and a Hind trainer. The Officers' Mess had a billiards room, ladies' room and a mess steward but, by then, some of the original regular officers including Ft. Lt's Odbert and Matheson, and some senior N.C.O.'s had departed to pastures new.

Although nationally the build-up in training had gained considerable momentum, it had been realised for some time by those in authority that, if peace efforts failed, Britain's needs could not be met with the aircraft available, either in type or quantity. Moreover, production capability did not exist in the aviation industry alone to build the additional aircraft envisaged necessary to cope with the threat posed by Germany. Extra capacity could be provided only by the utilisation of factories the peace time products of which would, if war came, be classed as non-essential items: for instance, motor cars and luxury goods; and, also, by the supplementary construction of 'shadow' factories: establishments built away from existing manufacturing bases, preferably at locations more difficult for enemy aircraft to identify.

In line with this thinking Roy Dobson (later Sir Roy), then General Manager of A.V. Roe & Co. Ltd., was charged with the task of finding such a site in Yorkshire. On a visit to Yeadon, near to his former

Overture to War

home at Horsforth, he met Captain Worrall to whom he mentioned his quest, adding that Doncaster was a possible location. "Why bother going there, everything you want is right here", came the reply, and that chance remark by 'Skipper' Worrall not only 'willed' the factory to Yeadon but, similarly, (albeit inadvertently) assured a postwar future for Leeds/Bradford Airport. **(Photo 6 front inside cover)**

Ministry officials agreed that the site was suitable., and plans for a factory located immediately to the north of the aerodrome, adjacent to Coney House Farm and alongside the A658, Bradford - Harrogate road, were submitted to, and approved by, the Wharfedale Rural District Council at Otley in the early summer of 1939.

Bearing in mind the grave situation developing in Europe at the time it does, with hindsight, appear incomprehensible that details of such an important (and, then, secret) aircraft factory should be required to go before the Planning Committee of a small, Rural Council; but, as Britain was still at peace, - albeit tenuously, - normal procedures had to be followed: such is democracy!

Some readers might question the involvement of the Wharfedale Rural District Council, rather than that of Aireborough U.D.C., with which, thus far, this narrative has been concerned. Contrary to popular opinion, however, the factory was sited within the boundaries of the village of Carlton which, at that time, came under the jurisdiction of the former authority; nevertheless, the factory was and continues to be, invariably referred to as being in Yeadon.

During that final summer of peace, when Gracie Fields and George Formby were voted Britain's top entertainers, and Wakefield born Noel Gay was enjoying tremendous success with his song 'Lambeth Walk', No. 609 Squadron began to anticipate the arrival of the Spitfire. Such aircraft were in very short supply, however, and conversion onto monoplanes was done in Fairey Battle's or, onto type, by occasional forays in Spitfire's of No. 72 Squadron from (or at) Church Fenton. **(Photo 6a - centre pages)**

The first Spitfire to reach the squadron [1]: Mk.1. L. 1082, was flown to Yeadon from the Vickers-Supermarine factory aerodrome at Southampton (Eastleigh), on 19th August 1939, by Squadron Leader Ambler - C.O.'s perks!? - the aircraft surviving, thereafter, almost to the end of the subsequent Battle of Britain. On 27th August L. 1082, accompanied by one Fairey Battle: N.2098 (which returned to Yeadon on 7th September), plus some elements of the squadron, moved to RAF Catterick - this having been designated its 'War Station'. One other Spitfire Mk.I:1086 arrived there two days later and three more: L.1058, L.1064 and L.1071 on 6th September. A less than dramatic beginning to what would become an illustrious record of achievement, culminating in '609' becoming the RAF's highest 'scoring' fighter-squadron and making the call-sign 'Tally-ho' its very own.

During the month, the people of Britain, facing almost certain conflict with Germany - for which they were ill prepared - responded in inimitable fashion by making "Yes, we have no bananas" the most popular song of the day!

More ominously, Herman Göring, leader of the Luftwaffe rallied his forces: "I have done my best during the past few years to make our air force the largest and most powerful in the world. The creation of the greater German Reich has been made possible largely by the spirit of the German airmen in the First World War, inspired by its faith in the Führer and Commander-in-Chief -thus stands the German Air Force today, ready to carry out every command of the Führer with lightning speed and undreamed of might".

Early on the morning of Friday, 1st September, Nazi troops stormed across the Polish frontier and by Sunday the 3rd, in Britain every able-bodied man between 18 and 41 was liable for immediate call-up. All club and private flying ceased; club aircraft being 'Impressed' into service with the R.A.F.,[2] and Leeds/Bradford Municipal Airport (Yeadon) was Requisitioned into No. 13 Group Fighter Command. Two Anson I's stood outside a hangar but were not flown.**(Photo 7 - centre pages)**

The 'On Strength' establishment of No.609 Squadron (<u>at Yeadon</u>) stood at Officers: 10, Other Ranks: 115. Also present were 4 Officers and 58 O.R.'s of No.5 Company, Womens Auxiliary Air Force (WAAF) - all pre-conscription volunteers - commanded by Mrs Carby Hall and her Senior Leader, Miss Senior-Smith; the WAAF's being billeted in

---

1 See Appendix B
2 See Appendix B

the Yorkshire Aeroplane Club clubhouse: On aerodrome defence duties were two Officers and 62 O.R.'s of 1st/6th Battalion, The Duke of Wellington's Reg't.

On that fateful Sunday morning, when Prime Minister Neville Chamberlain gravely told the Nation that it was at war with Germany, and countless families - whose lives would be changed irrevocably - wondered what lay before them, the banner headline of one national newspaper ran:

DON'T PANIC DIG !

Photo 4d. Official entreaty issued via various publications - in this case 'Good Housekeeping magazine' - to urge people to realise the desperateness of the situation.
credit 'Good Housekeeping 1940'

War

"Under the Shadow of War what can we do that matters?"

At 3.25 a.m. on Monday, 4th September, the people of Aireborough were awakened by the wailing sound of the first air raid sirens of the war. Many went sleepy-eyed from their beds to the shelters fearing that bombs would fall any minute, but, in fact, it was a false alarm, and the long, welcome, blast of the 'all-clear' came at 3.57 a.m.

Although in this corner of West Yorkshire the outbreak of hostilities was greeted with "a quiet and sober reception", according to one local newspaper, things were, nevertheless, moving onto a war footing. Two days before Chamberlain's dramatic announcement, the Territorial Army had been mobilised and, when war was declared, it's anti-aircraft units were already at their gun sites; including some in proximity to the Aerodrome.

The painting of white stripes on street corners, lamp posts, and other obstructions was completed just in time before 'Black-Out' restrictions began. Thereafter it became an offence to emit light from *any* window after the hours of darkness, or use vehicles with headlights not diffused effectively. Trains ran with blinds drawn and they and buses travelled with interiors unlit, or illuminated only by a dim, blue bulb. Even to light a cigarette, cigar or pipe outdoors after the hours of darkness was, similarly, prohibited. Britain became a dismal, gloomy, place and road accidents increased dramatically.

The 'Black-Out' was so much disliked, however, that the Government allowed one small concession when it permitted the use of torches, given that they were diffused by two layers of tissue paper. This, ironically, generated the first 'shortage' of the war when small batteries became almost unobtainable; and it is little wonder that bright, moonlit, nights were widely welcomed; that is, of course, until enemy bombing began.

Cinemas, theatres, dance-halls and other places of entertainment were closed, but when this was found to be detrimental to morale the authorities relaxed restrictions up to 10.00 p.m. and, from March, 1940, to 11.00 p.m.

Air raid precaution was taken very seriously: Aireborough being divided up into areas covered by 46 'Posts', each controlled by a volunteer Warden, complete with a black tin-hat upon which was painted in white: 'A.R.P.' (Air Raid Precaution). At the outset, Wardens wore everyday clothes but, ultimately, each was equipped with a navy or black Battle-dress uniform.

One of the local A.R.P. posts was located at the Aerodrome Garage (Warden A.W. Lamb), an establishment situated, as its name implies, close by the aerodrome. It was thought that, in the weeks immediately following the outbreak of war, this would prove to be one of the busier - and less healthy - places to be; but, in fact, there was little activity, and none if it by the enemy.

No.609 Squadron had taken up residence (temporarily) at Catterick and, as all club flying had ceased for the duration of hostilities, it was left to the Whitley bombers of No's. 51 and 58 Squadrons, whose parent station was at Linton-on-Ouse, and a number of aircraft from other No.4 Group Squadrons similarly deployed in the Vale of York, to boost local morale by their presence when using Yeadon as a detached 'scatter base'.

At 4.30 p.m. on 17th October, 'F6+PK' (WNr. 2728), a Heinkel HeIIIH-1 of 2(F)/122,[1] operating from Munster on an armed reconnaissance to try to locate H.M.S. Hood, was intercepted and shot down 20 miles east of Whitby by Green Section Spitfires from No.41 Squadron at Catterick, flown by F/Lt. H.P. Blatchford, F/Sgt. E.A. Shipman and Sgt. A. Harris. Of its crew of four only the Heinkel's pilot, Oberfeldwebel Eugene Lange and his radio operator, Unteroffizier Bernard Hochstuhl survived. After spending forty-three hours in a rubber dinghy without food and water, they were carried ashore by the current at Lythdale Sands near Sandsend where, almost at the end of their endurance, they were brought up the cliffs by two local men to become the first German prisoners of war to be captured on English soil. Forty years later they would return to the area to meet up again with their rescuers!

1　The 'F' was an abbreviation of 'Aufklärungsgruppe' : i.e. Reconnaissance unit.

War

Meanwhile, at Yeadon, a little way to the north of the aerodrome, theodolite encumbered surveyors were to be seen tramping the lush fields between Coney House Farm and the A658, and their presence prompted growing interest and speculation. Notwithstanding approval for the factory having been obtained details thereof were not common knowledge; particularly so now that a state of war existed and, with the need for secrecy in the country being paramount, few talked openly about anything which might be passed on to the enemy.

In private, however, there was considerable conjecture as to what was developing alongside the aerodrome, with ideas ranging from the accurate to the fanciful, adding to a popular belief that the area would soon become a prime target for the Luftwaffe..

Such fears were unfounded, however, for during the first weeks of the war, action by it and the R.A.F. was confined to attacks against targets, mainly shipping, through which it was intended no harm would come to the civilian population.

During December, at the height of what had become known as the 'SITZKREIG' - the phoney war [2] - the first turf was removed from the site alongside the A658: work had begun on what was to become the largest factory under one roof in Europe.

The Kelvin Construction Company Limited of Glasgow, regrettably no longer in existence, won

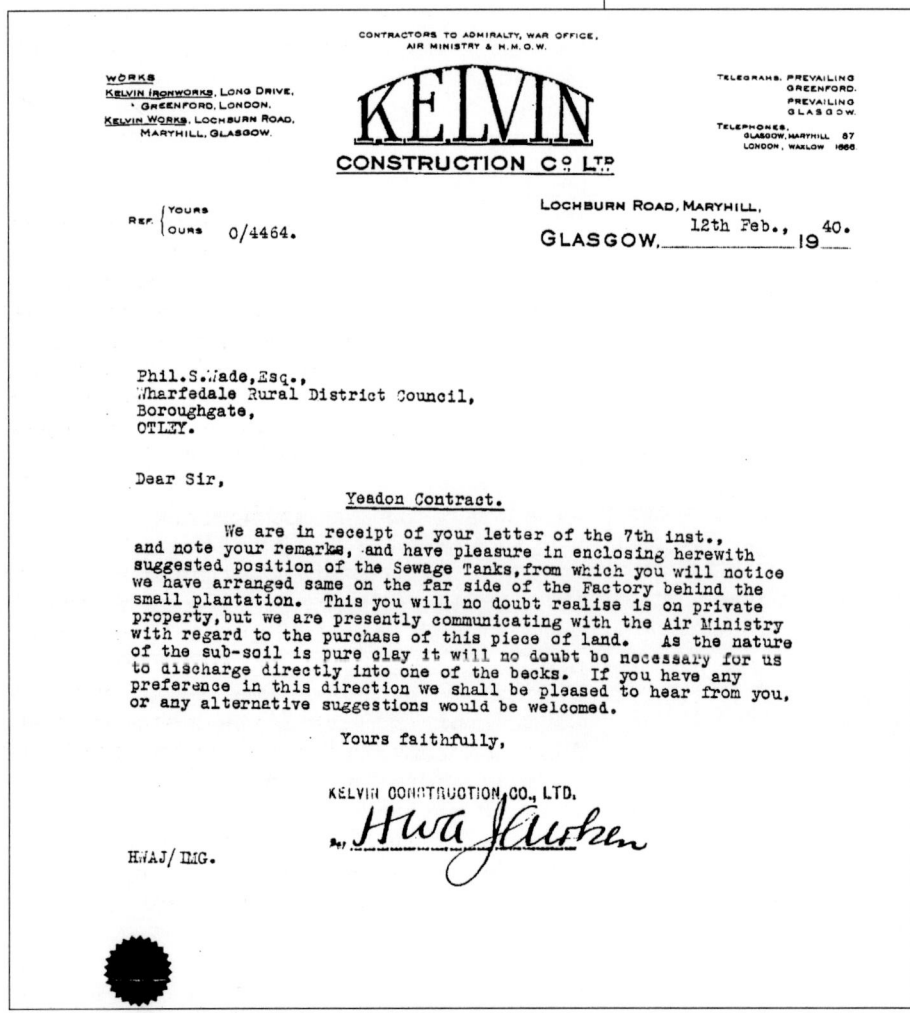

Photo 9.

A letter from the company to the Wharedale Rural District Council regarding the siting of the sewage tanks. Latter day environmentalists would be appalled at such a suggestion for disposal !

---

2   This was something of a misnomer for although land forces were not engaged, aerial activity in the French-German sector and in the North Sea Triangle (North German coast, Norwegian seaboard, the Shetlands, East coast of Scotland and England) was an everyday occurrence and losses in aircraft, shipping and men, on both sides, were substantial.

the contract to build the factory and, through the desperately cold winter of 1940, the worst for more than fifty years, a veritable army of its men and equipment descended on the site. They found considerable excavation was required, particularly at the northern perimeter, where it was necessary to level an area of steeply rising ground. Interestingly, in a depression just beyond this extremity there runs the track of a roadway along which, during the Roman occupation of Britain, Macedonian conscripts to its Legions marched en-route between Eboracum (York), Olicana (Ilkley) and beyond.

The contractors had to overcome severe physical obstacles which included the draining of several streams and the filling-in of a substantial pond; work also being hampered by areas of marshland and a sub-soil of heavy clay.

Beset by such engineering problems and extreme weather conditions, the workers and their families were less than enthusiastic about the introduction, on 8th January, of Food Rationing which restricted every adult in Britain to 12ozs (340gms) of sugar and 4ozs (113gms) of ham, bacon and butter per week. More severe controls came into being on 11th March when meat was reduced to a maximum of 1/10d (9p) worth per week, with the allowance of tea, margarine and cooking fats cut to just 2ozs (57gms) per week.

Gradually, as the months went by, food rationing was extended (as was the rationing of petrol which began on 22nd September, 1939) and, eventually, all food commodities excepting bread and vegetables grown in ones own garden or 'allotment' were affected. Included were basics such as milk and eggs, the latter allowance, by 1941, being one egg per week, per person! Sweets and chocolates (which remained 'on ration' until 1953) became almost unobtainable, as did cigarettes (then 7d (3p) for 10) pipe tobacco, cigars, and wines and spirits. Beer was often 'sold out' and, when not so, was generally of poor quality. Hardly, one would think, the ideal sustenance on which to fight a war, yet far worse deprivation, and heartache, was to come.

At 09.40 hours on 3rd February, the broad acres of Yorkshire were again involved in the making of a piece of history, when Hurricane's of Blue Section No.43 Squadron, led by F/Lt. Peter Townsend [3], supported by F/O 'Tiger' Folkes and Sgt. 'Jim' Hallowes, took off from Acklington to attack a Heinkel HeIII - 'IH+FM' (WNr.2323) of II/KG26 (the Löwen Geschwarder - Lion Squadron) 26 miles east of Whitby. The stricken bomber, which had flown from Schleswig, then turned inland, where it crashed to become the first enemy aircraft to be brought down on English soil. Its pilot, Feldwebel (FW) Hermann Wilms, and his radio operator Unteroffizier Karl Missy were the only members of the four man crew to survive.

As the terrible winter gave way to Spring, across the Channel Nazi forces began an inexorable progress towards the conquest of Europe. On 9th April, Denmark and Norway were invaded and, on 10th May, the Low Countries. Meanwhile, in France the B.E.F. was learning a sharp lesson: that, irrespective of high morale and good intentions, outmoded military thinking and equipment was no match for modern armour and aircraft as that possessed, in apparent abundance, by the enemy.

On the 10th May, Chamberlain resigned; a Coalition Government was formed, and Winston Churchill became Prime Minister.

Throughout the month, Allied forces retreated towards the Channel ports and, finally, between the 26th May and 4th June the greatest escape in military history was accomplished when 340,000 mainly British troops were evacuated from Dunkirk. The B.E.F., however, left behind it either dead, or as Prisoners-of-War, 68,111 men and virtually all its equipment while, in the unsuccessful campaign, the Advanced Air Striking Force (A.A.S.F.) and other elements of the R.A.F., lost 931 aircraft, of which 477 were fighters.

The 9th June brought the surrender of Norway and, on the 10th, Italy entered the war alongside Germany. Thus when, on the 21st, French representatives signed an armistice with Hitler, Britain stood alone; alone, and desperately ill-equipped, to continue the fight against a triumphant and seemingly invincible adversary, waiting confidently just twenty-one miles away across the sea.

> For all we have and are,
> For all our children's fate,
> Stand up and take the war:
> The Hun is at the gate.

These few words by Kipling grimly echo the desperate circumstances.

---

3   Currently Group Captain CVO., DSO., DFC., RAF (Ret'd).

War

The situation was indeed dire, not just for Britain but for democracy itself and although, ultimately, the gallant 'Few' saved the day, their victory in the Battle of Britain was, to quote the Duke of Wellington,".....a damned close run thing".

The mood of that period portrayed in films such as 'Mrs Minniver' and 'Dangerous Moonlight', with its haunting theme music: 'The Warsaw Concerto', might now appear dated but, then, the events were all too real for thousands of people.

Not surprisingly, throughout the summer, construction of the factory progressed with an increased urgency, and it became an everyday event to see long lines of lorries (so called then) almost nose to tail, en route to and from the site. Given the substantial number of vehicles involved and the size and variety of the loads they carried it was inevitable that some of their contents would get spilled; and, indeed, more than one local household found itself the recipient of an unexpected (but welcome) windfall which had, quite literally, 'fallen off a lorry!'

During August, despite it being only partially completed, operations began in the Machine Shop, situated at the northern end of the factory: the first section of the burgeoning building to be roofed. One of those involved at the outset was Jack Rowbotham, a native of North-East Derbyshire, who arrived at Yeadon after attending a Government Training Centre at Kirkstall, Leeds. This, and similar establishments elsewhere, was set up to train workers with engineering skills to gain an understanding of aircraft production. Later, the Centre also trained many who possessed no engineering background.

Jack Rowbotham lived, firstly, in 'digs' near the cricket ground at Headingley, but soon moved closer to the factory, lodging with a family in Rawdon. He was chosen for his job by Teddy Nield, one of several highly skilled specialists who, to assist in its early build-up, were sent to Yeadon from AVRO's Newton Heath facility.

"When I arrived at AVRO (virtually all former employees refer to the Yeadon factory simply thus) Tom Golding [4] and a chap called Stonehouse and myself were its first precision fitters", recalled Jack, "and our first job was to set up the bogey-jigs for Anson wing assembly, although the factory was far from finished at the time. In fact we could see daylight through the roof and the walls were just temporary lean-to's of corrugated iron sheeting. All in all the place looked like a giant builders yard".

Photo 10.

MACHINE   SHOP

Heraldic Emblems and their descriptions were the work of a former Avro Inspector at Yeadon, Joe Bruce, and were in colour.
copyright Joe Bruce.

Machine Shop

This is in the form of a question mark, which contains the answer to its own question.

The design gives the impression that a bit of juggling goes on in the machine shop, this is of course a thing unheard of.

The comparitive size of the balls have been carefully worked out mathematically. The word Rex of course means Royal or Good.

**On a ribbon at the bottom runs a slogan in pigeon Latin, supposed to have originated amongst the machine shop foreman and chargehands.
An interseting table, refering to bonus is also included which seems to work out quite correctly.**

---

[4] The spelling may be Goulding

Concurrently, alongside in the fledgling tool room, then in similar disarray, millwrights were assembling a variety of machine tools, acquired mainly via a national 'machine tool pool': a facility set up prior to the advent of the British-American lend-lease scheme through which, later, a huge quantity of war material was obtained. Ultimately, 800 or so belt-free machines, each driven independently by an electric motor, were utilised: a very modern feature for a British factory at that time.

On Saturday, 7th September, Göring changed his mind and, arguably, the outcome of the Battle of Britain, when he instructed the Luftwaffe to desist, very largely, from its daylight attacks on fighter airfields, to concentrate on the night bombing of London (primarily) and other cities and towns, with the intention of breaking the morale of the British people. The residents involved were far from being enamoured with this turn of events for it was upon their heads and property which the bombs began to fall, but it did provide a very hard pressed Fighter Command with the opportunity to repair, re equip and reactivate airfields which were in grave danger of being rendered inoperative.

The first belligerent act performed locally by the Luftwaffe had come more than two weeks previously when, during the early hours of Monday, 19th August, a lone raider dropped bombs on Otley Chevin, a six hundred feet (182 metres) high stretch of the Pennines, less than a mile to the north of the partially completed factory; the event being described in the Wharfedale and Airedale Observer as follows:

"The destruction of a rabbit, two gaps in stone walls and a few craters in a field were the sum total of damage caused by an enemy plan which unloaded its cargo of four H.E. bombs and about 60 incendiary bombs on a hill top in the North East of England in the early hours of Monday ...... one of the bombs which fell in a field had a delayed action and it exploded some time later. It made a crater 25 feet in width and 12 feet deep".

(During the war the media was strictly censored to obviate the possibility of the enemy inadvertently gaining useful information. Thus the location of all but the most trivial of events was identified in a similarly ambiguous way.)

In a private report of the incident the former Otley Fire Chief, Captain N.L. Barker, O.B.E. added "..... the first oil bombs dropped by the Germans in England. These are now in the care of the Police and National Fire Service. They did not ignite, and were sent to the Home Office".

Another piece in the same edition of the Wharfedale and Airedale Observer referred to a further incident: "Reports were received in a district of North East England last night (Thursday) that whilst a lone plane was passing over a whistling noise was heard, followed by a thud. A search was made and this morning a crater was discovered on a hill in proximity to where bombs were dropped on a previous occasion. This crater was 14 feet deep and 30 feet in diameter but, as the bomb was dropped in heavy clay soil this muffled the explosion, and no other damage has been reported".

Thus, within four nights, two individual raiders had dropped bombs on Otley Chevin; firstly, in the vicinity of the Royalty Inn and then between it and the village of Carlton, both of which, in terms the trajectory of a swiftly falling missile, are but seconds away from the factory. It is, therefore, understandable that, at a time when rumour was rife and 'fifth columnists' were seriously (*very* seriously) considered to be around every corner and with invasion expected at any minute, many in the district became convinced that 'they' - the enemy - were determined to destroy the factory there and then; irrespective of the fact that it was unfinished. Plausible as this seemed at the time, the facts of the matter were very different, as is confirmed by copies of Luftwaffe records supplied by the Bundesarchiv in Freiburg. These show that, in August 1940, the emerging factory and the adjoining aerodrome were not intended targets.

One document headed 'MELDUNG' is a summary of de-briefing reports made by the crews of seven Heinkel HeIII aircraft of I/Gruppe/Kampfgeschwader 53 'Legion Condor' (1/KG53) based at Lille in Northern France, on their return from taking part in raids on steelworks (no mention of a factory or an aerodrome) in Sheffield, Leeds and Hull, during the night of 18th/19th August, 1940; the night bombs first fell on Otley Chevin. **(Photo 11)**

The report shows the time of take-off and landing back at base, (all seven aircraft returned), time aircraft were over targets: 0010 - 0135; the height (in metres) at which they flew: 2700 - 3500 metres (8,900 feet - 16,500 feet); bomb loads carried - all were released ('alles geworfen'), ammunition carried, and the defences (Abwehr) in evidence en-route: 'Flak along the coast, searchlights near Leeds and Hull in strength, and five night fighters seen but no attacks developed'.

Two of the seven bombers raided Sheffield, two Leeds and the remaining three Hull, but the report indicates that due to mist and low cloud the crews found it 'scarcely possible' to locate targets (they were navigating by visual methods: 'ERDORIEN-

TIERUNG') and that, despite observing fires *near* Leeds, the success of their attacks could not be confirmed. Put another way, what the men of 1/KG53 were saying was that at the precise moment they released their bombs they - like many other aircrew during the Second World War - were unsure of their exact position!

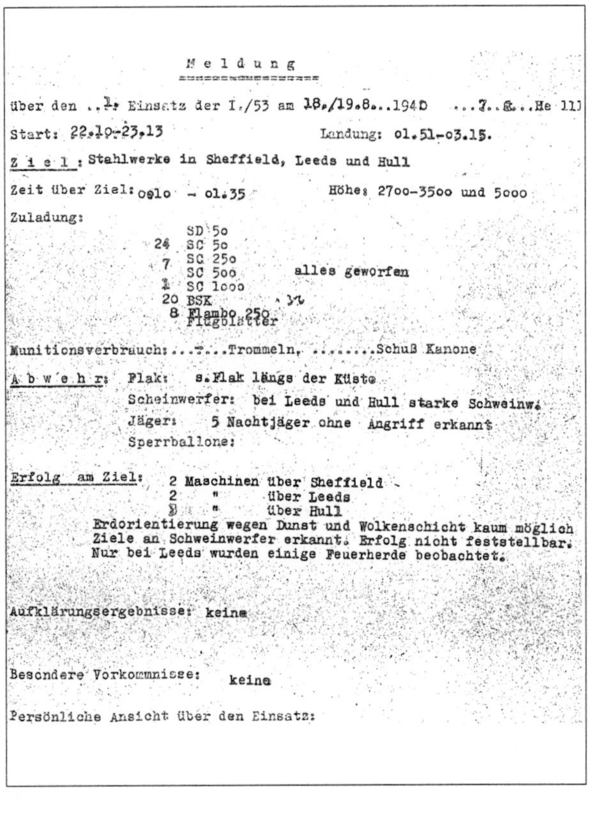

```
                    Meldung
                    ========
über den ..1. Einsatz der I./53 am 18./19.8...1940 ...7.&...He 111
Start: 22.19-23.13          Landung: 01.51-03.15.
Z i e l : Stahlwerke in Sheffield, Leeds und Hull
Zeit über Ziel: 0010 - 01.35    Höhe: 2700-3500 und 5000
Zuladung:
          SD 50
       24 SC 50
        7 SC 250
          SC 500    alles geworfen
        1 SC 1000
       20 BSK
        8 Flambo 250
          Flugblätter
Munitionsverbrauch:...7...Trommeln,........Schuß Kanone
A b w e h r: Flak:   s.Flak längs der Küste
             Scheinwerfer: bei Leeds und Hull starke Scheinw.
             Jäger: 5 Nachtjäger ohne Angriff erkannt
             Sperrballone:
Erfolg am Ziel: 2 Maschinen über Sheffield
                2    "       über Leeds
                3    "       über Hull
         Erdorientierung wegen Dunst und Wolkenschicht kaum möglich
         Ziele an Scheinwerfer erkannt. Erfolg nicht feststellbar.
         Nur bei Leeds wurden einige Feuerherde beobachtet.

Aufklärungsergebnisse: keine

Besondere Vorkommnisse:  keine

Persönliche Ansicht über den Einsatz:
```

Photo 11.

Summary of Bombing attacks carried out by 7 HE 111's of I/KG53 over Northern England on 18th/19th August 1940.

copyright : Bundesarchiv.

As Leeds was but two or three minutes flying time away from the area in which the bombs fell and, as no other enemy aircraft was in the vicinity on the night of 18th/19th August, it is, therefore, reasonable to conclude that one of the two Heinkel HeIII's detailed to attack the city was, inadvertently, responsible - its crew obviously believing they were closer to their target - and the fact that they came so near to hitting the aerodrome or factory was purely coincidental.

Similarly, there is no evidence of a planned enemy raid in the area during the night of 22nd/23rd, for bad weather had continued to obscure much of Britain during the week, and this restricted the Luftwaffe to hit and run attacks. De-briefing reports fail to identify any German aircraft which operated in the locality that night although individual bombers were active throughout North-East England; thus, again, given the adverse weather conditions, it is reasonable to assume that the fifth 'H.E.' bomb which fell onto the Chevin was dropped by a crew as unsure of its position as that from 1/KG53 and, likewise, as unaware that a war factory and aerodrome lay nearby!

Conclusive proof that, at the time, the Luftwaffe did not consider these to be of primary importance is contained in a copy of a target map used by GRUPPEN I, II and III of KG4 'General Wever', operating from Soesterberg, Eindhoven, and Amsterdam (Schipol) respectively, in raids on the North East of England during the night of 24th/25th August.

As can be seen, Leeds was detailed for attack at 0300 hours by 4 Heinkel HeIII's of III/KG4, flying from what would become Amsterdam Airport, carrying 15 SC 250kg bombs (these were, in fact, dropped in the Whitehall Road, Geldard Road and Copley Hill areas of the city) but, importantly, there is no mention of Yeadon Aerodrome, or the factory, nor is Yeadon even shown on the map. **(Photo 12 - end of chapter)**

Had the Luftwaffe considered them worthy targets, there is little doubt they would have been scheduled that night in the widespread attacks carried out by more than 40 HeIII's from KG4, or during two subsequent raids made by the same unit on Leeds and Bradford on 27th/28th August and 31st August/1st September (of which more later) but this was not the case. Even so, bearing in mind the very close proximity of Otley Chevin to human habitation, it has to be accepted that possible tragic consequences were avoided only by pure good fortune and the narrowest of margins! **(Photo 13 - centre pages)**

Regarding the incident in the early hours of 19th August, the Newspaper report and that of Captain Barker appear to conflict, in that a journalist made mention of 4 HE (High Explosive) bombs and 60 incendiaries, whereas Captain Barker stated ".....the first oil bombs dropped by the Germans on England....". This can be explained by the fact that the German SC 250Kg (560lb) HE bomb and the Flambo 250Kg (Flam: short for Flammenbomben or Fire-bombs) were similar in size and general appearance, thus it is safe to assume that two of the latter were those described by Captain Barker; the remaining two being of the SC 250 HE type, one of which was fitted with a delayed action fuse.

The 60 incendiaries were of a magnesium filled 1kg (2.21lb) type and a fin from one of them and a piece of shrapnel from an exploded shell, fired by a local anti-aircraft battery, are on display in the Otley Museum, at the Civic Centre in the town.

A section of one former A.A. Battery is still extant, looking similar to a number of air-raid shelters, in a field just to the north-east of Carlton village; almost alongside East Chevin Road.

Another piece of wartime history is contained as part of the pavilion of Otley Town Cricket Club, in Pool Road, for this housed a searchlight when it was 'off duty'.

Photo 11a. There being no street lighting during 'Black Out', this poster urged the public to use their torches in a sensible manner.

War

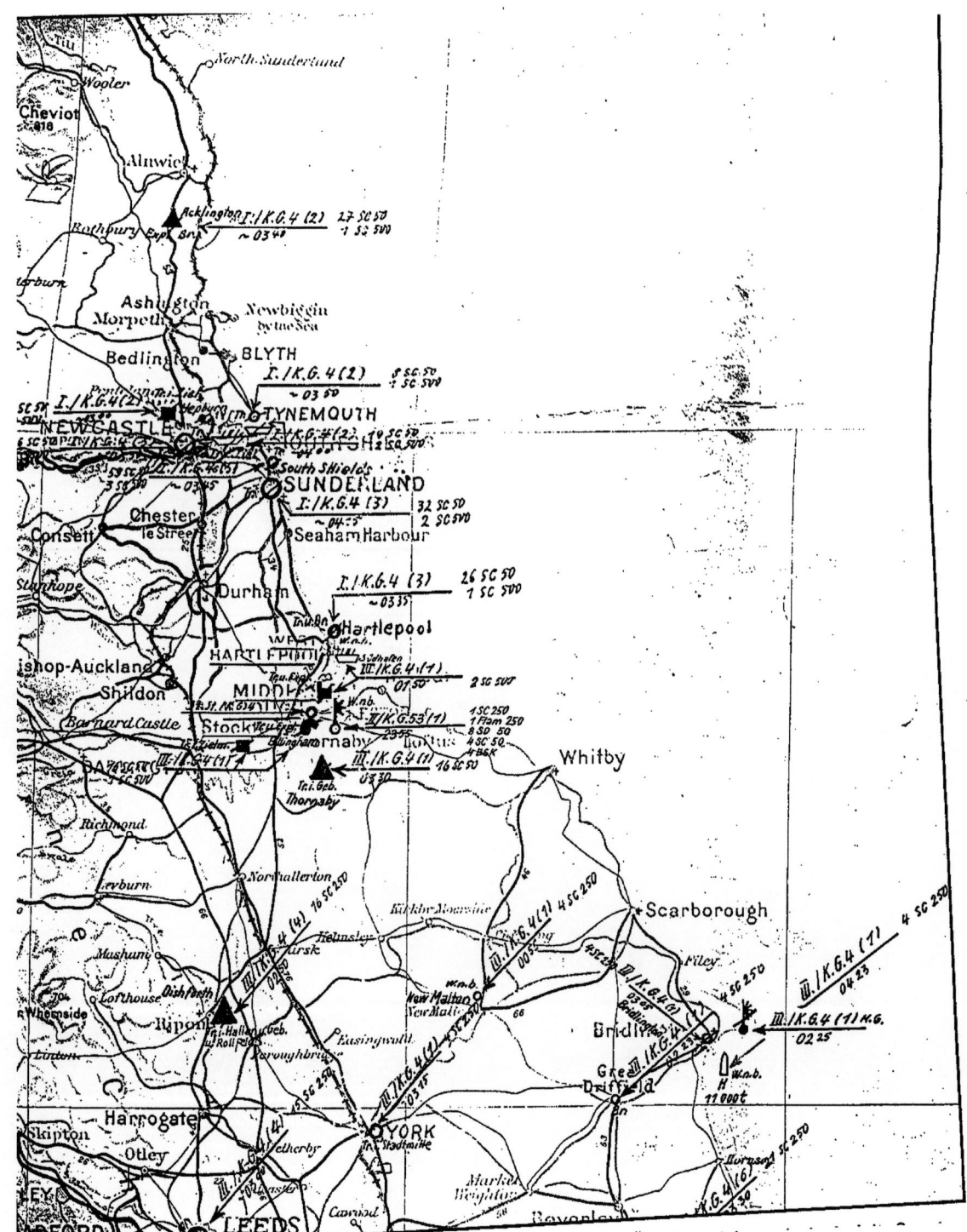

Photo 12.

Operational schedule for attacks by units of KG4, on Northeast England on 24th/25th August 1940; The date bombs first fell on Leeds. Yeadon is not detailed, nor is it even shown on the map !

Copyright: Bundesarchiv

Build Up

On 1st September, 1940, control of the airfield transferred from No.13 Group to No.12 Group Fighter Command but, on 6th October, No.4 Group Bomber Command established its Communications Flight and Central Maintenance Organisation at Yeadon to facilitate extensive overhaul and repair work. Shortly thereafter, five Armstrong Whitworth Whitley V's and five Vickers Wellington I's were to be seen bogged down in the marshy ground on the south-west side of the field.

Although Hitler postponed Operation Sealion - the invasion of England - on 15th September, the aerial battle continued; and it was indeed fortunate that the Luftwaffe remained unaware that ".....at the Vickers works in Sheffield, stood the only steam drop-hammer in Britain capable of forging crankshaft stampings for the Rolls-Royce Merlin engine. This 15 ton machine was kept running for months by an eight man team working around the clock, to achieve 84 stampings per shift....."[1] Had the drop-hammer been bombed out of existence who can say what the outcome might have been; not only for the Battle of Britain but of the war itself!?

Those at Yeadon were as ignorant of this situation as were the enemy, and as construction work on the factory progressed so an increasing number of key workers arrived. One was Leslie Stott from Brighouse who, later (as did Jack Rowbotham), became an AVRO Inspector - given Inspectors Number: 'RY33' - who was greeted on his first morning in the works by Bill Wellings, who had been sent from Newton Heath to organise the lay-out of production.

Another early arrival from Newton Heath, was Sam Ashworth, a Senior Inspector, whose task was to supervise the setting up of the Anson wing assembly. Leslie Stott recalled that "..... at that time it was all very haphazard; we were there a good time before the long-haired chap from the film studios came to comouflage the place.

Randall Paine, originally in textile design, joined AVRO in the Stores department of its Chadderton factory in September, 1939, "..... I soon formed an opinion that as far as raw materials and finished machine parts were concerned everything had been planned, but no thought seemed to have been given to the storage and subsequent assembly of these parts. In other words it had always been customary

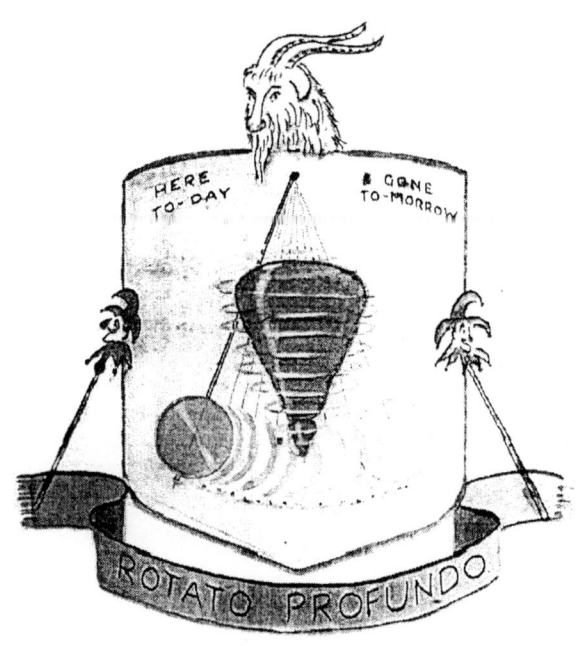

STORES

Photo 14.

This would seem to have very little meaning and appears to have no connection with stores.

A rotating top and a swinging pendulem surmounted by a goats head and supported by two jesters dolls, just don't mean a thing and neither does the motto.

(We understand this design has been dedicated to a Manchester gentleman named Mr Green). copyright J. Bruce.

---

1   Quoted in 'Harvest of Messerschmitts' D. Knight. See Bibliography.

Build Up

to store parts in number sequence, no consideration being given to size variation, which was alright for pre-war conditions when output was nominal but, with the changed conditions, immediate improvements in procedure were needed.

I was able to make drastic changes which, fortunately, worked successfully ..... and, out of the blue, C.J. Wood, my Head of Department, who had been very courteous and responsive to my plans, asked me to transfer to the Yeadon factory - which, until then, I had never heard of! - where my pay would rise to £4.10.0d (£4.50) per week (Manna from Heaven, indeed), to put into practice the new system. This turned out to be much easier than I had expected as a result of new workers coming fresh to this kind of work and, ultimately, the system was completely put into practice, Mr. Harper insisting on a professional approach to everything. The routine was, briefly, this: various stores were set up, *each being pertinent to and sited alongside a specific area of work*, e.g. tail section, nose or wing assembly and so on, with the overall system being known as Kit Marshalling. The Storekeeper, usually a female, held a chart for each kit which indicated its drawing number, and the full description of each item in the kit, and the quantity of every item required. The kits were prepared by the storekeeper - who stored everything as conveniently as possible - and when, say, a fitter, arrived with his ticket to draw D1/24: kit to equip the nose section of an Anson, that is what he received; no more and no less; with no time being wasted as would have been the case had he, and hundreds of others, been required to walk to and from a Main Store at the other end of the factory, and queue for individual items! Any shortages in the kits were dealt with on a Red ticket - IMMEDIATE ACTION - by the Progress Manager, Ken Goodman, whose job, I always thought, a real thankless task. **(Photo 14 see previous page)**

Everything, yes every single item, no matter how small was numbered. Nose section became D1, front fuselage D2, centre section (fuselage and stubs of wings on a Lancaster) F1, D3 and D4 being separate parts of the rear fuselage of an Anson and so on all the way down the assembly line, with even the smallest piece of machined metal having its own number. It was a huge job sorting it out to begin with but, without doubt, Kit Marshalling more than proved its worth .....".

The 'Mr. Harper' mentioned was Henry William Harper, appointed Chief Executive and Works Manager at Yeadon. A Londoner, he first moved north to serve as Chief Engineer with the Lancashire Aeroplane Club at Woodford, prior to joining A.V. Roe & Company Limited, with whom he was put in charge of engine installation. Thereafter, for seven years, he travelled extensively in South America and the Middle East representing the Company at demonstrations of its aircraft to foreign Governments, and in supervising the carrying out of ensuing contracts. Subsequently he spent some time at Newton Heath and, on taking up his duties at Yeadon, had been fifteen years in the service of 'AVRO'.

**FLECTERE SI NEQUEO SUPEROS
ACHERONTA MOVEBO**

PROGRESS

Photo 15.

Here we have the pen and pencil, symbols of a lot of spilled ink.

There are superimposed on a drab circle of the weekly round, while standing as upright as possible, is a corkscrew.

We are in some doubt as to the meaning of this. It may refer to an instrument used by progress chasers, or it may suggest the possibility that chasers are so crooked that they could hide behind one.

The motto is one which sums up the outlook of the indomitable progress chaser:

If I cannot move the Gods, then I will stir up hell. copyright J. Bruce.

Henry Harper was, undoubtedly, a very forceful character who brooked no interference with his

- 26 -

way of doing things. One former subordinate, who thought him a martinet, stated that workers feared rather than admired him, and that even his family took second place to his work. To be fair to the man, however, it has to be said that, in wartime Britain, the pressures and demands placed upon those at his level of management in the munitions industries, were enormous and constant; and one needed to be a very strong individual to withstand the strain, and yet run a successful enterprise. For his efforts he was awarded the M.B.E.

Appointed as Assistant Works Manager and Harper's deputy, was twenty years old Edward R. Holdsworth, a graduate of the Airspeed College;[2] a man of quite disparate character and background who, at times, found himself being required to act as a 'foil' to his superior. There were, of course, others who played a key role in the top management of the factory.

"Perhaps the most influential person in the whole organisation was Morgan Harris, the Chief Buyer," said Jack Kell, formerly a jig and tool Design Draughtsman at the factory, "his was a most vital, complex and unenviable job. Similarly, the Chief Accountant had an awesome responsibility. He was K.B. Crewe who, for some reason which I cannot now recall, became commonly known as the Mad Karoo!"

Such was the urgency to get things under way appointments were taken up piecemeal, with numerous managers, staff and shop floor workers, arriving to commence duties before their respective departments were fully operational; the first official work undertaken by the factory beginning many weeks before the building was completed.

The initial job contract involved the processing of designs for the Armstrong Whitworth Albemarle: a twin-engined reconnaissance aircraft, the construction of which had been specifically earmarked for factories which had no previous experience in the manufacture of aircraft. This plan was soon shelved, however, when it became necessary to introduce a modification to its wings, and thus no Albemarles were built at Yeadon.

The Ministry of Aircraft Production (MAP), under whose jurisdiction the factory came, then allocated it a contract for the construction of the Tornado: a Hawker designed, single engined fighter (conceived to fulfil Air Ministry Specification F.18/37) to be fitted with the Rolls-Royce Vulture V engine, driving a Rotol or de Havilland propeller, with the engine rated at 1980 h.p.

During the year beginning October, 1940, five Tornados, and 100 sets of drawings thereof were produced at Yeadon; one of these aircraft being flown at Woodford on 29th August 1941. **(Photo 16 - centre pages)**

The Vulture engine, design of which had begun in 1935, was also intended to power the Handley Page Halifax, the Vickers Warwick and the AVRO Manchester, but it soon became apparent that it had inherent faults and only the Manchester saw service with the engine. Ultimately, the Vulture proved so troublesome it brought about the withdrawal of that aircraft and the cancellation of the Tornado contract.

The Typhoon, Hawker's successor to the Tornado, inherited not only obvious design characteristics from its ill-fated predecessor but, also, some completed wings and components manufactured at Yeadon. Thus, bearing in mind the illustrious record achieved by the Typhoon later - not least of all when flown by members of No.609 (West Riding) Squadron - it could be argued that the time spent on the Tornado by personnel at Yeadon was not entirely unproductive!

Throughout the Autumn and Winter of 1940/41 an increased effort was made by the Contractors to finalise construction of the factory, and this was ultimately accomplished during February, 1941; twenty-one months after planning permission had been sought from the local Authority.

On completion, the building stood 1,740 feet (530 metres) long and 740 feet (225.5 metres) wide, containing therein (including a basement) an area of 1,514,190 square feet (140,724 square metres), the base of which was composed of concrete 7" (17.78 cms) thick; the overall structure being built of brick and reinforced concrete on a steel frame. On the inside the only walls were of the 'blast' variety - erected to afford protection during anticipated air attacks - and those used to partition offices; thus the very long, flat roof was supported, except at its extremities, solely by steel pillars.

---

2   An old boy of Bradford Grammar School, he had obtained initial flying lessons at Yeadon (with the Y.A.C.) before gaining his civil aviation certificate in a DH60G Moth, at Portsmouth, on 28th May 1939

Build Up

The author has been unable to ascertain details of the cost involved but, given that the AVRO factory at Chadderton, completed three years earlier, which covered an area almost exactly half the size of that at Yeadon, involved an outlay of £1,000,000, conclusions can be drawn which might not be too far from the mark; even though there were considerable differences in the topography, and requirements, at each site.

The general layout of the factory, viewed from its northern end, began with the machine shop and tool room - the first sections to be completed, and the first to commence operations - followed by others devoted to sub-assembly, various stores, and a blanketed-off area, officially termed the Spray Shop, but more commonly known as the 'Dope House'. The remainder of the ground floor, a considerable area, was given over to the main assemblies. A huge canteen, comprising several separate dining rooms for the different echelons of the workforce, with seating for 7,000 was positioned on the western side, above which were situated the management, design, purchasing and administration offices, from the inward side of which ran a balcony, from where a comprehensive view of the works could be obtained. At the opposite, eastern, side of the building, but below ground-floor level, a basement contained the important wood stores. Around the whole building ran the aforementioned roadway, wide enough for two vehicles to pass, on the outside of which but still within a deeply sloping outer roof, were air-raid shelters and toilet facilities for in excess of 8,500 people; albeit that, in the latter case, not all at once! **(Photo 16a - page 32)**

In an era when air-conditioning was virtually unknown in British factories and where, in the main, very rudimentary heating was the norm, it came as a pleasant surprise for new employees to find on arrival at Yeadon that, under the supervision of a resident engineer, Jack Lunnas, they were provided with an extremely up-to-date, American style, heating and ventilation system. This comprised a series of water sprays through which air was passed to be 'cleaned' as it circulated throughout the factory via metal ducts. Additionally, adequate piped water heating was provided by large 'Lancashire' boilers situated, as were the water filters, on the eastern side of the building, from where smoke emissions were channelled underground to a chimney, partially hidden by trees, alongside Coney House Farm (both farm and chimney remain to this day).

At the southern end of the main assembly area, large hangar-type doors opened onto a 30ft (9.14 metres) wide, metalled road, built to facilitate the

Photo 18a

Leeds born F/O Jarvis Blaney.

Jarvis Blaney was posted to No.20 E.F.T.S. as an instructor, on 12th April 1941, having served throughout the Battle of Britain with No.609 Squadron-which he had joined as a founding member, at Yeadon, in 1936. During June 1940, he flew a Spitfire as escort to the aircraft carrying Winston Churchill, when the Prime Minister made dangerous flights to Orleans and Tours, in vain attempts to persuade the French to fight on !. Blaney was promoted Flight Lieutenant while at Yeadon but, on 4th January 1942, was posted to No.4 E.F.T.S., at Brough. He was awarded the A.F.C. in 1943 and survived the war. He died aged 84, during February 1995 at Otley, within the sound of activities at the airfield he knew so well.

movement of partially completed aircraft across to final assembly; this being more popularly known as 'Finals' of 'Flight Sheds', contained in an existing pre-war hangar, opened in 1938, and several others, specifically constructed on the northern perimeter of the aerodrome (in an area now covered by the terminal building and car parks of Leeds/Bradford Airport), ultimately occupying almost 210,000 sq. feet (19,516 sq. metres) of floor space.

To have built what, at the time, was considered to be the largest factory under one roof in Europe was no mean achievement. To attempt, thereafter, to hide it from the prying eyes of the Luftwaffe was thought by some to be asking a great deal, for had not that wise sage Confucious said; "Nothing is more obvious than that which man attempts to conceal?". Nevertheless, the safety of the factory and its workforce were paramount and, under the auspices of the M.A.P., the responsibility for undertaking this complex, and daunting, task was indeed given to the aforementioned "long haired chap from the film studios".

He, and his staff, more used to the demands of the silver screen, aided in their task at Yeadon by local labour, conceived a veritable masterpiece of deception. To eliminate tell-tale shadows, grassed earth was banked at 45° along the sides of the building up to the level of its flat roof upon which was laid out a replica of the fields to the west of Coney House Farm, as they had appeared before construction of the factory began. Imitation farm buildings, stone walls a duck pond and dummy animals were added - and moved around from time to time - and fabric and wire 'bushes' and 'hedges' were foliated or de-foliated according to the season. **(Photos 17 inside rear cover, Photo 18 - centre pages)**

The factory covered some 30 acres (12.14 hectares) yet this impressive camouflage was achieved for an outlay of £20,000; even so, a tidy sum for those days. That it was successful is borne out not only by the comments of Allied airmen who invariably found the factory extremely difficult to locate but, more convincingly, from the fact that the enemy were unable to do so: a subject to which we shall return later in the narrative.

One local man involved in the work of camouflage was Newton Storey, a one time demolition and haulage contractor who, postwar, was landlord of the Crown Inn at Yeadon. Sadly, he died in 1962.

On 17th March, 1941, soon after completion of the factory, No.20 Elementary Flying Training School formed at RAF Station, Yeadon, it having been transferred to No.51 Group, Flying Training Command.

This brought about the departure of No.4 Group Central Maintenance Organisation; firstly, to RAF Station Dishforth, thence to RAF Station York (Clifton) where it would remain, under the jurisdiction of No.48 Maintenance Unit (48 MU) and Handley Page, until the cessation of hostilities.

On 24th March, the first aircraft to be employed by No.20 EFTS: eight DH.82 Tiger Moths, were flown in from No.12 EFTS Prestwick, on the disbandment of that unit. Unfortunately, their identities were not recorded! [3]

Seven days later, Squadron Leader N.J. Capper AFC, arrived to assume command of the School; being followed, within two weeks, by Flight Lieutenant S.P. Richards AFC, appointed his deputy, and seven other flying instructors (five officers and two sergeants); one other officer to be Link Trainer instructor and Flying Officer R.W. Hemsley, who was appointed adjutant.

On 6th April thirty pupil-pilots arrived from No.10 ITW (Scarborough), to form the First Course: their training began next day.

The 'On Strength' establishment (on that date) was RAF: 17 Officers; WAAF: 3 Officers; Other Ranks: 365, of whom 30 were under training (u/t) pilots, 155 on 'Starfish' detachment (personnel detailed to maintain 'starfish' decoy-flares, locally), plus 3 Officers and 104 Other Ranks of 'C' company, 7th Battalion, The West Yorkshire Regiment, engaged on Station defence duties.

All ranks (and their ground activities) were accommodated either in the former No.609 Squadron cantonment within the aerodrome perimeter, or in a hutted camp built on fields west of the aerodrome, immediately to the north of the Dam. Personnel deployed at several heavy anti-aircraft batteries, situated in the immediate vicinity, were billeted in a camp in Carlton village.

The first solo-flight by a pupil of No.20 EFTS took place on 22nd April but, frustratingly, once again, no details of his identity or that of his aircraft were recorded! He was soon followed by others and the first successful (thirteen) cadets were posted away on 16th May.

On 8th July, Squadron Leader Capper was transferred to RAF College, Cranwell, to become its CFI, being replaced as O.C. No.20 EFTS by Wing Commander J.B. Stockbridge. Six days later "......Messrs Blackburn Aircraft Co. Ltd., assumed responsibility for all services in connection with the School, with the exception of flying training of pupils..." Thus, No.20 EFTS ceased to be an exclusive preserve of the RAF: a fact confirmed by Vera Marland (née Houseman):

"I was employed at Yeadon by Blackburn Aircraft as a timekeeper. At first I had the use of an office in a little hut which also contained the crew-room. The hut was next to the officers, by the hangars, but because it was low down we couldn't see all over the aerodrome (due to undulating land the eastern edge of the airfield was, and remains, hidden from view at ground level at this point: Author) so we were moved to the top floor of a building that became known as the Watch Office (the top floor of the 'Club House': Author). One of my jobs was to log details of all the flying training done, and to mark the progress of each student. Poor lads, they

3   See Appendix C.

Build Up

remained unaware that I knew before they did which of them would fail!

I spent many hours alone in that hut, and later, the Watch Office on dark mornings and evenings when no flying was taking place, and everyone else seemed to have disappeared. Not all that pleasant in wartime I can tell you.

There were quite a few lads at Yeadon who serviced the training planes who, like us, were civilians employed by Blackburns and if anybody disputes this tell them I've still got my Blackburns official pass to allow me onto the aerodrome, and we were there until 20 EFTS was disbanded in January, 1942!"

Despite the shortcomings of Yeadon as the location for a flying training School [4] such was the desperate demand for pilots that, throughout the summer of 1941, activities increased at a pace. During August the unit was upgraded to a type 'B' School - three Flights - ultimately utilising in excess of fifty Tiger Moths (see Appendices); and staff and pupils believed the importance of the School had been recognised when, on 17th October, Marshal of The Royal Air Force, Lord Trenchard (The 'Father' of the RAF), accompanied by the Air Officer Commanding No.51 Group Flying Training Command, Air Commodore B.E. Baker DSO., MC., AFC made a visit of inspection.

Within a week (on the 23rd), however, instructions were received for the closure of No.20 EFTS in two stages: "....first portion on 3rd December, the second on 3rd January 1942. The Station to be transferred to the Ministry of Aircraft Production.."

The final day on which flying by pupils took place was 22nd December: 8 hours (Dual), 1 hour 05 mins.(Solo). Two days later fifty-one pupils were sent on leave, with orders to report, thereafter, to other units.

During its short, but busy, existence No.20 EFTS provided initial flying instruction to more than two hundred and fifty would-be pilots, many going on to gain their 'wings' (one can but wonder how many of them survived the war?). While at Yeadon they flew a total of 11,684 hours - 7,072 Dual and 4,612 Solo - the highest in any month being: Dual 1,248 in September and Solo 854 in August. Thirty-three of the School's aircraft were involved in flying accidents - four of them at least twice - several 'prangs' resulting in severe damage. Fortunately, however (and unusually for this type of unit), no fatalities or serious injuries were sustained by instructors or pupils..

After its disbandment, No.20 EFTS was no reformed elsewhere [5]. The final entry in it's records (9th January 1942) stated that all RAF personnel had been cleared from the Station and that "...staff of Messrs Blackburn Aircraft Co. Ltd.....remained to dispose of all equipment according to instructions..."

Although the existence of No.20 EFTS was of short duration its activities were, nonetheless, important - especially when one considers the fortunes of the war at that period and deserve to be recorded here; and, not least of all, because the unit was extant during the months when the factory was engaged in building its first 100 Ansons!

Another largely forgotten contribution to the war effort in Yeadon, was made in a small cluster of buildings situated to the west of Novia Plantation. This tiny unit, tiny that is in comparison with the factory 600 yards (546 metres) away to the east, was utilised throughout the period of hostilities for the testing and overhaul of Bristol aero-engines; a number of which were built by sub-contractors in the Leeds/Bradford area - one such being situated in what is currently the Hammonds Sauce Works at Apperley Bridge on the outskirts of Bradford.

'Bristols', as the small complex in Cemetery Road became widely known, was not involved with its larger neighbour, having been built for a different purpose but, nonetheless, its presence was such a continuously noisy factor in local life at the time, it is worthy of brief mention here.

For security reasons, no weather forecasts were available to the public during the war, and it gradually became the habit to listen to the volume of noise emanating from the unsilenced engines being run-up at Bristols' (which operated 24 hours a day, 7 days a week), to try and gauge the direction of the wind and thus the type of weather to be expected.

---

4   Up to October 1942 when Davidstow Moor, Cornwall, became operational Yeadon was located at the highest point above sea-level of any Service aerodrome.

5   No.20 Elementary and Reserve Flying Training School (No.20 E & RFTS) formed at Gravesend on 1st October 1937, but was disbanded in September 1939.

Not an infallible system, of course, but in those grim days it served as a useful and, sometimes, amusing method for attempting to outwit Mother Nature!

At times the cacophony of sound was very intrusive but, as far as the author can recall, there were few complaints that sleep was being disturbed or that the environment was being destroyed; and the few who did object were quickly reminded: "There is a war on!"

Back across the A658, the first substantial contract awarded to the factory was in respect of the AVRO Anson, so named after a former British Admiral, a twin-engined monoplane derived from a six passenger civil transport: the AVRO type 652. The Anson was 42ft.3" (12.80 metres) in length with a single span, fabric covered, wooden wing of 56ft 6" (17.22 metres). The Mark I, of which 7,000 were ultimately built in Britain was powered, initially, by two Armstrong-Siddeley Cheetah IX engines producing a maximum speed of 188 m.p.h. (300 k.p.h.) and weighed, empty, 5,000lbs/5500lbs (2265Kg/2491Kg). Jigs for the Anson were transferred to Yeadon from Newton Heath in May, 1941, under an initial contract: B61695/39 for a total of 1,000 Mark I's of which the final 50 were allocated to Yeadon; and, ultimately, through further contracts the factory was responsible for the production of more than 4,000 Ansons, in several variants. **(Photo 19,20 & 21 - centre pages)**

Captain Worrall[6] said of the Anson that it was ".....slow, placid and stable and, if trimmed correctly and left to its own devices, would fly on until its fuel ran out, before going into a glide and then, if the ground was level, would probably make a reasonable job of landing itself". Hugh Bergel, who reached senior rank in the Air Transport Auxiliary, also gained considerable experience of the Anson. He recalled it was "..... perhaps the best of all bad weather machines, with its low speed, its Spitfire-like stability, and its almost Beaufighter forward view ....."

The Anson was the first low-wing monoplane produced by AVRO and, similarly, the first to employ a retractable undercarriage. On 6th March, 1936, it became the first monoplane to enter service with the R.A.F. when Anson Mk.I. K6153 joined No.48 Squadron at Manston and, thereafter, the type was destined to serve with the R.A.F. for thirty-two years: a remarkable length of time for an aircraft considered obsolete as an operational type as early as 1940!

Such was the desperate shortage of front line aircraft at the time, however, the Anson was pressed into service in a variety of rôles, including that of making attacks on enemy shipping (for which it was certainly not designed), in addition to its intended coastal reconnaissance and communications duties. As the war progressed the diversity of its workload, and that of its variants, increased to cover radio countermeasures, air-ambulance and air-taxi operations, and, in this latter capacity, when flown by the Air Transport Auxiliary (ATA), the type logged almost ten million miles with a safety record second to none.

It was, however, in the training of thousands of Allied aircrew, at various locations at home and overseas, that the Anson really discovered its raison d'être and, today, there are still hundreds of men [7] of many nations, who can point, with some affection, to a 'Faithful Annie' in their log book.

Of the 11,020 Ansons built - 8,138 in the United Kingdom and 2,882 in Canada - half the domestic output, and spares enough for 900 more, were produced at Yeadon. That this was achieved in less than six years is remarkable enough, but even more astonishing when it is realised, that the task was accomplished by a workforce which, very largely, was unskilled. Thus it is pertinent here to consider how, and why, such workers came to Yeadon, and in what way did they react to the situation?

---

6   Who was appointed Aerodrome Controller and Chief Test Pilot at Yeadon.
7   Many women too!

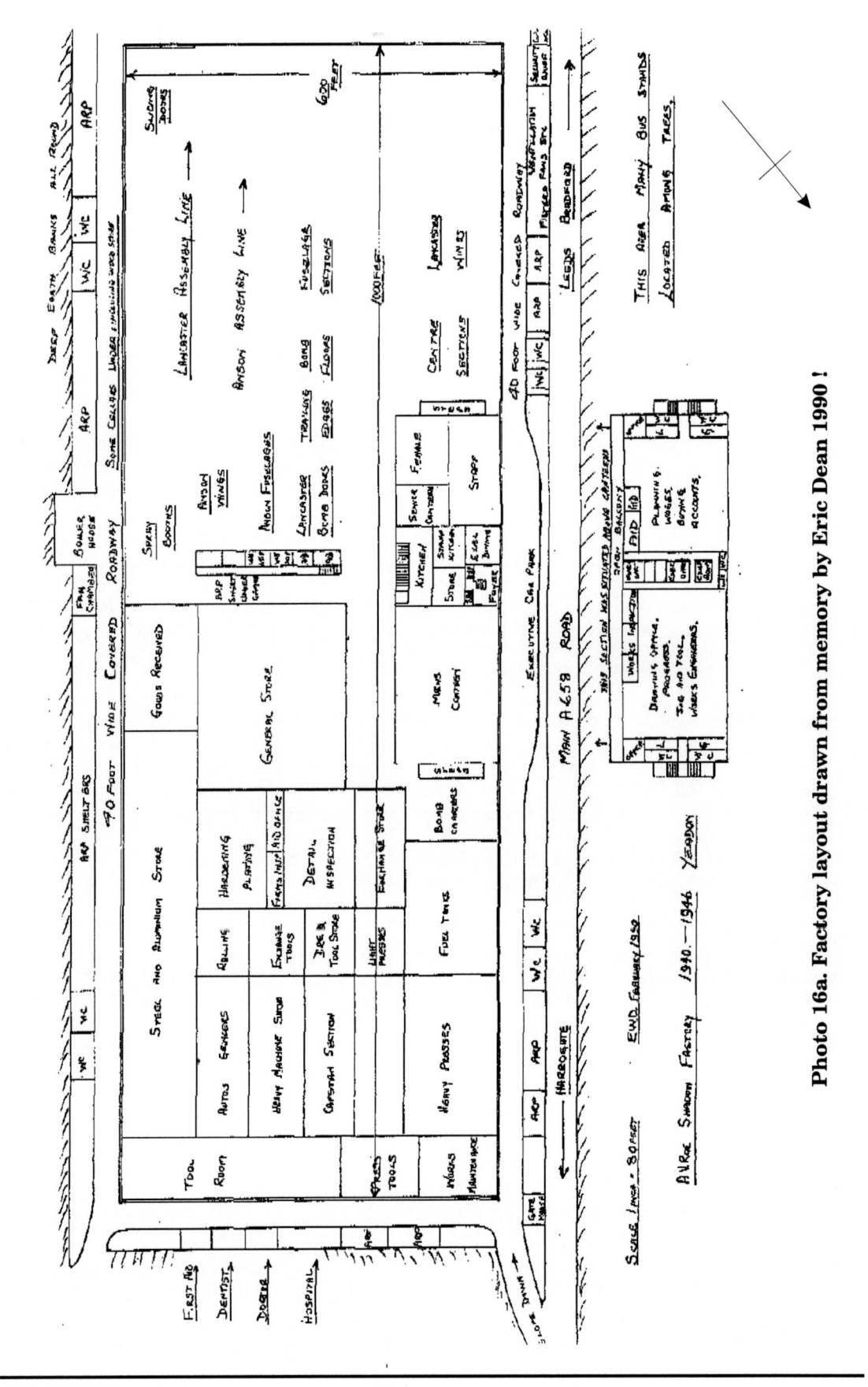

Build Up

Photo 16a. Factory layout drawn from memory by Eric Dean 1990!

Conscription

'From quiet homes and first beginnings, out to the undiscovered ends.' Hilaire Belloc.

'GO TO IT' was a slogan issued by the Home Secretary, Herbert Morrison, to urge those engaged in war work to greater effort. This was followed, on 17th March, 1941, by a further entreaty put out via the BBC and the National Newspapers which proclaimed:

"Womanpower for the war-effort" - 'that was the call today from the Minister of Labour, Ernest Bevin, as he announced the first step in a massive mobilisation plan. Registration of 20-21 year old women will begin next month (men from 18-41 had been so liable since the outbreak of war) with the aim of filling vital jobs in industry and the auxiliary services .....'

'..... Only a few days ago Mr. Bevin urged 100,000 women to step forward and volunteer, with the words: "I cannot offer them a delightful life, I want them to come forward in the spirit that they are going to suffer some inconvenience but with a determination to see us through. Women are desperately needed to take over all kinds of jobs to free men for active service ...."

Call for 100,000 women to do war work

Photo 22.

Poster issued by the Ministry of Labour and National Service, 15th March 1941.

Out of the kitchen and into the factories for Britain's women at war.

'As yet, married women with young children are exempt but those who can do war work locally will be backed-up by a huge expansion in day and night nurseries, and child-minding systems'.

"Transfer of women from their home is one of the biggest industrial problems of the war", said Mr. Bevin, "I am putting pressure on management to give greater attention to the reception of women and facilities for their comfort. The first month in a new job will be the worst". Prophetic words indeed, as many ex-munitions workers could testify.

The drive for young women coincided with one for men aged 41 and 42; the male trainees to earn £3.0.6d (£3.03p) and female £1.18.0d (£1.90) per week! By August, 1941, 2,000,000 women in Britain had registered but only 87,000 had gone into the uniformed services or the factories. Organisations for dealing with this influx simply could not cope. Many women felt let-down, and there was a poor response to further appeals.

The situation was not helped by the attitude of some management and trade unions who still held prejudicial views on the employment of women, - albeit for different reasons.

Pre-war, women employed in teaching, banking, nursing (and some other professions) who left to get married were not, normally, reinstated thereafter, and the employment of women in vast numbers during the war was not done for any altruistic reasons but, simply, one of necessity. Calculations had shown that by the end of 1941 more than 3,000,000 additional personnel would be required in the services, and essential industries, and up to half that number would have to be women, as not enough men would remain available.

The end of 1941 saw the conscription of unmarried women, between the ages of 18 and 30, into the uniformed services, essential industries and civil defence, and even those between 30 and 40 years of age were required to register for war work, although married women were exempted and those with children under 14 could not be 'directed' into a job which took them away from home.

By 1943, 1.5 million women were employed in essential industries; 600,000 of them in engineering, and *no other country* conscripted female labour. Had it not been so, it seems doubtful if the war effort in Britain could have been sustained, and the debt owed by the Nation to women, - not least to those who, though exempted, nevertheless volunteered, - is enormous. 'Bevin Boys', became the popular name for young men conscripted to work

Conscription

in the coal mines but, equally, 'Bevin Girls' might have been applied to their female counterparts involved in other industries, - they undoubtedly earned it.

The Bevin mentioned was Ernest Bevin, Minister of Labour and National Service, who hailed from the West Country: creator and General Secretary of the Transport and General Workers Union (TGWU) who, during the General Strike of 1926, had said "It will be the greatest Godsend to this Country if Mr. Churchill is out of office for evermore". Yet, in May 1940, when Winston Churchill assumed the mantle of Prime Minister, it was Ernest Bevin, not then an M.P., for whom he sent to request him to take on the daunting, but absolutely vital, responsibility of running the Ministry of Labour and National Service, within the Coalition Government. Fortunately, after initial misgivings, Bevin accepted and soon proved he was both brave and fair-minded enough to be the ideal choice. **(Photo 23 - centre pages)**

Under the 'Emergency Powers Act' of May, 1940, he held awesome powers to *'direct any person in the United Kingdom to perform any service specified'*. In addition, he could decree what wages would be paid, what hours would be worked and under what conditions. Within the legislation any worker could be directed to do any work, in any part of the country. What Bevin decided was essential work became such, and employees in essential industries could not leave their jobs without written approval of an official of the Ministry of Labour!

Both Churchill and Bevin fully realised that without the full backing of the working class people of Britain the war could not be won. Bevin had an instinctive understanding of people, and earned their respect, - if not affection, - by his tough, uncompromising, capabilities; recognised earlier by Churchill. It is to their everlasting credit that, despite class and political differences, they were prepared to work together for the greater good of the country.

When Ernest Bevin took over his Ministry he was given a virtual free reign by Churchill, but Britain still had 1,000,000 unemployed despite more than that number having been called-up for active service. The engineering industry, including that part of it involved in war work, was critically denuded of many skilled men, who, of necessity, during the days of depression in the 'thirties had taken jobs elsewhere; thus, in May, 1940, the nation faced the probability of an industrial disaster just as much as a military one.

It was then that Bevin showed his real mettle: he brought Employers and Unions together as never before, getting them to accept, among other things, better working conditions for employees, and an agreed rate for the job; plus the consent of the craft unions, - though not without a struggle, - to allow skilled jobs to be broken down into several operations, thus enabling the use of semi-skilled and newly-trained operatives, including women, to be used.

This latter move was a real break-through in industrial co-operation and was, undoubtedly, the main ingredient which made possible the production of a vast number of aircraft, and other war material, by a largely unskilled workforce.

It was under these circumstances that an ever increasing number of workers - the majority unskilled - arrived at Yeadon and, during 1941, what had been a trickle became a steady flow of new faces; of whom by far the largest number were conscripts, directed - in some cases despite their protestations - to work there for as long as was deemed necessary. Some arrived via the Kirkstall Training Centre, but a greater number of men and women commenced duties at the massive, man-made cavern alongside the A658 knowing little about engineering or aeroplanes, and even less about their manufacture. Incredible as it now appears, most were to learn their new 'trades' as they went along; gaining experience from the few specialists available or, more often, by following the example of fellow workers who had been at the factory just a few weeks longer than themselves!

This very basic, but successful, system was made possible by manufacturing processes being broken down, where possible, into operations which could be handled by the 'greenest' new recruit, with no-one being expected to run before they could walk. Jack Rowbotham remembered that "Initially we few skilled workers were employed doing jobs anywhere on the 'planes, and teaching those who were newly arrived - some of them even had to be shown how to use a screw-driver - but, later, as things progressed, we were moved to specific tasks on wing, tail-plane or fuselage assemblies, depending on our special abilities. The three men who bore the brunt of responsibility, were Horace Cooper, who was in charge of Anson wing assembly, Leonard Baines who similarly looked after the fuselage, and Dick Cliff who was in charge of Anson detail-fitting. Pre-war Dick had been a shop-fitter with Curtis of Leeds, and all three were highly skilled tradesmen, and there is no doubt that without the likes of them the place would not have functioned".

One of the very first unskilled female workers to be employed was Marion O'Neill (nee Fish) who recalled: "When I started work in the wire-splicing department (wire was used for the controls of an aircraft) the only others there were two or three men, and one of them had been a tram driver before going to AVRO, but it was he who taught me to splice. What a huge place AVRO was - not very welcoming at 7 o'clock on a dark winter morning, when you had travelled on a cold smokey bus from Bradford. We worked the clock round, doing twelve hour shifts six, and sometimes seven days a week and, when we were fully trained we worked six weeks on days and then three weeks on nights. Youngsters today couldn't cope with that".

Those early days were also recalled by eighty-two years old Mrs. A.M. Cooper who, as Miss Bennett, "..... first went into the splicing department and apart from Marion Fish and myself, there were only three other girls: 'Lucy' (later Mrs. L. Camp), Miss E. Hall (Mrs. E. Dennison) and Alice Hutchinson. Our charge-hand was Syd Wood, and they were a nice bunch to work with but, Oh dear me, those hours we worked were long .....".

What Mrs. Cooper omitted to say was that, at 35 years of age, and although not required to do so, she volunteered for war work. Sadly, she was to suffer a serious illness precipitated by the constant noise and long hours.

Marion O'Neill added to the story of the splicing department "..... the number in our little section grew to about thirty, and there we were hour after hour banging away with mallets at wires placed on wooden blocks. Sounds boring, and it was, but they were the nicest lot of workers I've ever been amongst .....".

Not everyone, however, was thought of similarly, as Norman Sherburn readily admitted: "..... I have a reputation for being a troublemaker, not being afraid to argue with the bosses about the way things were being done, or in respect of workers' rights .....".

He was 'directed' to Yeadon, having previously been involved on war work at Fowlers, the world renowned engineers in Hunslet and at English Electric at Thornbury, following a period spent as an Instructor at the Government Training Centre at Pontefract. "..... at AVRO I had charge of two shifts of four jig-boring machines, my main job being all trig' working out the co-ordinates from drawings. All the jig-borers had to do was put the piece of steel on his or her machine, square it up and work to my figures, calculated down to two-thousands of an inch. In our shop and the tool room it was absolutely essential to keep things dust-free, a near impossible task with all that 'green' labour about ..... I've always held strong political views and there was a time when Special Branch were asking questions about me, but no matter what I said about Communism and Russia I always tried to do my best to win the war .....".

After being 'moved' several more times, Norman Sherburn finished the war at the Sunbeam car plant having, in the meantime, worked at more than thirty establishments "..... they obviously thought that by keeping me on the trot I couldn't really undermine authority at any one place, ..." he added with a wry smile.

One who followed a completely different, and more permanent path was Roland Scatchard - whose photographs and encouragement were the catalyst for this book - who recalled "I was the sixth wood-worker taken on at AVRO, being involved at first in building the jigs for the Anson. I was then moved into the new Pattern-making Shop where eventually between fifty and sixty men were employed doing very skilled work. I say men because ours was the only department in the whole works never to employ women". **(Photo 24,25 - centre pages)**

Before introducing other reminiscences of that early period, it is, perhaps, sensible to take a wider look at life outside the factory - irrespective of the demands of war - as it affected the people of Britain at that time. For those not then alive and, in particular, those born since the 1960's it must be almost impossible to comprehend what 'normality' meant, even in peacetime, during that era. The whole attitude of society was very much more strictured as to acceptable standards of morality and behaviour; respect for ones elders and to authority, and in dealings with ones neighbours. Money, in any quantity, was a great deal more difficult to come by; especially for the working class, and the youth of the nation had neither the financial wherewithal, nor the freedom from official and parental control to 'do their own thing' to a degree that is the norm today. In this very much more affluent and technological age it is difficult to appreciate that good housing (with *inside* toilet facilities); central heating (even to have more than one warm room!); state of the art kitchens; automatic washing-machines; the telephone; T.V.; hi-fi; the Health Service; holidays abroad (indeed *any* holiday, *anywhere*, for more than one week); ones own car; supermarket shopping; money enough to buy (reasonably often) up-to-date clothes and to eat out as a matter of course; the Welfare State and all the other 'benefits' of modern society; including instantaneous world-wide communications via the

Conscription

This design depicts on one half, the happy welcome awaiting new arrivals to the Avro Convalescent home.

The idea is further carried out by the smiling old gentleman surmounting the circle.

The other half is unimportant, and only represents the view of the 12000 employees of the factory.

The surround of padlocked chain seems to have no significance and is probably added to complete a pleasing design. The motto however is very apt and sums up the average trainee: *Soon Ripe, Soon Rotten*

copyright J. Bruce.

EMPLOYMENT OFFICE

telephone, radio and satellite T.V., were just a pipe dream.

Considering these huge differences it is, perhaps, somewhat less difficult to understand why many of those who, during the war years, were compelled to leave home and family for the very first time, found the prospect far more daunting than do their grand-children who, today, set off on journeys taking them half way around the world!

One who underwent considerable apprehension was 'Amy' - her reasons for requesting anonymity will become obvious - who, at the time she was required to register for National Service, was barely eighteen years of age with a staunch, non-conformist, dales farming background.

"The countryside in those days was much more remote, in every way, from the city and town than is the case today. Women, who lived on a farm, seldom left it except on Market Day, to pop to the shops or to go to the Village Church or, in our case Chapel, on Sundays.

From leaving school at fourteen I helped mother in her duties around the farmhouse, and I also did odd-jobs around the farm. But I was not 'employed' and when my papers came my father could not convince the authorities that my presence on the farm was essential, (i.e. a Reserved Occupation [1]). He always had a temper and I suspect this must have made him upset so, in turn, he got the wrong side of some petty official and, not long afterwards, I was notified that instead of being sent into the Land Army [2], as I had expected, I was told I had to go to AVRO at Yeadon. By today's standards it was not that far away but, then, it seemed an awful long way away.

When I went down into the factory on that first morning I had more than butterflies I can tell you. I was so naive (we all were in those days) and it was so big, it just seemed to go on and on forever, and all those hundreds of people, and the noise! To say it came as a shock is not even the start of it, but the biggest shock of all was the terrible language, some of the worst of it from girls no older than myself. It took me weeks to come to terms with it all, and my brother said I was never the same again .....".

To be strictly chronological, Amy's reminiscences should have been inserted a year or so later in the narrative, but as we are currently concerned with the advent of 'conscripts', and as hers is a not too dissimilar story to that of hundreds of other young women who were entering Britains war factories at that time, it is included here. Amy, however, had additional problems to contend with:

"..... I suppose I had been at AVRO about six or seven months when we had a visit from some aircrew from a nearby R.A.F. station (probably one of the No.4 Group Bomber Stations in the Vale of York, from where such excursions were a fairly regular event) [3] and I looked up from my machine to see this pair of startlingly blue eyes looking at me ..... he, John his name was, said 'keep up the good work, we're relying on you', and he chatted on for a few more minutes, but I could only blurt out 'Yes' and 'No', and make silly laughs. Afterwards, I realised he had made a big impression on me, but when I enquired where I could get in touch with

- 36 -

him one of the other girls said I was to forget it as she was already writing to him! Some time later, possibly two months or so, I plucked up courage to ask her how he was, and she hardly looked up from her machine to say 'Oh, he's dead - he was shot down, or something'. I was so shocked I became angry at the matter-of-fact way she had told me, and I rounded on her, but she just looked me straight in the eye and said 'Look, there's a war on, he's the third one I've had whose gone and got himself killed. If you go for boyfriends who fly, this is what can happen'. This really upset me, but for the first time I realised what my work was all about, and afterwards I grumbled less and worked harder to win the war. You never forget those times, you know, and even though I became happily married after the war, I have often wondered what might have been if it had been me that had nerved myself to ask John if I could write to him, and on Remembrance Day it's his face I see when someone says 'We shall remember them.'".

Yet meet we shall, and part and meet again
Where dead men meet, on lips of living men.

        Samuel Butler.

At Yeadon, as in other war factories, the advent of conscripted labour brought together Tories, Socialists, Liberals, more than a sprinkling of Communists and many with no political affiliation whatsoever. Never before, not even during the conflict of 1914-1918, had the different classes of society been brought together in a common endeavour. The catalyst for this seemingly impossible homogeny of diverse talent into what became a highly competent, and successful, enterprise was, simply, necessity. The forces of evil (for that is what they were), under the guise of the Axis powers, had to be repulsed: the alternative was too horrible to contemplate.

The workforce at Yeadon was drawn to a large, but certainly not exclusive, extent from the West Riding of Yorkshire but, given the size of the County, this still meant that many employees were required to make a round trip from their homes (day or night shifts) of many miles: up to 80 miles being involved in some cases. In the early days journeys were made by existing, but war-restricted, public transport, which gave rise to inevitable delays. To obviate a situation which otherwise could have become critical the authorities organised a special bus service for the workers which, ultimately, involved in excess of 150 vehicles; these becoming a familiar sight as they journeyed in long lines to and from the factory. Not surprisingly, their presence caused their drivers, and the Police, many a headache, especially during the 'black-out'. When not in use the buses were parked on specially built roadways within, and partially hidden by, the trees of Novia Plantation, situated across the A658 immediately opposite the factory.

1   This applied to men and women whose civilian occupation was considered to be vital for the good of the Country: essential services including electricity, gas, water, sewerage, coal mining, the medical profession and agriculture (to name but a few) although not everyone employed therein was automatically exempted from call-up for National Service elsewhere. Surprisingly, the oldest of all 'professions' was considered a 'Reserved Occupation' (or, at least, it somehow became accepted as such) and some quite shameless women, rather than suffer what they considered to be the indignity of having to work on the shop floor of a factory, were not above claiming themselves to be 'ladies of the night'. Fortunately, Personnel Managers were quite adept at weeding out those who were, from others who were simply attempting to avoid doing war work; as is confirmed by the following story: At the end of the day of interviews, one of the personnel staff at Yeadon emerged from his office to be told he looked very pleased with himself. "So would you be", came his reply, "if you had just been propositioned by seventeen young ladies and had taken them all on !".

2   The Women's Land Army was one of several modes of war work to which women between the ages of 18 and 31 were conscripted. Those involved went where they were sent and were paid, not by the Government, but by the farmer for whom they worked. By 1943, the WLA numbered 80,000 (a third of whom came from the cities); its members being dressed in a 'uniform' of dark green jersey, jodhpurs (or dungarees) and old-type Boy Scout hats. The 'Land Girls', as they affectionately became known, were a familiar sight in the countryside where they worked 50 hours a week (extremely hard) as replacements for their male counterparts who had gone into the Armed Services. Regrettably, the girls gained an unwarranted notoriety through the innocent, but often naughtily misconstrued, wording of a wartime poster which described them as 'Having their backs to the land'!

3   One of those involved was Fl.Lt. Robert J. Sage of No.77 Squadron, Elvington, later Wing Commander R.J. Sage O.B.E., A.F.C., ultimately Chairman of the Squadron Association and, also, President of Yorkshire Air Museum, until his death in May 1994.

Conscription

Thousands of workers came from much further afield, and this influx of labour created an acute housing problem, which was only resolved - and certainly not overnight - by the mutual co-operation of the M.A.P; the billeting organisations set up by the local Authorities and, not least of all, by the local people who became directly involved.

This simple statement hides the prodigious effort required to overcome massive logistical problems, which included the building of two estates of brick bungalows - totalling 300 dwellings -: one at Westfield, Yeadon; the other at Nunroyd, Guiseley, and a hostel for 700 'single' workers constructed at Greenbanks, Horsforth. In addition, several thousand employees were 'billeted-out' with families in Yeadon, Rawdon and Guiseley, despite the fact that the householders chosen to receive them had little say in the matter!

An unforeseen problem arose in respect of the M.A.P. bungalows which, due to what some people (particularly the younger members of local society) considered to be a similarity in design, were unkindly dubbed the 'Pigeries'. In truth this was an undeserved epithet yet, for many residents, particularly the children involved, the name proved an embarrassment not resolved by the ending of the war, nor the subsequent closure of the factory.

Photo 27. A pair of the MAP bungalows on the Westfield estate, Yeadon, prior to being demolished 1955.

As to the housing of the large, itinerant, workforce there is no one better qualified to comment than Mrs. Judith Murray; formerly Chief Billeting Officer for Aireborough Urban District Council, who was directly involved in the work from 1941 until the end of the war. Her reminiscences were legion but, due to the limitations of space, it is possible to include only the following:

"The authority to billet was vested in the Clerk to the Council and was granted through the Minister of Health. His directives were discussed and then acted upon by local Councillors. At first, in 1940, only one billeting officer - Mr. R. Haley - was appointed but, when it became apparent that the task would prove much bigger than envisaged earlier, two more officers were appointed but they, and Mr. Haley, went on to other things. Then, in 1941, a female officer was appointed (Mrs. J. Murray) at a salary of £200 per annum; an appointment made despite the misgivings of some members of the Council who felt it was not a task to be undertaken by a mere female! Despite this the office was run by a woman, supported by other women, until its closure. Those involved (in addition to Mrs. Murray) included Mrs. Amy Longbottom, Mrs. Peggy Pringle, Mrs. Ann Wickham, Mrs. Kathleen Sharp and Mrs. Margaret Graham.

Every householder in the districts of Yeadon, Rawdon and Guiseley, was required to fill in a form giving the exact number of rooms in the house, the number of occupants and their occupations, and there was a penalty for non-return. It was feared that it might be necessary to resort to compulsory billeting and the circulars gave authority for this; the only excuse, other than lack of room, being a Doctor's certificate for ill-health. However, although it was felt expedient to let the rumour run in the district that compulsory billeting would be used, it was felt that only in the very last resort would this be applied, as the only cover in this case would be a room, with access to light, water, and sanitation, which would have been a pretty unhappy state of affairs for war workers, working the long hours they did, and having to rely on getting their meals at work. As it happens we managed to avoid this, and only in one case did we have to ask a householder to appear before members of the sub-committee to say why he did not wish to have a war-worker lodger. This had a happy ending.

We were in daily contact with the AVRO Billeting Office which did not have carte blanche to go around the district commandeering accommodation as we did. The area was known as a red area, which meant that it was very important from a war effort point of view, and we had to keep in mind that there were other local firms engaged in war work (such as Blackburn Aircraft in the old Tram Sheds at Guiseley) which might also need help with housing.

It was hilarious to see the reaction of very important visiting officials, in one case a Brigadier, calling at our 'outhouse' office, housed in the old stable block at Micklefield House, Rawdon, furnished with an old trestle table, three rickety chairs, an old wireless cabinet, used as a stool, an old kitchen dresser and a wooden cupboard, and warmed only with a spluttering gas fire. Eventually, though, we did get a telephone!

Every billet was inspected, the householder was assessed, and as far as we were able, we tried to 'fit' the billetee to the household. Councillor Fred Jackson was the official Billeting Officer at AVRO helped, largely, by Miss Ruth Layfield, and her staff, who worked long hours; and we made it a rule, that no one was left without a bed for the night even if they arrived after official hours.

We had one bad blob when we prepared for 60 girls and 30 Irish navvies arrived! No way could we cope with them and after feeding them, the Housing Office, Leeds City Council, came to our rescue and housed them in Shaftesbury House, Beeston. The navvies came to help build the MAP houses.

Joe Kubaschewski - a young Polish Air Force Officer, speaking very little English, worked at Avro. We billeted him with a Mr. & Mrs. Ferguson in Rawdon as Mr. Ferguson spoke Gaelic, and they understood each other quite well. Another unusual request came when we were asked to find a home for an Eskimo working for a period at the factory.

House requisitioning

The authority was vested in the Clerk of the Council (AUDC) to requisition houses for transferred war workers. The house had to be empty before we could stick a notice on it, saying it was under requisition; and then put a family in. A proper rent was charged, this being estimated by Mr. D. Smallwood of Dacre, Son and Hartley, after survey of the property and, eventually, when it was returned to the owner it had to be in good structural condition. Houses to rent were few and far between, and very rarely for sale, so we had to move fast when we were told of one coming empty. Quite often a coal merchant would tell us, and we also had to watch obituaries. I was once accused of sitting all day in a dustbin, watching removal men at work, and dashing out immediately they closed the door the clap the notice on!

One householder alleged that a child had wet the bed. We collected the bedding, emptied it into a clean tick, sprinkled it with crushed mothballs and sewed it up. The delighted householder *knew* we would see justice done!

One hot summer day, a soldier and a young woman; she clad in a mousy fur coat and winter boots, came to ask us if we could find "'im" for, if we could, "'ee" (the soldier) was willing to marry her if she could get a divorce. "'im" had worked at the Chadderton factory - the one with the long chimney - before being sent to Yeadon some two years previously, and she hadn't seen him since. We found 'im out of 12,000 workers, and also found that he was a very senior employee happily housed in Bramhope, with his *other* little 'family'!

I also recall another gentleman who came to be billeted asking for somewhere where he might practice on the piano. We placed him in a house where this was possible but, after a week or two, he came back begging to be moved (he brought his luggage with him) as his landlady was making unacceptable demands on his manhood!

The rumours about AVRO were legion: lazy workers, bad workmanship, foremen who waylaid young girls into quite corners, etc., and I was officially informed to let such rumours proliferate as they helped to put the enemy off the scent regarding the importance of the place.

We, involved in billeting, could claim our bus fares but the Council Treasurer (West Riding County Council), Harold Wilson - yes, the very same - was so keen not to pay one halfpenny more than we spent that we kept all our bus tickets and filed them on a spike.

From Mrs. Murray's illuminating recollections it is obvious that a large capacity for hard work, and a sense of humour of similar proportions were prerequisites for the vital work in which she and her colleagues were involved. It is equally apparent, that the successful organisation and functioning of a war factory would not have been possible without the considerable involvement of the local community.

The siting of such a large manufacturing unit as that established at Yeadon, in what was then a semi-rural area, was bound to create problems; not least of which was the marked distrust shown by local residents to the newcomers who came to work and live among them. To get this in perspective, however, it should be borne in mind that prior to the Second World War the vast majority of the people of Britain lived and worked in the area in which they were born. Few, outside the privileged classes, owned a motor car and, for most folk, a journey of more than ten or fifteen miles was quite an event - perhaps once a year for a holiday of one weeks' duration. Thus, contact with others outside ones family, friends or workmates was severely

Conscription

restricted: this resulting in a far more narrow and parochial outlook than is the case today. Not surprisingly, a substantial number of those who were directed to work at 'AVRO' found themselves received in the locality with a distinct coolness; and this problem was not restricted solely to the adults, for similar feelings were much to the fore in local schools where the offspring of the 'incomers' were accommodated. Many of these children were dragged, metaphorically (although, in some cases, almost certainly literally), from other homes and schools, many miles distant and, understandably, some of their number took to this enforced transportation with ill grace.

Integration of the itinerant war-workers was a gradual and not entirely successful process, although some friendships - and marriages - forged with locals have lasted to this day.

* * *

On 3rd January, 1941, Leeds University Air Squadron formed: Yorkshire's only representative among twelve such units set up within the auspices of the Royal Air Force Volunteer Reserve (RAFVR). Its first C.O. was Wing Commander Ridley D.S.O. Ninety-three students enrolled of whom fifty-six were, subsequently, accepted as being "... fit to be aircrew or temporarily unfit...." Thereafter, with the exception of absences between 1946-1947 and 1948-1954, the Squadron was to be present at Yeadon until 1959. **(Photo 27a - centre pages)**

Although technical training was undertaken at H.Q. (34 University Road, Leeds), cadets gained air experience, at Yeadon, in DH82 Tiger Moth: BB673' acquired 13th December. However..." because of snow and bad weather was not flown until February 1942....". The aircraft served until July 1944 when, because "... the airframe was old and fully non aerobatic...., it was disposed of to Rearsby to be broken up; being replaced by another Tiger Moth:T5616, obtained from No. 8 E.F.T.S. at Woodley..

Anson production began in earnest at Yeadon during May, 1941: the first trickle which would become a veritable flood. On the 4th of the month the Government instituted 'Double Summer Time' to give the hard pressed agricultural industry two hours extra daylight. On the 12th the House of Commons was bombed and, two days later, Hitler's Deputy, Rudolph Hess, descended by parachute from his Messerschmitt Me110 into a field south of Glasgow in a vain attempt to meet the Duke of Hamilton and, through him, Winston Churchill, to sue for a peace-pact between Germany and Britain.

On the 15th, unknown to all but a small group of people, Gerry Sayer, Chief Test Pilot of the Gloster Aviation Company, first flew the Gloster Whittle E28/39, precursor of the Meteor, thus launching Britain into the jet age.

Early on the morning of the 24th, in the Denmark Straight between Iceland and Greenland, the German battleships Bismarck and Prince Eugen were intercepted by H.M.S. Hood and H.M.S. Prince of Wales. At 05.45 hours the Hood and the Bismarck commenced firing almost simultaneously and, seconds later, having received a direct hit in her Magazine, the Hood blew up and disintegrated amid a sheet of brilliant orange flame. Three minutes later the huge, 40,000 ton (40,640 tonne) ship was gone, taking with her all but three of the 95 officers and 1,324 men aboard.

Photo 28.

Ray Myers inspecting work done in the Bomb Aimers position in a Lancaster.

Agnes Ludlam (nee McNally) was then 17 years old and working in the canteen at the factory; she recalled: "I will never forget that dinner-time when the news came over the wireless that the Hood had gone down. One of our girls dropped all her plates, and fainted, her sailor husband being on it. We just couldn't believe it. The Hood sunk? We were stunned for days ....."

Indeed the whole nation was stunned, but there were many war-workers (and others) with loved ones away on active service who braced themselves at *every* news broadcast, prepared for the worst, but hoping and praying that any subsequent knock on the door would not herald the dreaded telegram. One was Ray Myers, an Electrical Inspector at the factory, whose husband was in the Royal Navy. "..... the constant fear and worry got you down at times but you carried on. In a funny sort of way when your husband was facing danger it made you all the more determined to see the job through ....."

Donald Winn, a Senior Inspector at the factory, had a very high regard for the positive way women workers faced such stress, and yet succeeded in doing their share of tough war work. "..... they had to contend with the regular physical problems that men are not bothered with, and hundreds of them had the additional burden of husbands or boyfriends who they feared would get killed or maimed on active service. I had a lot of admiration for those girls, they had a tough war but, regardless, they buckled down to it ....."

Donald Winn knew what he was talking about in the context of a 'tough war' for he had been through the 1914-18 conflict at the sharp-end, having served with the Flight Battalion of the Royal Engineers prior to joining No.24 Squadron when it formed in the Royal Flying Corps (RFC) in 1915. When the Squadron went to France a year later (as the first DH2 fighter unit) he witnessed the loss of many young pilots - then earning 2/-d (10p) per day -and their Observers, through lack of training, inadequate equipment, or faulty aeroplanes. At the outbreak of the Second World War, Donald tried to re-enlist in the R.A.F. but was told he was too old, so he worked as a joiner for Kitchen & Hodgson of Bradford on a building contract in Hull "being bombed almost every day - it was like being back on the Western Front". He then volunteered to work at the Yeadon factory but, at the time, there were vacancies only in the Pattern Making Shop. Somehow, he convinced the staff at the Labour Exchange that he was suitably qualified and they issued him with a 'Pattern Makers Certificate'. Nevertheless, once at the factory, he persuaded those in authority to put him in a position more suited his specific skills, and he was appointed an Inspector (later a Senior Inspector) on woodworking assembly, mainly on the Anson. He added:

"I could never forget those young lads who were killed in the First War because something wasn't as it should be with their 'planes. So my motto at AVRO was always 'If it's not safe enough for me to fly in it's not good enough for anyone else.' This got me into all sorts of arguments with those who were constantly pushing for faster and faster production; very often those clever b————s from Manchester who always considered themselves superior beings ....."

The latter remarks are similar to ones expressed by a number of former employees at Yeadon, and the subject is one which merits further consideration as the story unfolds.

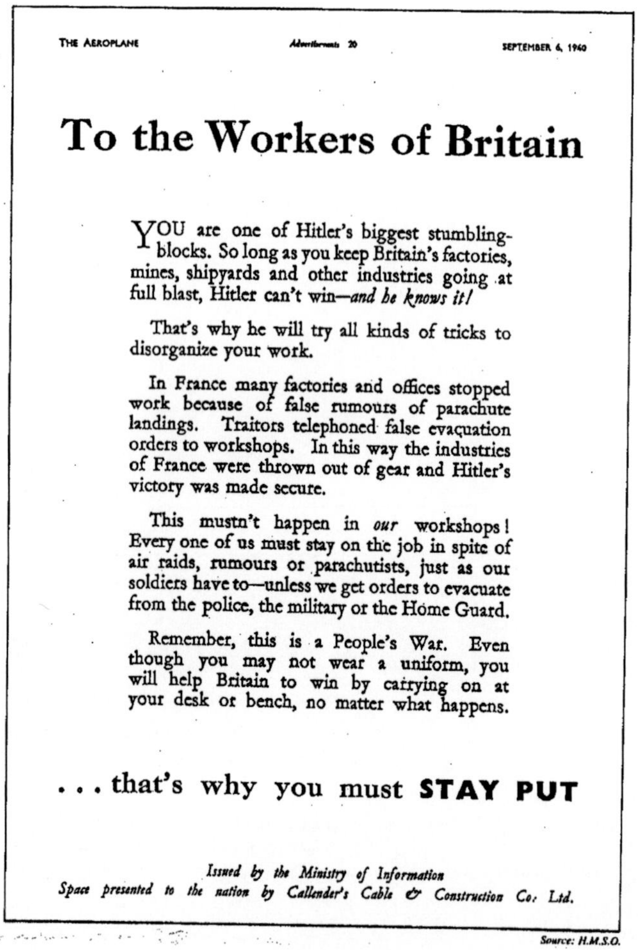

THE AEROPLANE Advertisements 20 SEPTEMBER 6, 1940

To the Workers of Britain

YOU are one of Hitler's biggest stumbling-blocks. So long as you keep Britain's factories, mines, shipyards and other industries going at full blast, Hitler can't win—*and he knows it!*

That's why he will try all kinds of tricks to disorganize your work.

In France many factories and offices stopped work because of false rumours of parachute landings. Traitors telephoned false evacuation orders to workshops. In this way the industries of France were thrown out of gear and Hitler's victory was made secure.

This mustn't happen in *our* workshops! Every one of us must stay on the job in spite of air raids, rumours or parachutists, just as our soldiers have to—unless we get orders to evacuate from the police, the military or the Home Guard.

Remember, this is a People's War. Even though you may not wear a uniform, you will help Britain to win by carrying on at your desk or bench, no matter what happens.

... that's why you must **STAY PUT**

Issued by the Ministry of Information
Space presented to the nation by Callender's Cable & Construction Co. Ltd.

Source: H.M.S.O.

Photo 28a. Originally issued by the Ministry of Information, this entreaty was used by various magazines, periodicals and advertisers to put over the message of the dangers posed by Fifth Columnists.

Production Begins in Earnest

"......till lathe and hammerblow release their wings, and through cell-windows small we see them fly the lucid life-and-death way of the sky."

Hubert Nicholson - 'War Factory'

On Saturday, 21st June, 1941, the day before German forces attacked Russia, Anson Mk.1 W2612, the first of more than 4,000 of the type to be built at Yeadon, was test-flown by Captain Worrall. On the flight he was accompanied by the now well respected aviation journalist and author, John Stroud, who recalled: "It was my one and only visit to Yeadon and although I remember it was the first Anson to come from the factory I don't think there was anything extraordinary about the flight. I do recall, however, that it was a very wet and murky Saturday morning."

Just two months later, on the 19th August, W2612 accompanied by the next three Anson Mk.1's built at the factory: W2613, W2614 and W2615, began a journey intended to take them to Australia where they were to join the Royal Australian Air Force (RAAF). On 10th September the ship in which they were being transported was torpedoed off the West Coast of Africa, thus denying Yeadon's first Ansons active service.

Of the first 50 of the type manufactured at the factory, 9 subsequently reached Australia, 8 went to Canada to serve with the Royal Canadian Air Force (RCAF), and 4 were shipped to South Africa where they were taken on strength by the SAAF. Such was the attrition rate, however, particularly at training units, that of the remaining 25, only W.2641 was to survive through to the end of the war and, even so, it existed only until 12th January, 1946, when it met its nemisis on crashing in France.

After the first batch of 50, many more 'Yeadon' Ansons were shipped to Australia, and South Africa, with a smaller number going to New Zealand and Rhodesia. The majority were used by various training establishments set up under the terms of the Commonwealth Air Training Plan [1], more commonly known as 'The Plan': an agreement made on 17th December, 1939, for the training of aircrew within the various Commonwealth countries: a development which necessitated the ready availability of a large number of suitable aircraft.

The Anson, in various configurations, fitted into the scheme of things admirably and, before the requirement for such intensive training came to an end five years later, several thousand of the type - the majority having been built at Yeadon - had been used at one or other of the 333 flying training schools set up throughout the Dominions: Great Britain 153, Canada 92, Australia 26, South Africa 25, Southern Rhodesia 10, India 9, New Zealand 6, Middle East 6, U.S.A. 5 [2] and Bahamas 1.

Although not, of course, privy to this information, employees at Yeadon were made fully aware of the growing urgency to complete aircraft under construction; this becoming particularly evident after the arrival from Newton Heath of a senior foreman, Jack Stoker, whose prime function was to see that the job was done more quickly. He entered into his task with some relish and, being what one ex-colleague described as "a real b..... livewire", he succeeded; albeit that, at times, he did not endear himself to some of those he 'chased'!

Others involved in the burgeoning production included Charles Simpson, who was in charge of the wood-working machine-shop, and Harry and Henry Marshall: two brothers much respected for their expertise with engines - large and small - gleaned from many years spent, pre-war, in the travelling fairground business. Hubert Whiteley, formerly of Glenway Coaches and Reg Berry, who were employed as engine-fitters, also utilised skills developed during their peacetime employment.

Throughout the second half of 1941 Anson production steadily increased from the 7 per month achieved in June and July to 30 per month by

---

1   Known as "The Empire Air Training Scheme" up to 1st July 1942
2   These were establishments run by the R.A.F., as distinct from the American organisations which also trained Commonwealth aircrew.

Production Begins in Earnest

December; yielding a total of 96 built by the end of the year, by which time the whole works had taken on an air of activity and purpose not seen, or felt, before.

Whether one was employed in the noisy press and machine-shops, where row upon row of millers, automatic lathes and multiple drills were in constant use cutting and drilling metal to pre-marked angles, contours or holes; or in the nearby shops making tools and patterns; or preparing and lining-up wooden stringers, formers and longerons; or constructing the wooden wings, fuselage and tail-assemblies, rudder fittings and other control surfaces; or inserting radio and electrical equipment, turrets, engines, fuel tanks, landing gear and wheels; wire-splicing, shaping, stitching and applying fabric and upholstery; paint-spraying and doping, designing, modifying, planning, buying, warehousing, calculating wages and a host of other clerical duties; inspecting, progress-chasing, fuelling, testing, test-flying, policing, driving, working on the airfield, preparing and/or serving thousands of meals, or being involved in a multitude of other jobs - not forgetting those extra duties on Fire-Watching, Air Raid Precaution or in the Home Guard - each and every employee from top management to the newest recruit knew they were part of a massive and still developing, enterprise.

Because the majority of war-workers were unable to 'read' standard engineering drawings (few of them had even seen one, previously) copies in greater detail were prepared by a small group of draughtsmen who, on occasions, in the early days were required to obtain information by crouching in cramped spaces within a completed aircraft. The resultant larger scale drawings, printed on parchment-like paper, were prepared for *every* component, including hundreds of subsequent modifications, irrespective of its size; the requirement being that the drawings should be understood by the newest 'green' recruit and, additionally, even the tools to be used for each job were specified.
(Photo 29 - centre pages)

Every component, no matter how small, was allocated its own specific number, and as small parts were assembled to become larger ones those, too, received an individual identification; almost as if the exercise was the putting together of some giant model kit. Numbers allocated at Yeadon were prefixed 'RY/LW' to signify 'Roe-Yeadon' (work from the three Manchester factories: 'R3/LW') and the final identification for a completed aircraft was the attachment of a brass plate, containing its airframe number, to its wings and fuselage.

During construction, each aircraft gradually took shape as it moved along the assembly lines, and its progress was logged on 'history (or record) sheets' (contained in a ring-binder) on which all work carried out was signed for: firstly by the person who had completed the job, then by a chargehand or foreman, followed by a Company Inspector and, finally, by an Inspector from the Aeronautical Inspection Department (AID - which had an establishment at all aircraft factories) when he or she deemed the work as being up to the required standard. Sub-assemblies and engines and, on occasions, larger fuselage and wing sections built by sub-contractors were, similarly, issued with - and never moved without - their own 'history sheets'.
(Photo 30 - centre pages)

On its completion, an aircraft was issued with a log book for the airframe and one for each of its engines, containing copies of all individual 'history sheets', plus details of the running of the engines - every minute - on test, whether flown or ground-run.

In the early days all finished work was checked and approved by a member of the A.I.D. Staff but, as their number never exceeded 40 at Yeadon (divided roughly 50% men/50% women, among whom were Mrs. Sutton and Messrs. Denton, Kermode and Dean), when the factory began to expand, demand considerably exceeded capability. Thus it became the practice for A.I.D. personnel to make daily 'spot checks' on batches of production and, at less regular intervals, undertake complete and thorough inspections of work being done in the various departments. This meant that one day an A.I.D. Inspector could be checking the quality and finish being achieved in the electro-plating and anodising section, and the next making an in-flight test of various equipment on board a newly completed aircraft; followed, perhaps, by a visit to one of the many outside subcontractors, and so on, right through each facet of aircraft production.

This would appear, at first glance, to have been a most interesting and rewarding way of earning ones living in wartime Britain; but, as is so often the case, this was only partially true. Undoubtedly, the men and women who made up the staff of the A.I.D. were, of necessity, high calibre technically but, additionally, by their terms of reference they were required, on occasions, to undertake work and make decisions thereon, which required a great deal more than practical ability. Such was the case when the factory was under pressure (frequently) to increase production,[3] and some item of faulty workmanship made it necessary for them to say 'NO', when all around the others were crying 'YES' - this can never have been easy.

Photo 31. A.I.D.

A plain shield emblazoned with the tools of the trade, a magnifying glass and inspection mirror, is crossed by a blue band donating the dual capacity of the gentleman.

The idea is further carried out by the rather queer headgear which is a type favoured by deer stalkers.

These air ministry men have to be very athletic as shown by the acrobatic act at the upper left.

The motto is a gift from production and inspection:

They Condemn What they do not Understand
copyright J. Bruce.

One of the A.I.D. Inspectors involved at Yeadon was Eric Dean, a native of Hull who, prior to being 'directed' to the factory on 7th July, 1941, had been on A.I.D. detachment at other factories of the AVRO Group within the Manchester area. Earlier he had attended the Kidbrooke and Milton Training Schools after service with Blackburn Aircraft at Brough, having first 'served his time' as a fitter and turner with Messrs. Rosedown and Thompson of Hull. He recalled:

".....My specific job at Yeadon was as an 'Interchangeability Inspector' making sure that any part or component - no matter where it had been made - would fit into any aircraft of the same type. This was the secret of successful wartime production and, despite all kinds of snags, it worked. In addition, I had to inspect various completed sections: wings, fuselages, tail-planes, etc., and later, the finished aircraft after which, if all was up to standard, I would sign and date form '1090'. which showed that the aircraft was satisfactory for onward delivery to the R.A.F. ....."

Eric was accommodated at three different locations during his five year tenure at the factory, and his reminiscences make it quite clear that belonging to the A.I.D. - a Government Organisation - was no guarantee that ones wartime 'home' would be of a high standard. He, his wife, and young daughters, were first quartered at an address in Wharncliffe Road, Shipley, on the outskirts of Bradford. "..... the house had to be scrubbed from top to bottom with very strong disinfectant before we could move in, and even though it got rid of some of the smells we still found the property infected with bugs. We called the authorities and men were sent to apply sulpha-cyanide and the bugs disappeared but then, to top it all, as soon as we go the house warmed-up it was overrun with mice which came in out of the cold!....."

Having spent several weeks thereafter getting the house into a reasonable condition, Eric arrived back from work one day feeling desperately ill: "..... we had endured weeks of Lancashire Hot Pot (supposedly) for dinner in the canteen - God only knows what was in it - with Pilchards equally regularly for tea, and when I saw Rabbit on the menu that day I couldn't resist having some, even though we were told it had come from Australia. I ate it as if I was starving - others were doing the same - after all, Britain was almost meatless at that time, but it was my last proper meal for a long while because, within an hour or two, I became very ill, and I finished up being off work for five months! ....."

Eric's illness led to complications and even when he was supposedly recovered he was unable to walk without the aid of a stick. This convinced his Doctor that he must be accommodated closer to the factory; thus Eric and his family came to be the tenants of a M.A.P. bungalow, built two years previously, situated at No.5 Bacon Street, Nunroyd, Guiseley.

"..... We found that most of the windows were broken, and the floor was covered with dead leaves and other debris, and the whole place was filthy. We managed, after a while, to clean it up but, even then, I soon came to agree with a neighbour who described the bungalows as 'having been designed

Production Begins in Earnest

by an idiot, and built by 'morons' for the buildings had really been flung together. They were built in pairs, of brick, with metal-framed windows and they had a concrete floor that was obviously thinly laid on top of ash-cinders, straight over the original grass. The walls contained no plaster on the inside and no cement rendering on the outside - it was just plain brick. The roof was flat and constructed of what appeared to be panels of shredded-wheat covered with tarred roofing-felt. Because the foundations were so minimal the walls soon began to sag; some at the extremities, others in the middle. The fortunate residents were those whose walls leaned outwards, as then any accumulated rain water ran *away* from rather than *into* the rooms!

Residents who were employed at the factory as fitters were in constant demand from their neighbours to realign pipework and water tanks that had been displaced, or sprung leaks, due to the subsidence.

The bungalows were ice-cold in winter and like ovens in summer. Condensation on the walls and ceilings required constant attention if mildew was not to form on clothes, bedding and curtains. In the colder months, with the floor always being damp, it was not unusual to get up in a morning to find the rugs had frozen to the concrete beneath ....."

It was in these awful surroundings that Eric's youngest daughter was born, and things were not improved by the attitude of some locals towards members of his family:

"..... I have no fond memories of Guiseley. To start with we were ostracised to a large extent - and my daughter also found the same when she started school there later - my wife used to get very upset at the way she was treated in the shops, where she was nearly always ignored until the shopkeeper had served all the locals - despite the fact that some of *their* husbands were also working at the factory! Looking back I am convinced that those of us who came from outside the area to work there, irrespective of our position in the works, or our previous background, were all tarred with the same brush as far as Guiseley folk were concerned ....."

That war workers could be treated in such a way: badly housed and unwelcomed, is lamentable but the nation at that time was in a parlous state: there was neither the time, money or resources to make provision for more than basic necessities and, sadly, as had been touched upon earlier, newcomers to the district found barriers to friendship a good deal more difficult to break down than would be the case a generation later.

To a very large extent it became a matter of gritting ones teeth and although, perhaps, grumbling a good deal, simply getting on with it. As if to compensate for this black side of things, however, as the war progressed there developed a 'we're all in it together' attitude which, although not evident in every circumstance, became prevalent enough to help ease the difficulties and privations experienced by many.

The hit songs of the period give some indication of the desperate attempt by 'Tin Pan Alley' to lift the nation's morale: 'It's a Hap, Hap, Happy Day', 'Up Housewives and at 'Em', and 'It's a Lovely Day Tomorrow', being just three of many which enjoyed considerable success during what was the most grim period of the war for the people of Britain.

There was, of course, no television and it was to the radio which people turned for their home entertainment. The B.B.C. (and only B.B.C. was available until late in the war) provided just two daytime only services: 'The Home Service' and 'The Forces Programme' - precursors of Radio's 4 and 2 respectively - and, with the exception of 'The News' broadcasts on the former (much less frequently issued than today) the largest audiences were enjoyed by several weekly comedy shows including Tommy Handley's never to be forgotten 'I.T.M.A.' (Thursday's 8.30 p.m.) - which remains unsurpassed for its volume of listeners (twenty million) - with its crazy humour and loveable characters: Mrs. Mopp ("Can I do yer now, Sir?"), and the Colonel Chinstrap ("I don't mind if I do!") to mention but two, becoming a veritable national institution which few missed deliberately. Other shows such as 'H.M.S. Waterlogged' (which, after the war, became 'Waterlogged Spa'), 'Stand Easy', and the ever popular 'Much Binding in the Marsh' (with Kenneth Horne and Richard Murdoch) along with 'Happidrome' (Sunday's 8.30 p.m.) what a name to conjure with if you recall those days! - with the inimitable 'Ramsbottom, Enoch and Me' - 'Me - being a certain Mr. Lovejoy, performed by Harry Korris, all played their part, and a very substantial part it was, in raising morale.

The characters and catch phrases from these, and several other wartime shows, became so popular and evoked such strong feelings that on their phrasing out postwar, millions of listeners likened it to the passing of a member of their family !

Readers might be beginning to wonder what all this has to do with building aeroplanes? Well, the simple answer is a great deal; for the radio and, outside the home, also the cinema and the dance-hall provided a much needed escape to 'switch-off' for a little while, from the grim reality of war, and the relentless day by day grind, necessary to meet ever-growing demands for higher output.

There is no doubt that humour, whether it be on the radio or on the shop floor, made a tremendous contribution to the emotional well being of Britain's war workers; as has been confirmed through correspondence and conversations with many former employees at the factory.

Agnes Ludlam (nee McNally) remembered that "..... at break time we would take our big wooden tea-trolleys onto the factory floor - my round included the Tool Room, Machine Shop and Dope House - it took over half an hour to get round with everybody singing along to 'Music While You Work', and many a time I would get back to the kitchen to find that some joker had put a dish-cloth or a block of Monkey-Brand cleaner in the tea urn: you couldn't help laughing ..... later in my service at AVRO I must have pleased someone as I was promoted to the staff canteen, and then to the Executive dining room. There we had a uniform which consisted of blue dress, lace cap and white apron, and we were trained to carry five soups, dinners or puddings on one arm and three on the other. Before we got used to it many a diner's head was shampoo'd with soup, gravy or custard .....!"

Margaret Birkbeck, worked in the Machine Shop on a milling machine and among more serious reminiscences recalled "..... the funny little man who made our tea. After we had drunk it he dipped our cups in a bucketful of filthy water and then joked he wanted a tip for giving us something extra - foot and mouth! Then there was our foreman Billy Baldwin who lived quite near the factory. He wore glasses with thick lenses, and when he had to tell us something unpopular like doing more work in less time - a quite regular thing - we would all pull faces and some of us would make gestures when his back was turned. He would laugh and shout above the din 'Yer don't fool me, I can see yer in mi glasses,' and we would all laugh."

The Chief Inspector of the A.I.D. establishment at Yeadon when Eric Dean arrived was W.L. Amer, who loved to play practical jokes on those around him. Eventually some of his staff grew tired of being on the receiving end of his tricks so they decided to get their own back. "He and his wife had been invited out to a special dinner, somewhere in Leeds; full dress, etc., and being a boss he had the limited use of a company car. Someone brought in a weary looking kipper and, unknown to Mr. Amer, we tied this to its exhaust manifold. Apparently the effect was so nauseous that he and Mrs. Amer had to abandon the car and proceed back from Kirkstall by taxi. We, of course, were highly amused but the Amers' were certainly not impressed! We didn't stop at that, however, for we used to buy things from a small joke shop in Bradford, one of which was a thing like a small thimble which could be fitted over the plug terminals of his car. Depending upon the type of 'thimble' used, after a few minutes driving, clouds of white smoke would emerge from under the bonnet, or loud bangs would proceed clouds of black smoke. We used this ruse periodically on Amers' cars and he became so suspicious that he took to lifting the bonnet to look at the plug leads before every journey ....."

Mrs. Emmie Hardwick (nee Lambert) a former Inspector on the bomb-gear production line remembered, "We all had a good laugh when condensation dropped from the ceiling and someone shouted 'It's those animals on the roof up to their tricks again."

Hubert Winchester, who worked in the Machine Shop, recalled: "Card Schools proliferated from time to time, particularly on the night-shift, and one night four workers were sat round an upturned wooden box intent on a game when a voice from the shadows called out 'Have you got a good hand Joe?' 'Yes', came the reply, 'Well make the most of it, its going to be your last in this place.' The voice was that of the senior night foreman making an unexpected check and he caught them redhanded."

These few amusing reminiscences, selected from a considerable number provided by former employees, show an almost childish sense of humour which, perhaps, fifty years on, appears out of place. The opposite was, however, the case for the humour, irrespective of the fact that it was juvenile, was a very essential antidote to the tedium; the dirt; the noise; the blackout; the rationing; the stress and fear engendered by having loved ones absent on active service and, not least of all, from not knowing for how long it would continue. The daily, or nightly, shift expected of war workers was indeed extremely long, even for those more used to a longer working week than is the case today, and many recall 'a week seeming like an eternity!'

Joe Walton was 21 years old when he was interviewed for a job in the Pattern Shop with the terse words: "Are you a member of the UPMA (United Pattern Makers Association)? Have you got your own tools? Right. Start Monday.' He vividly remembered the lengthy shifts and the additional hours spent travelling to and from the works:

"I used to get up around 5.30 a.m. and go down to the Bus Station in Keighley to catch the 6.30 a.m. Andertons Bus and, sometimes, we had to wake up the driver who, if he had been on the beer, slept in

Production Begins in Earnest

it overnight. If, on the other hand, I got up late, and missed it, the only alternative was to catch a service bus to Greengates (on the outskirts of Bradford) and there get another one going to Harrogate which stopped en-route at the factory. Doing it that way could take well over an hour (a good half-hour by Andertons) which was not funny in bad weather and, of course, it meant you were late for work; very much frowned on I can tell you. At the factory gates we had to show our AVRO passes to the AVRO police who, if you were late, would 'phone your department to see if your foreman wanted you in ....."

Regular 'lateness' offenders were required to appear before an Absentee Committee, made up of representatives from Management and Unions, which met in a hut situated in Novia Plantation. The Committee could, and did, impose fines and continued absenteeism, without a good cause, was severely dealt with; this being considered a very serious offence in wartime.

Joe Walton continued: "..... I worked from 7.30 a.m. to 7 p.m. and, if I was lucky enough to get across the road in time, I might catch the express bus back to Keighley which meant I would be home for about 8 o'clock [3] but, if not, it could be much later, and some others on my bus had to go onto Skipton or outlying villages after that. [4] I worked five days one week followed by Saturday off then, starting Sunday, I worked seven days having the next Sunday off. I did this for three weeks, followed by three weeks on nights working 7 p.m. to 7 a.m., and so on ....." There were slight variations among the employees in different departments but, overall, the total hours worked per week averaged out more or less the same.

One young Bradford lad was unconcerned with such considerations; all he wanted to do when he left St. Bedes Boys Grammar School in the city was to work on aeroplanes.

"I was fascinated with aeroplanes so I offered myself for a position at the AVRO and, although I didn't know one end of a piece of machinery from another, I was quite thrilled when they offered me a job right away. It wasn't until later that I realised they were desperate for workers ....."

So wrote Bernard Hepton the now internationally known and respected actor "..... I started at Yeadon as a fitters mate, working on Anson's, and being made the butt of the usual apprentices jokes but, then, after a successful application, I went up to the Jig and Tool office where I learned engineering drawing; together with an afternoon - or was it a full day? - at Bradford Tech. I learned what a Jig and Tool was, and what it did and, from there, without signing any papers, it was agreed that I should be apprenticed and sent to work in the various departments - tool room, tool tryout, lathe setting, milling and shaping machine operations and, finally, into the Design Office. A wonderful training which I thoroughly enjoyed. There is no doubt that if I hadn't gone into the theatre this would have been my career ....." **(Photo 32 - centre pages)**

The Spray Shop, more commonly known as the Dope House was, without doubt, one of the more

Photo 33. The Drawing Office at Yeadon   copyright AVRO

---

[3] The daily exodus of 8,000 workers (11,000 at peak production in 1944) rushing to 'catch' their buses like some frustrated football crowd - particularly during the hours of black-out - caused very real problems, and for those who worked furthermost from the bus park the operation became something to be dreaded.

[4] Some employees were required to make very long journeys: as much as a four hour round trip in a number of cases; and, with the exception of a minority who walked to and from the factory, most workers could add at least one hours' travelling time to their eleven or twelve hour 'shift'. Thus it is not surprising to learn that many of those involved recall those days as being a marathon containing little more than work, travel and sleep.

unpleasant, dirty and least healthy places in the factory. Here, assemblies received a coat of celon (amyl-acetate) 'dope', and the 'seams' of air-frames were packed with cotton wadding and sealed with red-lead paint. These functions produced an almost permanent smell of pear-drops which permeated the immediate atmosphere, and even further afield, despite the place being curtained-off. In much earlier times, the inhabitants of Northern Britain had been known as Picts - 'The Painted People' - and those unfortunate enough to be consigned to the Dope House could, quite justifiably, have used such a name.

"During my AVRO days during 1941-42," wrote Mrs. L.M. Winterbottom, "I worked in the notorious Dope House spraying Ansons. We wore long green overalls and had wool 'snoods' over our heads to cover our hair. Most of us wore clogs, rather than shoes, and I can remember mine being bright red ones. Due to the fumes, the factory Doctor, Dr. Outhwaite (who also had a surgery in Yeadon), ordered that every Dope Sprayer had to drink two pints of milk, and take one Adexelin tablet every day. Eventually, I couldn't cope with the dope or the milk, and the capsules were only slightly more bearable, so I asked to be transferred into another department ....."

Doreen Varley (nee Watson) worked on Anson wing assembly but vividly recalled the Dope House: "When the fuselage of a plane was assembled it was taken to the middle of the factory and huge curtains were drawn around it. Then it was sprayed with dope and, needless to say, the smell was awful. It lasted for hours afterwards and it gave you a headache, and what it did to those who worked permanently in the Dope House I dread to think ....."

Another with similar memories was Mrs. E. Flesher who worked in the 'Bought-Out' Store situated almost above the Dope House: "The smell was awful, and although the men and women who worked in there richly deserved their extra milk every day, we who worked nearby were not unaffected, and we were a little put out that we didn't get the same allowance."

Margaret Westropp was one directly involved: "My sister and I worked at a tailoring factory in Leeds before being sent to the AVRO. At first we were put on the assembly line but we volunteered to work in the Dope House, as it paid more money. We worked twelve hours a day dressed in boiler-suits with a pair of scissors hung from our waist, and we carried a full roll of cotton wadding and a large paint pot and brush, to put on the red lead. The fumes were awful and they were bad for our chests but we drank a lot of milk, and we were young and, in a strange sort of way, we enjoyed it. We were given twenty-fours hours to do each 'plane - that was based on the time they expected it to take - and six of us worked as a team. As we had been used to piece-work in tailoring we were always able to beat the target in half the time, so we got double the money! The red lead took some peeling-off our hands, and it was difficult to get off the brushes but, above all, we had to be most careful not to get it into our eyes. It was long hours, and hard work; sometimes we were called over to the finals to put right something that had been missed and, believe me, working in the confined space of a plane which was nearly finished was always difficult - the fumes were really bad. It was tiring, hard, smelly, work but the worst thing of all was going down that slope into the factory each morning, knowing you wouldn't see daylight till goodness knows when.[5]

The 'Finals' (or 'Flight Sheds') a separate, but equally important, part of the factory, divorced from the main building by a 400 yard (364 metres) roadway - part of which is still extant - across which were taken the thousands of partially completed aircraft. This department was accommodated (as has been mentioned earlier) in hangars alongside the northern perimeter of the airfield, in which final fitting-out and pre-flight testing was undertaken.

Mrs. Dorothy Foster recalled her own experiences there: "When I went from the Training Centre at Kirkstall in 1941 I had no idea I would be at AVRO until 1946. I worked in the flight-sheds on the aerodrome where we did all the final assembly. Among the jobs I did was fitting landing lights, fuel gauges, oil systems and the clocks and dials in the cabin, and I even fitted sparking plugs in the engines. Sometimes we worked outside and it was very cold in the winter, but in the summer it was great. They envied us across in the works then. At first the men weren't keen on having women working with them, but as time went on they got used to us and in the end we were just one happy family. We didn't have much contact with the works only going across occasionally for parts we needed in a

---

5   After a visit to the factory, J.B. Priestley wrote 'Daylight on Saturday', (published by William Heinemann Ltd. in 1943), a novel roughly based on his findings at Yeadon.

Production Begins in Earnest

hurry, and I never saw any of the super shows that were put on in the canteen. I can only remember going there for supper when we were on nights - it was a longish way when it was pitch dark - but I wasn't scared for there was always a few of us.**(Photo 34 - centre pages)**

I was married in 1941 but my husband was in the Royal Signals and he was soon sent overseas. I didn't see him again for nearly six years, so I made myself get interested in my job to try and keep my mind occupied. It was hard at times, him being away, and the job was long hours too, but I got on with it, like most of the others, for there was a war to be won.

When I look at the photographs of my workmates I can remember them all, but not all their names. I often wonder what has happened to them?

One thing I will never forget, though, was the day Captain Worrall took me up for a spin!"

Ray Marshall was an AVRO Inspector on electrical systems who worked in the Flight Sheds. "My number (Inspector's) was RY150, and I recall the work well. At times it was tedious with the hours being so long, and sometimes we felt a bit cut-off from those across the road. We did have some advantages, though, for being much fewer in number we enjoyed more of a family atmosphere and we could always see the end product of our labours, and everything of interest on the aerodrome.

You got a special feeling when you watched Captain Worrall or Mr. Biggart take-off for the first time in a plane you had worked on, but I was specially fortunate in being at AVRO because it was there that I met my future wife."

When 14 years old (the school leaving age was not raised to 15 until 1945) Peter England began work as the Works Manager's office boy. "Mr. Harper's secretary was Miss McGuire, and Roy Dobson's office boy was Richard Gardner (who, to the surprise of the author, it transpired was one and the same as the 'Dick' Gardner with whom he played cricket some years later!). Eventually, I was transferred to the Lancaster hangar on the aerodrome,

where I was put in the 'Servicing Gang' consisting of Keith Davies, Billy Bjorck, George 'Podge' Modley - whose father and mine both worked elsewhere in the factory - Jimmy Ford and two older boys who began their proper apprenticeship whilst I was there: Phil Howarth and Marc ? Our job entailed dealing with the ground batteries and the chocks, and we sometimes went on air tests which, at our age, was a marvellous experience. There was a resident Rolls-Royce engineer, Cyril Howsley, and Norman Bird [6] was in charge of engine testing. I remember Taffy Thomas and Arthur Parker - what characters - and, of course, Arthur Marland who was in charge on the aerodrome."

There was actually a Marland family connection for Arthur, whose official title was 'Flight-Shed Superintendent', had his son Albert working in the same department and Vera Houseman, who would become his daughter-in-law, regularly made visits from the Tax Office in the main works, having transferred there from Blackburn's on the demise of No.20 EFTS.

Arthur Marland had been transferred to Yeadon from Woodford (where he was employed as a Chief Inspector) but son Albert made the journey across the Pennines from Newton Heath.

"I began with AVRO at Newton Heath as a bound apprentice, on a fixed wage of 7/6d (37½p) a week until I was eighteen, learning to be an aeroplane rigger - woodworker that is, - on Ansons. One day they asked me to volunteer to go to Yeadon and I put my name down, and soon I was on my way. In 1946, because I had volunteered and not been 'directed' there I was unable to stop them calling me up for the Army. A bit much when you consider I had done just as much war work as thousands of others who never went into the Services!

Of my time at Yeadon I remember best some of the characters: There was 'little' Joe Long who worked on the petrol bowser, he was always cracking jokes and making folks laugh (there were two Joe Long's in Yeadon at the time: 'Little' Joe and 'Big' Joe, both of whom were well known for their activities as amateur comedian and actor/producer respectively), and 'Taffy; Thomas and Arthur Parker for the foreman-engineer in charge of flight-testing -

---

[6] At the Farnborough Air Show in September, 1972, Raymond Baxter, commentating for the BBC, made an appeal for Lancaster instruments to aid the refurbishment of 'S-SUGAR' (R.5868) which now resides in the R.A.F. Museum. A certain Norman G. Bird, of Keighley, offered several items; included among which were a P4 Compass, an Astro Compass, bomb-switches, a Blind-Approach meter and numerous gauges. Might it have been the case that these items had an earlier connection with Yeadon?

one on Lancasters the other on Ansons - both very similar types of extrovert.

I remember one occasion we had a visit from some high ranking Army Officers - red tabs, the lot - and as they came round the corner of the hangar Taffy, who was up in the pilot's seat of a Lancaster, let go on the engines full blast. The officers were bowled over much to everybody's amusement, except theirs of course, and afterwards Taffy remained the picture of innocence, although from where he sat he couldn't have missed seeing them!

On another occasion, though, it was a very different story; one which could have ended in tragedy. Taffy was doing a flying - test with Captain Worrall when something went very, very, wrong and they scraped back by the skin of their teeth. Afterwards, a chastened Taffy said that had the pilot been anyone less skilled than Captain Worrell they would have 'had it'.

Photo 36.

The Lancaster Bowser.

This contained 100 octane fuel.

Photo credit R. Scatchard

Production Begins in Earnest

Photo 36a. Two cards reproduced actual size from a comprehensive list of 'Pilot's Notes' issued to A.T.A. In this case the 'Notes' are part of a series in respect of the Spitfire and Seafire.

Flight Testing and the A.T.A.

All newly built aircraft were flight-tested prior to onward delivery: an operation which commenced with the ground running of engines before take-off. Eric Dean recalled the procedure: "On an Anson a big handle was removed from a clip on the bulkhead behind each engine, and placed into socket at the back of the engine approximately two feet behind the propeller. You then wound the handle until the bod in the cockpit (sitting in a comfortable seat out of the wind, snow or rain!) waggled the throttles and booster switch and, hopefully, the engine started - they were Armstrong Whitworth Cheetahs. Then, with the props blowing a gale in your face you had to remove the handle, lift up a flap in the cowling, and place the handle in its clip-stowage, fasten down the flap, and crawl away under the wing - this needed to be done both port and starboard - *away* from the props. You then took hold of the rope attached to the wooden chocks held against the wheels, ready to pull them away at a signal from the pilot. One day a young woman was doing this job and after the engines were started she forgot the procedure by ducking out *forwards* - near disaster!! She required about forty stitches in her derriere, and she was unable to sit down for a long time; but she was lucky, she could so easily have killed herself!

On an aerodrome at nearly seven hundred feet above sea-level, as is Yeadon, this job in winter was the coldest I have ever known.

All aircraft awaiting collection - and, at times, there was a considerable number of them - were pegged down, with all controls locked. Before they could be flown off a full inspection was done by one of the AID Staff who, if all was O.K., would then sign Form '1090', remove the control locks, and allow the engines to be run-up.

When the pilot took over he, or she in the case of many ATA Staff (Air Transport Auxiliary), checked all controls and instruments and, if all was found to be in good working order they would sign acceptance on Form '700'. On occasions, however, even at this late stage, it was not unknown for the wrong lever to be pulled, resulting in the collapse and damage to the undercarriage, two or four engines and props, and an awful lot of lost tempers!"

Each new aircraft received a standard air test of engines, controls and equipment, with additional in-flight checks being carried out on the fifth and tenth aircraft from each batch. One such check involved diving an aircraft to its maximum permitted speed - 375 m.p.h. (603.37 k.p.h.) in the case of a Lancaster - a stress test which, on 11th September, 1944, at Woodford, sadly confirmed the inherent dangers of test - flying when a newly completed Lancaster failed to pull out of a dive, killing its pilot and flight engineer. Perhaps it was on a similar test that Captain Worrall and Taffy Thomas almost came to grief?

Despite there being a considerable number of production and ground checks, often faults were revealed during subsequent air tests and this resulted in aircraft being returned to the Flight Sheds for rectification. It was not uncommon to find individual aircraft going through this procedure several times (one former employee recalled an Anson having more than ten air tests) before the 'gremlins' were defeated. With an ever increasing number of completed aircraft coming from the factory this placed an impossible burden on Captain Worrall, thus he came to be joined by David G. Biggart; ultimately more commonly known by the appellation: 'Reckless' [1] a native of West Hartlepool, former Instructor at Bournemouth Flying School and, from January 1940 until April 1942, a Flight Captain with the Air Transport Auxiliary, who was detailed to share the test-flying duties. Such was the enormity of the operation that, by the end of 1946, when the factory ceased production the two men had, between them, taken Yeadon-built aircraft into the air on several thousand occasions. A remarkable record which was certainly not achieved without some danger to themselves; and a great deal about the character and capability of the men is revealed by the fact that, as far as the author is aware, this seemingly impossible task was completed without serious mishap.

---

1   This nickname was earned not through any shortcomings in ability, nor through a lack of proper caution; but as a result of his occasional impish behaviour: of which more in due course.

Flight Testing and the A.T.A.

By all accounts 'Reckless' Biggart was considered by the ladies to be a bit of a heartthrob, but being the cause of female infatuation was no guarantee of unreserved admiration by ones male contemporaries; as will be revealed. Captain Worrall on the other hand was no extrovert, being considered by many of his subordinates as pleasant enough but rather uncommunicative; and on the subject of his achievements which, over a twenty-five year period, were considerable he remained modest, stating that he never set out to be the best test-pilot: just the oldest!

Nevil Shute, writing in his autobiography 'Slide Rule' about the early days when Captain Worrall was CFI of the Yorkshire Aeroplane Club, said of him "..... our third pilot was the best of the lot. He was a stout, good-humoured man of forty-five, happily married, with three children at school, a little suburban house with a garden which he cherished, and a couple of dogs. He was an unadventurous man who never boasted of the time he flew the aeroplane through the hangar as all the other had done ..... he probably knew more about aeroplanes than any of them ....."

Later, Shute made mention of Worrall's wartime activities "he must have been one of the most successful, yet unsung, test-pilots, proving that the best of breed are not the dazzling, young, tearaways of the adventure novels with the string of glamour girl-friends, and the hot-rod sports cars, too ready to risk their lives and your aeroplane, but the happily married man, with a wife and family. A man who likes the thought of living to a ripe old age and, thus, will not damage himself or your aircraft to satisfy his vanity, but rather fly within the parameters of his instructions, and thus produce for the manufacturers the best of tests ....." Surely no test-pilot has ever received a better testimonial? [2]

Test flights differed in their type, complexity and duration. Some involved a trip as far as the Isle of Man and back to make a comprehensive check of engines and/or equipment. Others might involve a much shorter journey to ascertain if a fault discovered on a previous air-test (or tests) had been rectified. At the other extreme came the stress tests in which an aircraft was flown to its know limitations. These demanded of a pilot all his skill, experience and courage for, at such times, he quite literally put his life on the line.

Other AVRO personnel, principally the Flight Sheds engine foremen and senior inspection staff, were involved in air-tests, and on those concerning the Anson (prior to the advent of the Mk.X series 2 in 1944 which had an hydraulically operated undercarriage) young apprentices were taken along to manually operate a lever 144 times to raise or lower its wheels! One of their number, Peter England recalled, "We didn't complain though because, in those days, lads of our age had no other opportunity to fly. We sweated a bit getting the wheels up and down, but it was worth it for the sheer excitement of being able to go up in a plane, and the others who didn't get the chance envied us like mad."

An Inspector from the A.I.D. flew on one in every five air-tests after he, or she, had first done a full inspection of the aircraft and duly signed a '1090'.

These, and hundreds of other, quite repetitive tests performed day by day must, at times, have proved very boring for even the most phlegmatic pilot thus it is, perhaps, less surprising to learn that, on occasions, David Biggart was tempted to liven-up the proceedings. Jack Keel remembered: "Scores of workers were taken up on one or other of the test flights, but such were the horror stories told on their return by those who had endured being thrown all over the sky by 'Reckless' - that's how he came to get his nickname - when it came to my turn I declined but, do you know, I have regretted it ever since."

Vic Carter, a senior foreman-electrician, once returned home after a day spent on air-tests with indentations in his scalp which remained for days afterwards!

Eric Dean, however, had no option but to go along on the flights "..... the sense of humour - at times we likened it to sadism - of one certain pilot got the better of him, and a number of us required to go on air-tests were subjected to some pretty savage treatment. We found ourselves suddenly being pinned to the roof of a turret, or flung to the fuselage floor, or shunted backwards and forwards in an aircraft flown by a pilot who, nevertheless, sat motionless with a studied dead-pan expression on his face. With a notebook, pen, and other equipment in our hands, and encumbered with a hefty parachute pack [3] - particularly restricting as far as

---

2 Captain Worrall was awarded the M.B.E. for his war-time service at Yeadon.
3 Some six months after these were issued to AID staff at Yeadon - having throughout, been taken on air tests they were found to have their safety strings still in place; thus, in the case of an emergency the parachutes would not have opened.

our female staff were concerned - frozen stiff in winter, and boiled like a tomato in a greenhouse in summer, we were helpless against those responsible.

Obviously it gave the perpetrator some satisfaction and, probably, helped him relieve the tedium, but there were occasions when we considered he had gone a bit too far, and then, 'words' were exchanged. On reflection, however, although at times we 'got the treatment' there was never any real danger on the flights. Oh no, the devil was always fully in control and knew exactly what he was doing ....."

Not all amusing incidents occurred in the air, however, as is confirmed by the following, well authenticated story:

Some Ansons were fitted with a power operated Bristol gun-turret driven by an hydraulic system which, in turn, was activated by an electric motor located under the navigators seat. As the turret could not be rotated without power it was necessary to 'switch on' before commencing an inspection. One day a female member of the A.I.D. staff (who to spare her blushes, shall remain nameless) overlooked this and, once inside the turret found, to her dismay, that it could not be traversed; whereupon, in attempting to extricate herself to rectify matters, she inadvertently became hooked by her bra' straps onto the gun-mounting. Finding herself in a semi-prone position, unable to move in or out of the turret, she desperately shouted for a colleague to come to her aid, but the only one readily available was of senior rank, and male. What followed in the very restricted confines of a transparent turret can easily be imagined, and the red-faced embarrassment of the official, and his lady subordinate, was in no way mitigated by the wisecracks mouthed by a large number of garrulous onlookers!

The height about sea level at which Yeadon stands lends it to being prone to periods of low cloud. With the advanced technology available today this is less of a problem (although not completely so) to aviators, than was the case during the 1940's. Then, such climatic conditions led to days of inactivity resulting in large numbers of aircraft sitting around the airfield perimeter awaiting test, or onward despatch.

"The taxi Anson's piled with flying kit,
Each ferry pilot cons his morning chit,
When from the weather office comes the cry
That to the west black clouds bestride the sky.
Then out "Met's" head is thrust from windows wide
This dark portent to ponder and deride;
'Tis dull, 'tis dark, the clouds precipitating,
No weather this for us to aviate in!
But one more bold by far than all the rest
Out to the runway taxis, gazes west,
Raises an eyebrow, casts his eyes about,
Wriggles his corns, his shoulder blades, his snout.
Instincts at work - will it be wet or fine?
What does this Flying-Weather seer divine?
He turns about and trundles back to "Met"
To tell them that it really will be wet."   Anon.

On the first day when predicted weather (predicted *only* to 'official' sources) changed from 10/10th's cloud - "birds will be walking," to "expect a period of clearer weather" (or similar), Captain Worrall and David Biggart would commence flying just after dawn and continue unabated until sunset. Similarly, early in the morning, several 'taxi' Ansons from No.7 Ferry Pilots Pool (7 FPP) at Sherburn-In-Elmet would arrive to disgorge a number of ATA aircrew (on one such flight ' - though not at Yeadon - an Anson carried 15 passengers. It's lady pilot stated she did not fear it would be unable to get off the ground, only that it's floor might give way!) ready to fly the waiting aircraft to their various allocated destinations throughout the country.

Before this could take place, however, once again a thorough inspection of each aircraft was necessary, including loose instruments such as navigators clocks, and even leather belts used to tie down items on board, before the exchange of '1090's' and '700's' could be made. That this was necessary was highlighted on an occasion when the procedure was not fully followed: a young ATA pilot being lucky to escape with her life, when the Anson she was attempting to fly-off hit a pile of earth on the perimeter adjacent to the A658. On investigation it was found that a cock had been left open, allowing fuel to flow from one side of its wing to the other at the whim of gravity, and it was fortunate that this did not result in tragedy. Although badly shaken, the young pilot displayed tremendous spirit for, after a brief rest, she continued her journey in another Anson.

All aircraft, whether built at Yeadon or at other factories, remained the property of its manufacturer until signed for, on a '700', by the pilot making onward delivery. This led to problems when bad weather forced aircraft on air-test to put down away from home base. In such circumstances only personnel from its 'parent' factory were allowed to inspect it to ascertain any problem, or even to undertake its refuelling.

Flight Testing and the A.T.A.

Thus various types and grades of fitters, inspectors and even fuel (on occasions) were required to be transported, often by road, to the location where the aircraft had landed; for them to undertake the usual pre-flight measures and the issuing of yet another '1090': a frustrating and time consuming exercise which, in winter, was seldom welcomed.

When a ferry pilot 'collected' an aircraft he, or she, handed over one copy of a triplicate 'chit' to the officiating AID member present. A second copy was given (later) to, and receipted by, the recipient and the third was sent, as a telegram, to No.41 Group R.A.F.: it being responsible for the allocation and movement of all aircraft. In return, before the aircraft departed, the responsible AID official at the factory airfield handed the ferry pilot its log book (airframe, engine and airscrew) which stayed with the aircraft throughout its life.

The ferry pilot then commenced preliminary cockpit checks; started and warmed up engines, keeping an eye on oil temperature and magnetos et al (at some factories this procedure was carried out by the AID, to its own satisfaction, *first*) and when satisfied all was as it should be he (or she) would sign the '700' following which, usually, with a cheery wave of the hand, and the minimum of fuss, off they flew into what, in the smoke-blackened Britain of the 1940's, would often be a grey murk rather than the proverbial wide, blue yonder!

Form 700 was a simplified version of a Log Book which recorded, among other things, the quantity of fuel carried (a Fighter's tanks were always completely full; a Bomber's half full) and no pilot flew an aircraft until he had agreed its acceptance by the signing of it.

The history of any British aircraft factory extant during the Second World War cannot be told fully without an appropriate reference to the Air Transport Auxiliary (ATA); which came into being during 1939, under the initial auspices of British Overseas Airways Corporation (BOAC), to relieve the R.A.F. of a variety of non-operational activities: transportation of despatches, mail, certain medical personnel and ambulance work et al, with a Director of BOAC, Gerard d'Erlanger - who became the ATA's first Commodore - being put in charge of running the organisation.

He began by recruiting civilians between the ages of 28 and 50 who had a minimum of 250 hours flying time in their log books, at a salary of £350-£400 per annum (an amount equivalent to that earned by junior officers with BOAC) and provided them with a dark blue uniform complete with ATA insignia; thereafter, instituting a chain of command and structure of organisation. Pauline Gower, with more than 2,000 flying hours in her log book, took charge of the women recruits.[4]

As the war progressed, and an increasing number of R.A.F. personnel were forced, by circumstances, into a more operational rôle the task of transporting a growing number of newly built, and in-store, aircraft also became the responsibility of the ATA. From 1st January, 1940, No.1 Ferry Pilots' Pool was established at White Waltham (Berkshire), which became the Headquarters of the organisation and, ultimately, fifteen more 'Ferry Pools' [5*] were formed at various locations throughout the U.K., plus four Training Schools and a Communications Air Movement Flight at White Waltham. **(Photo 37 - centre pages)**

By the end of hostilities 153 personnel of the ATA, including 16 women, had been killed fulfilling their duties; among them being the renowned Yorkshire-born aviatrix Amy Johnson, who died on 5th January 1941, when the Airspeed Oxford: V3540, she was ferrying from Prestwick via Squires Gate to Kidlington, crashed into the River Thames, miles off course.[6] Her divorced husband, Jim Mollison, equally famed, was also a ferry pilot with

---

4   Lettice Curtis, who was the first female member of the ATA to graduate onto four-engined types, ferried a total of 1,467 aircraft; of which 222 were Halifaxes, 162 Spitfires and 125 Mosquitos. Recently she has written down her reminiscences in 'The Forgotten Pilots': a long overdue testimonial to the Air Transport Auxiliary. (See Bibliography). In the winter of 1995 she agreed to become a Vice President of Yorkshire Air Museum.

5   No.15 FPP, at Hamble, became an all woman pool: i.e., all its Pilots were female - men were involved as flight engineers - but there was one chauvinistic C.O. at another Pool who would not allow any woman onto his flying-staff! From 29th July 1943, selected members of the WAAF began flying training with the ATA (to which they were seconded) and, ultimately, 17 of them qualified as pilots. Postwar, several joined the WAAFVR, and flew a variety of aircraft, including jets, with a number of RAFVR Squadrons.

6   There is some current speculation that the Oxford was shot-down, inadvertently, by a local anti-aircraft battery or guns on board a R.N. vessel; the matter, subsequently, being 'hushed up'!

the ATA, being awarded the M.B.E. at the end of the war. He served as a Flight Captain, she as a First Officer. [7]

The advent of women into the ranks of the ATA had, however, its lighter moments and, not least of all, on R.A.F. Stations which were, in the main, staffed by young would-be Lothario's, only too pleased to welcome visits by female ferry-pilot's; as was revealed by one of their number who, when asked by her Mother "...Is it dangerous, dear?..." replied "...Only when I land..."

During its short existence the ATA was responsible for the delivery of 171,934 single-engined aircraft, 110,636 twin-engined (of which 8,528 were Ansons), 25,030 four-engined (9,805 Lancasters) and 967 Flying Boats. Additionally, 179,325 hours were flown by ATA Ansons (a sizeable number of which were built at Yeadon) collecting and delivering crews. Although the overall totals include individual aircraft 'ferried' more than once, this does not detract from the fact that this was a remarkable effort by a civilian organisation - and a typically British one at that - with no previous experience of supporting a war machine.

The ATA took to its task in such a proficient manner that, with the minimum of fuss, it succeeded admirably where some thought it would fail: in the job of getting much needed aircraft from the factories, to where they were most sought, in the shortest possible time.

The contribution made by its 1,515 aircrew and 2,786 ground personnel was so vital to Britains war effort that, denied their participation, the R.A.F. would, undoubtedly, have found itself very seriously disadvantaged.

---

[7] Sir Freddie Laker, of Postwar Aviation Traders and Laker Airways fame, was a Flight Engineer with the ATA.

Flight Testing and the A.T.A.

Photo 36b. The arms take the form of a heraldic banner, supported by a scythe, the symbol of time. The scythe is in pretty bad shape on account of the way it has been knocked about by ratefixers. At the top of the banner is a pair of scissors, symbol of cutting, (this pair was made in Manchester not Sheffield). Across the middle of the banner is a golden chevron, inlaid with tears of blood. (these are shown incorrectly, they should be shown on the shoulders of a ratefixer, rampant). Below is a special hourglass as used by ratefixers, with auxiliary vacuum attachment. copyright J. Bruce.

The Advent of the Lancaster

In June 1941 a firm contract for 450 Lancaster bombers was issued and, by the end of the year, the first three to enter service with the R.A.F: L7537, L7538 and L7541 had been received by No.44 (Rhodesia) Squadron at Waddington. Shortly thereafter, further contracts increased the number of Lancasters on order to 3,020 and as, 2,000 Ansons were already contracted for, it was obvious that the AVRO factories alone could not hope to complete the work in the time specified. Thus the 'Lancaster Group' came into existence, which comprised A.V. Roe & Co. Ltd. (Manchester and Yeadon); Metropolitan-Vickers(Manchester); Armstrong-Whitworth (Bagington and, later, Bitteswell); Vickers (West Bromwich and Chester) and Austin Motors (Austin-Aero, Longridge).

At that time, in its thirty year existence, A.V. Roe & Co. Ltd. had designed and built in excess of 80 different types of aeroplane - excluding modifications. Among them were single seat fighters, single and twin-engined trainers, bombers, sea-planes and flying-boats, deck-landing types and torpedo bombers, Schneider Trophy entrants, several types designed or adapted for operations on polar expeditions, civil aeroplanes from single to four-engined; even autogiro's and, with the '504' and the Tutor, AVRO had supplied the R.A.F. with its standard basic trainer in unbroken succession since the First World War.

By the time the Lancaster arrived on the scene a substantial number of its key workers had been with AVRO for a lengthy period and, among them, occupying positions as departmental managers, foremen and chargehands, were men [1] of outstanding ability and 'know-how' gained in a highly competitive industry through good times and bad. They belonged to no 'Johnny-come-lately' outfit; the firm had been around a long time, and they knew something about building aeroplanes!

This was an attitude which prevailed among some of the 'old hands' transferred, through the advent of the Lancaster, to Yeadon where a few of them did, on occasions, display an air of superiority. This was, perhaps, understandable, but it was hardly likely to endear them to their new, largely conscripted, colleagues.

Getting Lancaster production quickly under way, and maintaining it successfully thereafter, was the direct result of a comprehensive manufacturing programme initiated by Roy Dobson (by then Managing Director of A.V. Roe & Co. Ltd.) and the man who replaced him as Works Manager (Chadderton), C.E. 'Ted' Fielding.

The production programme was planned down to the smallest detail, and incorporated the careful organisation of labour, equipment and material supplies, including that from many sub-contractors. A major ingredient to the success of the plan was the 'breaking-down' of the manufacturing processes into, literally, thousands of constituent operations to allow assembly by unskilled workers: clear indication that AVRO's founder, Alliott Roe's dictum 'make it simple' was still writ large in the minds of his successors. Indeed, so strongly had be imbued them with this philosophy that production requirements must be an essential part of design, that the Design Office was known as Production Department No.1.

All factories within the Lancaster Group began production of the bomber similarly prepared, as is confirmed by Harold Penrose: ".... each firm was not only provided with every design detail, drawings of special tools and jigs ..... but also with a complete Lancaster, five structural sets of fuselage, wings and other major components together with assembly equipment ....."[2]

As stated earlier, in January 1942 The Ministry of Aircraft Production assumed control of the aerodrome at Yeadon. All personnel involved with No.20 EFTS departed except for a handful of civilians, thereto employed by Blackburn Aircraft, who were re-employed in situ at the factory.

The L.U.A.S. Tiger Moth: BB673 remained, however, and continued to give air-experience flights for the tyro cadets.

---

1   Pre-war, women on the shop floor were conspicuous by their absence.
2   'Architect of Wings': Airlife 1985. Such aircraft were serialed in the 'R' series and are credited to Manchester production.

The Advent of the Lancaster

Lancaster production at the factory began simultaneously, its workers having, in the seven previous months, produced 100 Anson Mk.I's. A commendable enough effort given that it was achieved from scratch by a largely unskilled labour force; which, to a substantial degree, had been required to learn the job as they went along. The Anson, however, was a comparatively small aeroplane built, in its early configuration, basically of wood and weighing, when completed, about the same as two average-sized motor cars.

The Lancaster was quite a different proposition (and, until mid-March, 1942, still on the secret list), albeit that it was smaller than the other four-engined 'heavies' then in service with the R.A.F.: the Halifax and the Stirling (appreciably so in the case of the latter) it was, by the standards then pertaining, a very sizeable aeroplane, being 69ft 6 ins (21.18 metres) long with wings which spanned 102ft (31.08 metres), standing 20ft (6.09 metres) above the ground. On completion a Lancaster weighed, empty, 16½ tons (16.76 tonnes) and, when fully loaded with 2,154 gallons (9,792 litres) of 100 octane fuel, guns and equipment, more than 30 tons (30.48 tonnes). Specifically designed to be built in 31 main component parts (see diagram) made up of 55,000 smaller components (excluding nuts, bolts and rivets), a Lanc' required approximately 500,000 individual manufacturing operations, taking up more than 70,000 man hours, and 7,140sq.ft. (663,57 sq. metres) of floor space to complete, having thereto consumed the best part of 20 tons (20.32 tonnes) of aluminium; each aircraft costing the taxpayer £42,000.

To accommodate the considerable additional workload created by the Lancaster, it was necessary to supplement the workforce at Yeadon (and at other Lancaster Group factories) with skilled and unskilled personnel in substantial numbers; the input of all grades rising from a steady stream during 1941 to a veritable flood by the end of 1942, by which time in excess of 100 new employees were arriving at Yeadon each week.

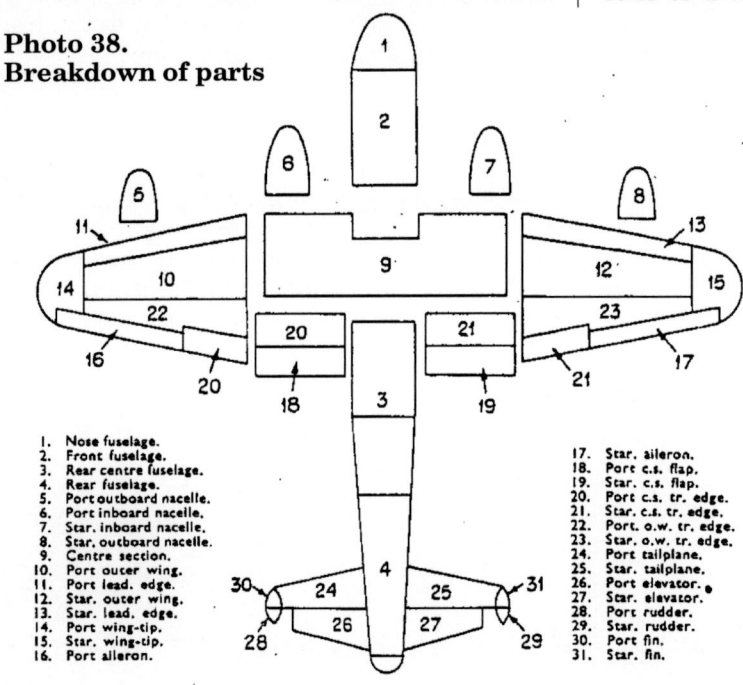

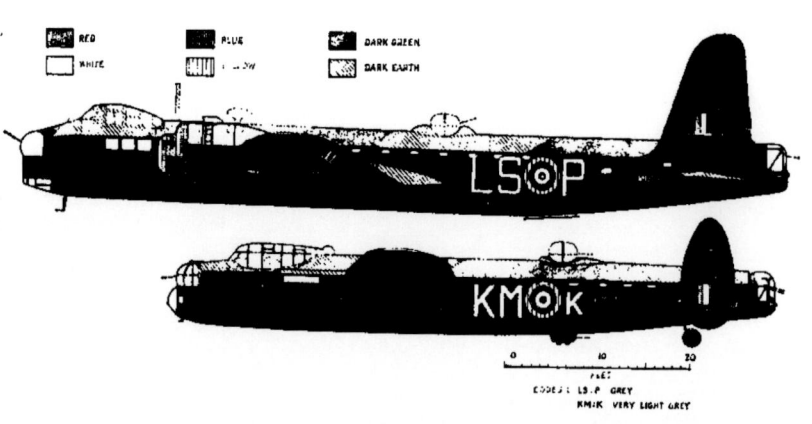

Photo 39. Comparison between the size of the Stirling (top) and the Lancaster. The Halifax came between the two.
Credit A.M. Alderson

Photo 38. Breakdown of parts

1. Nose fuselage.
2. Front fuselage.
3. Rear centre fuselage.
4. Rear fuselage.
5. Port outboard nacelle.
6. Port inboard nacelle.
7. Star. inboard nacelle.
8. Star. outboard nacelle.
9. Centre section.
10. Port outer wing.
11. Port lead. edge.
12. Star. outer wing.
13. Star. lead. edge.
14. Port wing-tip.
15. Star. wing-tip.
16. Port aileron.
17. Star. aileron.
18. Port c.s. flap.
19. Star. c.s. flap.
20. Port c.s. tr. edge.
21. Star. c.s. tr. edge.
22. Port. o.w. tr. edge.
23. Star. o.w. tr. edge.
24. Port tailplane.
25. Star. tailplane.
26. Port elevator.
27. Star. elevator.
28. Port rudder.
29. Star. rudder.
30. Port fin.
31. Star. fin.

Joe Munns was one of a number of specialist engineers recruited. He had begun his career with machine tool makers Alfred Herbert Limited of Coventry, where he was working when the Luftwaffe bombed the city in November, 1940. Later, when transferred to Yeadon, he was employed in the tool-room "..... marking off lines, angles, and contours on metals and castings prior to machining ....." He further recalled, "..... most of the things we marked out for were for jigs and tools; such as drill-jigs, press-bend tools and piercing tools. The largest job was working on the jig for the

Lancaster wings. The blue-print was so big we had to spread it out on the floor and crawl about it on our hands and knees until we found what we wanted ....."

The well organised AVRO bus service (eventually controlled by Mr. Nelson, formerly of the West Yorkshire Road Car Company) had not come into full operation when Joe began work at Yeadon. "At first I was on days but, as the work load increased, I went onto nights. My hours were 7p.m. to 7a.m., six nights a week. This meant I had to leave home about 5.30 p.m. then catch a service bus into Leeds and then another which went to Yeadon Fountain from where I walked the rest of the way ....." (The 'rest of the way' Joe mentioned was the best part of a mile. A walk which, of course, had to be repeated, but in reverse, at the end of his twelve hour shift!) "..... when I think back to those days now, I don't know how we managed it. It was all work and sleep, nothing else ....."

Photo 40. AVRO workers Tool Check.

Showing authorisation Number. 4960 allocated to Joe Munns.

Another specialist tradesman sent to Yeadon around that time was Alf Harris - 'Big Alf' to all who knew him - an electrician who, earlier in the war when employed at Port Glasgow, had also experienced what it was like to be on the receiving end of a Luftwaffe attack. Before going to Yeadon he spent some months at the huge underground ordnance complex at Thorp Arch, near Wetherby, so he was well used to the feeling of slight claustrophobia when entering a factory designed to appear, similarly, below ground level. (Which, despite many claims to the contrary, Yeadon was not). "..... I went first into 'F1' where the centre section of the 'planes were assembled then to 'D3': rear fuselage and tail-planes, followed by 'D2' where we worked on the cockpit section and then to 'D1' where the nose section was dealt with. Although I was a trained electrician I had never worked on an aeroplane before, but it came as an even bigger surprise when my instructor turned out to be a young lady. She was Eve Young from Rawdon who, before going to AVRO, had run a babywear shop in Leeds!"

During the early months of 1942, many new faces joined an every growing throng making their way to the factory. Some, particularly a number of the younger women who came from sheltered existences, pleasant homes and 'clean' jobs, felt that tending vicious, sparking, screaming machines was mans work; not meant for those of the fairer sex more used to clean finger nails and pretty dresses! Hundreds of others cared little for such memories - for that is what they had become - being more concerned with alleviating the tedium of their jobs and travelling to and from the factory on cold, dimly-lit buses. Sometimes, however, even such dark clouds could have a silver lining for it was on such a bus journey that Joe Munns met Elsie Glover, the girl who would become his wife. "..... after a while, though, Elsie got fed up with the bus trip and managed to get billeted out in Guiseley with a family named Busfield, and it made her day seem a good deal shorter. At AVRO she worked in the de-burring section, alongside May MacDonald and Miss Morrell - she has never forgotten them - where, for hour after hour, they sat at benches filing off rough edges from metal components after they had been machined. One of their most important jobs was in tackling and de-burring of the Lancaster bomb-bay doors, for nothing had to stop *them* from opening ....."

An interesting fact about this particular department is that it was the one to which all expectant mothers, other than those employed on non-manual work, were transferred to undertake 'light duties' and, although the mums-to-be never outnumbered the other staff employed there the place, nonetheless, became popularly known as the 'Maternity Ward'!

In the Nineteen-Forties, sex education if it existed at all, was minimal and the majority of young people were extremely naive about such matters. During the war years Britain experienced 300,000 illegitimate births (of which, despite a widely held belief to the contrary, little more than a quarter were the responsibility of U.S. Servicemen!), and the majority were neither planned nor welcomed. In the huge munitions factories, staffed with thousands of young women, forced into close proximity

The Advent of the Lancaster

with, often, somewhat older men (and many of both away from home and family) all working long hours, under the pressures and duress of war, the outcome was inevitable.

Clifford Stansfield who, like Alf Harris, worked on F1 Section at Yeadon recalled: "Practically every night at dinner-time (12a.m. - 1a.m.) there would be a show put on in the canteen. Anyone who didn't want to see it could go out into the field at the back of the factory for some fresh air and, as nearly everyone seemed to have an AVRO 'Sweetheart', it became a regular thing to say to the lady of your choice 'Can I take you out to see the AVRO moon' meaning, of course, let's go out for a kiss and cuddle!"

Without doubt there were hundreds of such liaisons and, not surprisingly, sometimes there was a price to pay. On one occasion, after the discovery of the body of a baby in a ladies toilet, a female worker was prosecuted for carrying out illegal abortions.

Evelyn Fitzgerald, whose maiden name was, most appropriately Lancaster, worked at the factory from 1941 to 1945, firstly wire-splicing on the Anson lines, and then on the Lancaster airframe. Her memories of those days were crystal clear: "I shall never forget my years at AVRO. To be honest it was the best time of my life. Something different seemed to happen every day but, above all the others, there are two memories that I shall never forget. The first was the time when a man got electrocuted - Oh, it was awful seeing him - and the second was the babies. It might be hard to believe but there *were* babies born at AVRO, and there were a lot of abortions too. Some of the girls were so innocent that they got themselves into trouble in no time. I can tell you (Evelyn added with a chuckle) if the lads from the 'Air Force had known what had gone on in some of their Lancasters - and not just on night-shift either - they would have been really surprised. Some babies were started in them and a few were born in them too."

To those unfamiliar with the sheer size of the factory, or of this period in history, such happenings might appear highly improbable, but the author has received corroboration that similar 'goings-on' (as one correspondent described such encounters) were not unusual in war-time factory life. One, well authenticated, story concerned a member of the nursing staff on duty at the factory clinic who, on opening the doors of a parked ambulance to admit a patient, discovered therein two workers embraced *flagranti delicto* who, far from being embarrassed, were most aggrieved at being asked to desist! **(Photo 41 - centre pages)**

Another factory liaison brought the wrath of an irate wife down upon the head of an innocent member of the AVRO Police. Arriving at his gate office the angry lady declared that 'they' should not allow her husband to be enticed into 'carrying-on' with that young hussy from assembly. "You should stop the married men being tempted," she said. The policeman smiled back at her and replied, "Eh, love, if we had to check every mans' marriage-lines, they would make such a pile we shouldn't be able to get down Harrogate Road for sweeping brushes."

Mrs. M. Wright, who began work at the factory shortly after the commencement of Lancaster production, recalled that not all romances were of an illicit nature. "I started at AVRO in 1942 and was there until it closed down. At the beginning I was on Ansons, where they trained me to do the electric wiring of the wireless operators lights - we ran wires to the terminals and we fixed wires into the radio transmitters - and we did the morse key and the roof lights. When I went onto the Lancaster I was given the job of wiring the bomb-release button and always worked a twelve hour shift, six days a week, with one weekend off in four, for which I was paid £3.2.6d (£3.12½p). My bosses were Vic Carter and Jack Brooks and our chargehand, Sam Pickard. All of them were good to work for, and Sam married one of the girls from the assembly-line called Doreen. The four of us, including my husband who was employed at AVRO as a welder, used to go out together - we had some lovely times - and Doreen and I still go out together twice a week!"

Mrs. E. Flesher who was employed, firstly, in the 'Bought-Out' store and, subsequently, on Lancaster fuselage assembly, remembered romantic breakfasts with her husband to be. "I have happy memories of AVRO for it was there I met my husband. We didn't get married until after the war because he was only there for about five months but, during that time, we used to have our breakfasts together - at 4a.m. - pineapple chunks and cold custard! Not very nice when you think about it now, but Oh so very enjoyable then."

Early in the war, when Britain stood alone with invasion imminent, many highly qualified tradesmen were, of necessity, called-up for service in the armed forces, thus denuding the war factories of their vital skills and experience. By early 1942, when the threat of invasion had receded, it was realised by those in authority that a number of such men would be of more value to the nation if gainfully employed in the munitions industries, and plans were set in motion for their transfer. Interestingly, however, the individuals concerned were not discharged to become civilian workers, but remained Service personnel throughout their subsequent involvement in the factories.

John Holbrook joined the R.A.F. in 1940 and received some of his early trade training at No.6 Service Flying Training School (6 SFTS) at Little Rissington, Gloucestershire, becoming a skilled fitter on engines and airframes. He recalled "In February, 1942, I was one of six R.A.F. lads 'seconded' to AVRO Yeadon. Three soon returned to Service duties but I, and at least one of the others, remained there for the duration (of the war). I worked exclusively on Lancaster 'finals', where my immediate superiors were Reg Bell and Jack Jagger, the latter having sold Rolls-Royce cars for a living before the war. Work in the 'finals' included fitting engines, propellers, fuel tanks and fuel systems, and the control systems - ailerons, trimmers, rudders, etc. The very first job I tackled was fitting fuel tanks - one large one and a smaller one in each wing - which were made in their thousands elsewhere in the factory. Eventually, I worked in every section in 'finals' and although I was technically still in the R.A.F., and was paid service rates of pay, I wore 'civvies' (civilian clothes) as did the other R.A.F. lads. We envied those who were being paid civilian rates of pay for doing the same jobs but we didn't qualify for it as, being servicemen, we couldn't join a trade union. We were subject to military rules and regulations, although being in a civvy place of work this affected us only rarely and, throughout all my time at AVRO, I lived at home with my wife in Pudsey!" **(Photo 43 - centre pages)**

Photo 42. Lancaster assembly.

copyright AVRO

Leslie Briggs was another seconded from the R.A.F. to Yeadon, but his was a somewhat more circuitous route.

"I joined the R.A.F. early in 1941 hoping to become a pilot but my hopes were dashed when it was discovered that I had slight colour blindness. I re-mustered and was sent to Melksham where I qualified as an instrument mechanic. During the course the gen was that those who passed with a mark in excess of 80% would be sent to America, 'in civvies', as they were not then in the war, to fit the new automatic pilot named 'George' into Liberators and Fortresses purchased for the R.A.F. I got the 80% alright, so you can imagine my disappointment when my posting came up and I found myself en-route to Snaith not Dallas'......"

Snaith, at the time, was the home of No.150 Squadron and, for several weeks, Leslie fitted and overhauled 'George' in its Mark III Wellingtons. Soon, however, he received orders to report to AVRO Yeadon where, supposedly, he was to undertake the same job on Lancasters.

"..... I went to Yeadon with another lad called Blore and we were very surprised to find we were to wear 'civvies' and, even more so, when we were issued with clothing coupons and ration cards which we didn't require in the R.A.F., and given a sleeping out pass and cost of living allowance of 30/-d (£1.50p) per week, so we could live out! I lived at home in Bingley with my family, and travelled to and from the factory on Andertons buses from Keighley, along with civilian employees, most of whom never knew I was still in the R.A.F. ....."

(It would appear that, where possible, personnel seconded from the Services into war factories were transferred to establishments relatively close to their homes).

Skilled and unskilled workers were needed as never before in Britains factories for, albeit that the events of this period have sometimes been overshadowed by others it is, nevertheless, arguable that these were the darkest days of the war, for Britain and her Allies.

On the 'Home Front', as it became known, Food Rationing, which had been introduced on

The Advent of the Lancaster

3rd January, 1940, was tightened, as was that of clothes and most household items (introduced in June, 1941) and, in February, 1942, even soap joined the commodities one could not obtain without enough 'points' (or 'coupons') in ones Ration Book, Britain was a grim, grey place and, elsewhere, the situation was desperate. The infamous Japanese attack on Pearl Harbour, on 7th December, 1941, precipitated the United States of America into the conflict but this did not, immediately, help turn the tide of Axis successes.

Earlier, during November, the pride of the Royal Navy, the aircraft carrier Ark Royal, had been sunk by a U-Boat and, in December, off the coast of Malaya the battleships Repulse and Prince of Wales met a similar fate at the hands of Japanese bombers. On Christmas Day, Hong Kong surrendered and, on 12th February, 1942, the joint forces of the Royal Navy and the R.A.F., admittedly hampered by bad weather, were unable to stop the German battleships Scharnhorst, Gneisenau and Prinz Eugen, from making an audacious and successful dash through the English Channel from Brest to Germany.

On the 15th, Britain suffered further ignominy and defeat when 'Impregnable' Singapore, like Hong Kong six weeks earlier, surrendered to the Japanese and, by the end of March, the armies of Imperial Japan had virtual control of South East Asia; and only 100 miles of the Torres Strait separated them from Australia.

On the Russian Front, although the German advance had been halted, no one could be sure if this would be maintained, for Hitler's armies stood at the gates of Moscow and had occupied cities as far east as Odessa and Kharkov. In the Western Desert, despite Tobruk having been relieved, the situation was one of stalemate and it was feared, in some quarters, that Rommel's Afrika Korps might not be contained. Meanwhile, in the Atlantic, a desperate struggle prevailed in which the convoys transporting vitally needed food and raw materials, were being decimated by U-Boats at a rate which could not be sustained if Britain was to survive; and, during the first three months of 1942, not one U-Boat was sunk by the Allies!

A grim time indeed and it could be argued, with some conviction, that this was not the most propitious moment for a Senior Officer to take up a new Command. Nevertheless, the situation demanded appropriate action and thus, on 22nd February, Air Marshal Arthur Harris [3] then forty-nine years of age, became Air Officer Commanding-in-Chief, Bomber Command. Subsequent events would prove (as had been the case with Winston Churchill two years earlier) that 'Cometh the hour - cometh the man !!

On the day Harris became its leader, Bomber Command consisted of 58 Squadrons, of which 7 were non-operational, comprising a total of 547 aircraft and, of these, only 62 - 29 Stirlings, 29 Halifaxes and 4 Lancasters - were 'heavies'. By May, on any

```
              AIRCRAFT FACTORY
                 SLACKNESS

             Reply to Otley M.P.'s
                  Criticisms

                (To the Editor)

Sir, With reference to your report of a speech made on
March 24th, in the House of Commons by Sir Granville Gib-
son, M.P. for Pudsey and Otley, in connection with a
particular aircraft factory.

The statements contained therein, both with regard to pro-
duction and conditions generally, are entirely without
foundation, and we, as the official representatives of the
workpeople in this factory, would appreciate the opportu-
nity of refuting the statements made by the honourable
gentleman.

It is regrettable that facts and figures cannot be quoted
publicly,as if this was possible a complete answer could
be given to the very loose and false statements contained
in his speech. -

Yours, etc.

J. DAVIS, Convenor of Works Committee;
T.W. NORTON, Chairman of Works Committee;
R. WARBURTON, ex-Chairman of Works Committee.
```

---

[3] Ultimatey; Marshal of the Royal Air Force, Sir Arthur T. Harris Bt.,GCB, OBE, AFC,LL.D (Born 1892, died 1984).

one occasion, there was an availability, on average, of slightly more than 400 aircraft, of which 136 were four-engined types. A further 71 were two-engined Blenheims, Whitleys and Hampdens, soon to be retired from front-line service, and the remainder were mostly Wellingtons.

It was recognised that to win the air war, substantially more four-engined bombers would be required: a total of 7,000 being deemed necessary by July, 1943, to allow for the inevitable losses, and yet be able to complete the task Bomber Command had been set. In the event, this proved to be a considerable under-estimate for, by the end of the war, more than twice that number had been built, and Lancaster production alone had surpassed it. By May, 1945, Bomber Command had at its disposal 1,609 Lancasters and 363 Halifaxes; almost fifteen times the number available three years previously, when, to the worker on the shop floor, such a development would have seemed as likely as sending a man to the moon.

The first Lancaster contract awarded to AVRO Yeadon (Contract No.1807) was for 350 of the type, of which the first 10 (Serial Nos. LM301-LM310) were designated Mark B.1's and the other 340 (LM311-LM756)[4] were planned as B.111's; the only difference between the two being in the type of engines used: the B.1's being fitted with Rolls-Royce Merline Type 20's built in Britain, and the B.111's with Merline Type 38's, manufactured under licence by Packard, in Detroit, U.S.A. Ultimately, the Yeadon factory produced 695 Lancaster, all but 54 of which (B1's) utilised engines built by the American Company, and only AVRO (Manchester) constructed more B.111's than Yeadon.

It is, perhaps, pertinent here to make specific reference to the ubiquitous Rolls-Royce Merlin engine which, in addition to the Lancaster, also powered the Hurricane, Spitfire, Mosquito, early series Halifax, later series Mustang and, in one configuration or another, several other types during the Second World War. Tens of thousands of Merlins were manufactured by the Rolls-Royce factories in England and Scotland, and by Packard in the U.S.A., and there is no question that the engine was a key factor in the Allies gaining air supremacy. The plaudits for achieving victory in the Battle of Britain have, quite rightly, been heaped upon the heads of 'The Few', but it has to be acknowledged that the future of the Free World hung, not only in their young hands, but also on the capabilities of this superb engine: and its ongoing improvement and development was of equal significance in the eventual outcome of the air war.

The Merlin engine has, quite rightly, become a legend but a large slice of credit for its ultimate success must go to F. Rodwell Banks, a fuel technician, who, during a successful career, became Director General of Engine Research at the Royal Aircraft Establishment (RAE), Farnborough. He pioneered the introduction of leaded fuel into Britain, and his work was invaluable to Supermarine in its successful bids for the Schneider Trophy. Subsequently, in liaison with Rolls-Royce, through the introduction of 87 octane and, later, 100 octane fuels, his researches brought about an enhancement in performance of the engine which was to prove decisive.

During the making of the film 'Battle of Britain' in 1969, in addition to the British fighters fitted with various variants, all the 'Heinkel 111's' and 'Messerschmitt 109's' (Spanish built) were powered by Merline 500/45 series engines and currently, the world speed record for a piston-engined aircraft of 517.06mph (831.94kph) is held by a specially prepared Merlin.

Concurrent with the first Lancaster contract, 600 more Anson Mk.1's were allocated to Yeadon and its workers, even if they had been ignorant of the fact beforehand, were now fully aware of the tremendous task which lay before them. This is not to say, however, that they were without their critics, as is evident from this extract from the Wharfedale and Airedale Observer of 3rd April, 1942:

Thus rumour and innuendo, those pernicious products of secrecy, were a threat to sustaining war workers in their endeavours. Nevertheless, it was absolutely vital that their morale was maintained for, if this was to fall (as had been proved elsewhere) production would follow suit. See opposite page.

Various methods were employed to obviate such a situation; including frequent visits by 'stars' of the stage, screen and radio; social get-togethers of various kinds and tours of the factory by a succession of V.I.P.'s; the latter, usually, given to making patriotic exhortations from the stage in the main canteen!

---

4   In an effort to confuse the enemy as to how many aircraft were being built, some numbers were omitted from a serial sequence.

The Advent of the Lancaster

'Team Spirit' was encouraged through the formation of the AVRO Institute through which musical, theatrical and sports groups were organised; and one of the first reports of the latter concerned a cricket match, played in aid of the Red Cross Fund on 19th July, 1942, between a 'North East Works X1' and a team from Otley. This took place at the (then) ground of Green Lane Cricket Club, Yeadon, which became the home venue for the AVRO factory team; on that occasion represented by Messrs. Bailey, Cooper, Farrer, Mellor, Elliot, Nottingham, Howard, Conroy, McAndrew, Bartle, Murphy, Carlisle and Swift. (Otley also fielded thirteen players).

Early in the war, for security reasons, any sports team, or theatrical or musical group representing the factory was described simply as coming from a 'North East Works'; but, as the war progressed, their origin became common knowledge and, ultimately, the name AVRO was used quite openly.

During a working week averaging almost 70 hours, it was obviously important for those involved to be able to escape for a while from the tedium and repetitiveness of their job. Thus, as a result of tests made in Britain and the U.S.A., which proved that music could mitigate stress, management wisely allowed for the more popular radio programmes to be relayed over the loud-speaker systems of their factories; but this was not achieved without a struggle in some establishments where certain managers were convinced, initially, that the intrusion of music would prove distracting to their workforce!

Soon, however, workers were happily singing along with their favourite artistes and bands of the day even though, in some departments, the performers could barely be heard above the din of the machinery! One former Yeadon employee remarked, "Even when I couldn't hear the wireless properly for the racket in our section, I could always tell when 'Don't fence me in' or 'Pistol-packing Mamma' was on because the girls used to laugh and do all the actions."

The BBC produced several radio programmes designed specifically for war workers: notably 'Music While You Work', a half-hourly medley of popular music, and 'Workers Playtime' a variety show of similar length transmitted to coincide with 'dinner breaks'. In addition, most munitions factories provided some 'in house' entertainment several times each week, and this is a subject to which we shall return.

War workers also enjoyed certain privileges denied to the man and woman in the street, in that they were given an extra allowance of food, made available as cheap meals in works canteens - where the provision of hot, cooked, food was a comparatively recent innovation - and although, of necessity, the fare was essentially plain it was, nevertheless, largely welcomed; not least of all because it was not subject to deduction from ones Ration Book!

Another occasional 'perk' came in the form of extra supplies of cigarettes - a commodity often unobtainable in the shops - and in an era when the majority of adults (and many who were not) were smokers, such a bonanza brought real pleasure. For the minority who were not addicted to the 'weed' its availability was a source of some profit, and a number of workers made quite a good side-line out of it.

In a more obvious attempt to promote increased production from its workforce, AVRO nurtured an active competitiveness within its factories, by publishing a league table of their achievements against set targets. From comments made by several former employees at Yeadon it would appear, however, that the scheme, far from generating the anticipated esprit-de-corps, actually accentuated any grievances or differences, real or imagined, which existed between them.

One form of morale boosting exercise which was a success, was that which involved visits to the factory by those who flew the aircraft built there. This was particularly evident within the ranks of women workers, many of whom recall the visits to this day.

Evelyn Fitzgerald (nee Lancaster) remembered: "I'll never forget how young they looked; just boys really, and it made you feel proud to think they were flying over Germany in 'planes you had helped build."

There is no doubt that, overall, such visits had the desired effect, for the workers realised that the young men in blue would be lucky to survive. "We weren't going to let them down" is a comment made to the author several times and many workers remembered the visits of Wing Commander Guy Gibson, V.C., DSO[*]., DFC[*]., and his crew after the 'Dams' raid in 1943,[5] and that of Flt. Lt Bill Reid

---

5   None of the Lancasters involved in the epic attack were built at Yeadon.

The Advent of the Lancaster

(of whom more later) and the survivors of his crew, when they went to the factory after he had won the V.C. piloting a Lancaster built there.

Visits to war factories by V.I.P.'s other than Service personnel were also important, and none more so that when the visitors were members of the Royal Family. Lord Louis Mountbatten made the trip to Yeadon before he was appointed Allied Supreme Commander in South-East Asia, and he made a tremendous impression, particularly on the ladies, when he spoke in the canteen. He told them that they should not think of their serving menfolk as gazing starry-eyed into the night sky dreaming of them back home, but rather that their thoughts were constantly on the enemy so that he could be defeated as soon as possible!

The much loved Princess Royal also visited the factory from her home at nearby Harewood House, as was recalled by her son, the Honourable Gerald Lascelles:

"My only recollection of AVRO and Yeadon was that my mother, the late Princess Royal, visited the factory some time early in 1942, and I accompanied her on this trip. I remember being fascinated by the size of the Lancasters which were being built there at the time, and was most intrigued by the gun turrets which I think came to the factory already assembled, and merely had to be fitted into the aircraft frame."

Donald Winn also recalled the occasion, but from a different standpoint. "Some of those so and so's from Manchester were, as usual, trying their best to be on the front row when a Royal paid us a visit and, just after we all lined up, round the corner came one of the lassies from the canteen with her tea trolley, completely unaware that anything out of the ordinary was afoot (in a factory so large this was not uncommon). As soon as she realised she tried to stop but not before she had jerked her trolley into somebody who, in turn bumped into somebody else and so on. As you are not supposed to speak unless spoken to when in the presence of Royalty, it was hilarious watching them trying not to curse as they almost fell over each other. The Princess just smiled in a knowing way, but said nothing, and I though it served the Manchester crowd right for trying to be one up on the rest of us again. The sad part was that the lass with the trolley got scalded with hot tea."

In the context of Royal visits a unique event took place at Yeadon on Thursday, 26th March, 1942, when Their Majesties King George VI and Queen Elizabeth toured the factory. They made the visit ostensibly to sign GEORGE and ELIZABETH on the fuselages of two Lancasters, presented to them as being the first to come from the production lines at Yeadon; but, as the King and Queen walked through the various departments to be greeted by cheering workers, it was obvious that their presence was of far greater significance in boosting

Photo 44.

Old newspaper cutting of H.M. King George VI and Queen Elizebeth pictured in Bradford. A little before they visited the factory, Thursday 26th March 1942.

- 67 -

The Advent of the Lancaster

morale. Details of the ceremony have been recorded by Harold Penrose,[6] and in a reference to what occurred immediately after the Royal signatures were appended, he states "..... then the King was conducted to the door of his machine and made his way to the cockpit where Roy Chadwick sat by his side, and they talked of their early flying experiences with AVRO 504's. Meanwhile, Her Majesty was listening with gracious dignity to Roy Dobson's bubbling enthusiasm on such subjects as welfare of employees, and how aeroplanes are made.

When the King rejoined her she turned from Dobson to the AVRO designer and said 'Tell me, Mr. Chadwick, how do you manage to design such huge and complex aeroplanes as these?' He gave it a moments thought, then smilingly replied, 'Well, Ma'am, you don't have to be crazy but it's a help!' At which Royal protocol collapsed in laughter ....." His Majesty, wearing the uniform of a Marshal of the Royal Air Force, and the Queen dressed in a long coat of fine woollen material in Parma violet colour, with a matching wide-brimmed felt hat, and a posy of pink flowers attached to her coat, had visited Bradford and the Royal Ordnance factory at Thorp Arch, before travelling by road to Yeadon. As the King and Queen drove to and from the factory, they were greeted by thousands of flag-waving, cheering, locals whose morale was, similarly, greatly lifted by the occasion.

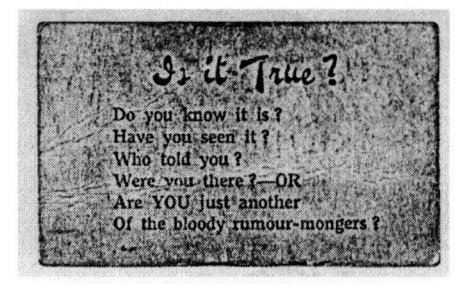

Photo 44a. One of the many cards issued to prevent loose talk.

Photo 44b. Two principal characters in the story of A.V.Roe and Co Ltd: Roy Chadwick (left) and Roy Dobson (pointing finger at model of York). photo credit AVRO

---

6   "Architect of Wings", .by Harold Pearce: Airlife 1985

Photo 1. Ist Lt. Max Dowden USAAF pictured beneath a Halifax Mk. II. credit Russell Margerison.

Photo 2. right, High Street, Yeadon, late 1930's. The 'New Picture House' is the white building on the left. A scene many AVRO employees came to know well.

Photo 13. botton left, A Heinkel He III of KG4: the unit involved in attacks on Leeds and Bradford August 1940.

Photo 18. left, Southern aspect of the factory, winter 1992. Note extreme right the un-camouflaged sloping roof and hangar door exit.
Photo 20. above, Anson Mk I's in paint shop (Dope House) at Yeadon. credit AVRO/MAP. Photo 21. below, The Anson electrical installation department. credit AVRO/MAP.

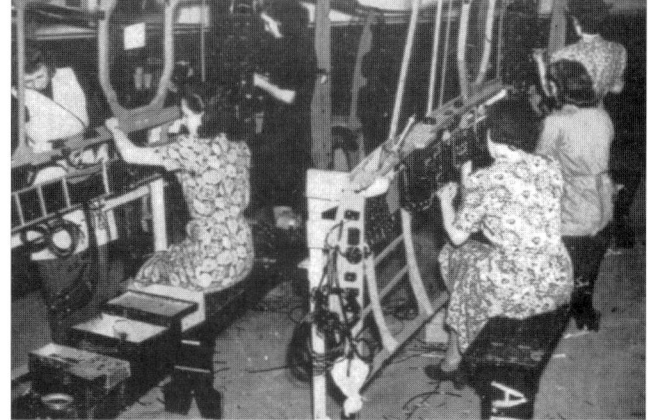

5. Two of No. 609 (West Riding) ron's Hawker Harts: K1420 & K839? of the Watch Office / Op's room.

J. Fawcett.

Photo 5A. Hawker Hinds: K5497, K5451 & 6845 of No. 609 Squadron pictured outside the Bessoneau hangar. Yeadon March 1938. See Appendix B. Credit Aireborough & Horsforth Museum Society.

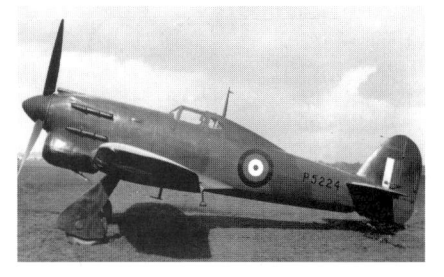

Photo 16. The ill fated Tornado, five of which were built at Yeadon. credit I.W.M.

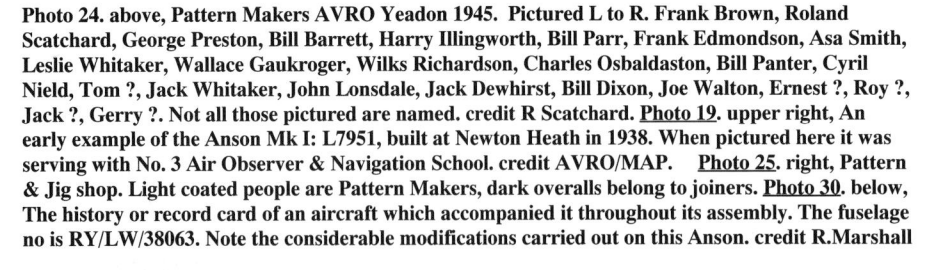

Photo 24. above, Pattern Makers AVRO Yeadon 1945. Pictured L to R. Frank Brown, Roland Scatchard, George Preston, Bill Barrett, Harry Illingworth, Bill Parr, Frank Edmondson, Asa Smith, Leslie Whitaker, Wallace Gaukroger, Wilks Richardson, Charles Osbaldaston, Bill Panter, Cyril Nield, Tom ?, Jack Whitaker, John Lonsdale, Jack Dewhirst, Bill Dixon, Joe Walton, Ernest ?, Roy ?, Jack ?, Gerry ?. Not all those pictured are named. credit R Scatchard. Photo 19. upper right, An early example of the Anson Mk I: L7951, built at Newton Heath in 1938. When pictured here it was serving with No. 3 Air Observer & Navigation School. credit AVRO/MAP.   Photo 25. right, Pattern & Jig shop. Light coated people are Pattern Makers, dark overalls belong to joiners. Photo 30. below, The history or record card of an aircraft which accompanied it throughout its assembly. The fuselage no is RY/LW/38063. Note the considerable modifications carried out on this Anson. credit R.Marshall

Photo 27A. The first volunteers to Leeds University Air Squadron, pictured outside No. 39 University Road, 1941. Back row: Snow, Crowther, Benson, Scargill, Eastwood, Bryant, Unknown, Kujundzic, Whitehead, Gartery, Centre: Aaron, Appleby, Lupton, Watson, Unknown, Braidwood, Willesden, Hanson, Chapman, Unknown, Denby, Horner, Porritt. Front: Mrs Davies(sec), Dyson, Staziker, Cpl Varley, Pilot Off. Ince, Wing Commander Ridley, Sgt Palmer, Cpl Stubbins, Hodsman, Bothom, Mr Crosland (driver). Only a handfull of those who subsequently qualified survived the war.   credit S.B. Hanson/ E.G. Appleby.

Photo 43. Some of the Lancaster/York 'Finals' personnel, including, centre rear, Alf Harris; and, tenth from right (in suit), Leslie Chorlton, who was in charge. Taken 1945. Photo credit A. Harris.

Photo 32. Bernard Hepton as he is better known today. Photo credit Bernard Hepton.

Photo 41. Three members of the AVRO Police Force. William Windross at right of picture seen outside Gatehouse No. 1. Note AVRO winged insignia on the caps. Photo credit Mrs Windross.

Photo 35. 'Some Yeadon Worthies' gathered in front of the aerodrome offices (Club House). Back left, Arthur Marland (Flight Sheds Superintendant), immediately to his front-left, Ted Sherring(Chief Inspector-Flight Sheds) whose deputy, George Barlow is on extreme left (hand on chair). 2nd row, 2nd from right, Captain Worrall (Airport Controller & Chief Test Pilot), back right with glasses, W Hyde (Snr. Foreman), Front row, extreme right, Pam Worrall (Captn. Worrall's daughter and secretary), extreme left, Mrs Eileen Southgate & to her left Kay Marshall, the wife of Ray Marshall, who was responsible for this photograpgh.

Photo 34. Some of the Flight Sheds personnel. Mrs Foster is pictured in boiler suite (with belt) below the Anson's port side propeller.   Photo credit Mrs D. Foster.

Photo 48. A rather severe looking J.A. 'Seamus' Stuart in RAF uniform. Photo credit Miss G. Stuart.

Photo 37. The all woman Ferry Pilots Pool (No.15) at Hamble. The gent on the right was a flight engineer. 'Peggy' Lucas right front row.   Photo credit Y. 'Peggy' Lucas

Photo 23. Ernest Bevin.

Photo 58. Gracie Fields surrounded by admirers after she had entertained a huge audience in the canteen, 30th August 1943.   Photo credit R Scatchard.

Photo 59. The former Peacock Hotel at Yeadon. Photographed in 1992 just before it was demolished. Photo credit G. Myers.

Photo 60. Low Hall, Nether Yeadon, used by AVRO to accommodate visiting V.I.P's.   Photo credit Aireborough & Horsforth Museum Society.

Photo 45. M2-AK, a Ju88A-5, of No.2 Staffel Kustenfliegergruppe 106 (2/106): identical to the M2-DK, which crashed at Idle, Bradford, 5th May 1941. Note: eight armourers were needed to deal with its bomb load.

Photo 47. Dornier Do.217E-4S. The type of aircraft in service with KG2 at the time of the Luftwaffe's last attack on Leeds on 27th/28th August 1942.

Photo 50. Yeadon built Anson Mk.1:MG19 No.1 Air Gunnery School.(1 AGS), Pembr 1943. Identical to those despatched to oth similar units.

Photo 64a. Fl/Lt Bill Reid VC, receiving silver model Lancaster from the works manager H.W. Harper on his visit to the factory December 1943. The four surviving members of his crew were L to R. P/O Les Rolton DFC, (Bomb Aimer), Sgt Jim Norris CGM (Flight Engineer), F/Sgt Frank Emmerson DFM, (Rear Gunner), Fl/Lt Bill Reid VC, F/Sgt Cyril Baldwin (Mid Upper Gunner). credit W Reid VC,BSc.

Photo 46. above, Copy of a rather creased Luftwaffe aerial target map of parts of Leeds; probably obtained aboard the airship Hindenburg during its visits in May and June 1936. Armley & Wellington Road at bottom left of picture. B,C &D were gasworks, A was Leeds Forge Albion works.

Photo 66. 'Survivors'

Yeadon built Lancaster III:LM509 'PH-M' Minnie the Moocher of No. 12 Sqdn, Wickenby, with some of its air and ground crew. Skippered by Plt/Off H. Trotter. The bomb symbols represent the 44 ops. 'Minnie' and her crew went on to survive the war. credit Wickenby Register.

Photo 65. Yeadon built Lancaster III:LM332 of No. 103 Sqdn. Elsham Wolds, which took part in attacks on Berlin on six occasions. Pictured here with some members of Tom Picketts crew (later Air Chief Marshall Sir Thomas-not photgraphed) On 16th Dec. 1943 when with No. 576 Sqdn it collided with Lancaster JB670 over Ulceby shortly after take off for Berlin. The crew who were all killed, comprised: F/Sgt F.R. Scott, Sgt S.V. Hull, F/Sgt P.M.C. Ellis, Sgt G.G. Critchley, Sgt G.H. Caldwell, Sgt B.P. Wicks, Sgt J.W. Ross.

Photo 69. The ambulance conversion of the Anson. As can be seen, the special hatch provided access for stretchers. credit P.H.T. Green Collection.

Photo 63. Some of the damage inflicted to Lancaster LM360, by the cannon fire of an enemy nightfighter. credit W. Reid VC, BSc.

Photo 64. Fairey Battle Bombers (R to L):K7638, K763 ? & K7629 used by No. 609 (West Riding) Sqdn. at Yeadon during Spring/Summer 1939, for the conversion of its pilots onto monoplanes in readiness for the Spitfire. Note new hanger under construction. credit J. Fawcett.

Photo 72. Factory Home Guard unit. The factory had its own Home Guard unit. Here is 'E' Company 3oth BN. W.R. Home Guard September 1944; Sgt Allen Modley 7th from right, 3rd row back. credit G. Modley.

Photo 75. Flg/Off C.C. Smith DFC pictured (in characteristic pose !) November 1944.

Photo 76. Lancaster III:RE118, HW-N^2 'Naughty Nan' of No. 100 Squadron, Elsham Wolds, 1945, pictured after bringing back ex-prisonners of War from Italy, May 1945. copyright R Pierson.

Photo 70. Powered by Armstrong Siddeley Cheetah XIX engines, NK870 was the prototype ambulance variant of the Anson Mk XI. Fitted with Fairey-Reed, fixed pitch metal propellers, hydraulically operated flaps and undercarriage, it first flew at Yeadon on 30th July 1944. copyright Philip Jarrett.

Photo 71. Originally built at Yeadon in 1943 as an Anson Mk I, MG159 was later converted to become the prototype Mk XII (as seen here) and served with AVRO's controller of research and development. During 1944 it was converted to an Anson Mk XIX and early 1945 was re-registered as an AVRO Nineteen. copyright Philip Jarrett.

Photo 85. Lancaster's being refurbished at AVRO's repair facility at Bracebridge Heath, Lincoln.   copyright AVRO/MAP

Photo 77. above, Lancaster Mk I:ME455 (built at Yeadon) of No. XV Squadron, Mildenhall, prior to flying home newly released British Prisoners of War from Germany, Summer 1945. credit Chaz Bowyer Collection.

Photo 84. left, Nancy Blezard and colleagues riveting Lancaster Bomb Bay Doors. The most vulnerable part of an aircraft, AVRO, Yeadon 1943. credit Miss Blezard.

Photo 83. The last Lancaster built at Yeadon MkIII:TX273. Captain Worrall at the controls, lifts off from runway 19, October 1945. credit AVRO/MAP.

Photo 78. Lincoln B.2:RE290 in Far East paint scheme. Not one of the six Lincoln's built at Yeadon, but identical thereto. The photograph well illustrates the differences between the type and the Lancaster. credit via Bruce Robertson.

Photo 87. Fl/Lt. 'Bill' Reid VC and crew, plus two unidentified personnel, under the wing of the AVRO York (also unidentified), on their visit to the factory.

Photo 82. The plaque placed alongside the Anson for Yeadon's Victory Parade read: A 25th of Britain's war production of 125,000 planes. The local Yeadon factory made 4,7000 Anson's, 700 Lancaster's   copyright AVRO/MAP

Photo 88. A group of Aerodrome/Flight Sheds personnel posed with one of the five Yorks destined for Fama in Argentina. Captain Worrell is in the second row (under the 'M'), his daughter and secretary Pam, front right, third from right Mrs Eileen Southgate, standing 8th from left, Ted Sherring (chief Inspector Aerodrome).   photo credit R. Marshall.

Photo 94. AVRO Nineteen:G-AGZT with Captain Worrell at the controls leaving runway 28 on air test. Note puff of smoke emitted by engines, the Clubhouse bottom left and runway 01/19 crossing at right angles. photo credit R Marshall.

Photo 91. AVRO Nineteen G-AGNI loaned by AVRO to the Railway Air Services for evaluation. credit J. Parke.

Photo 93. G-AGUX, G-AGUE, G-AGUD, the first three AVRO Nineteen's delivered to Railway Air Services. Seen here on completion at Yeadon late 1945. Note wartime firing butts in the distance. Credit A.V.ROE/MAP

Photo 89. Jig and Tool Drawing Office staff. L to R. Niad, Jarvis, Farrar, Poole, Green, Barker, Chomley, Hird, J Marshall, Asquith, G Grange, Richardson, Doreen Eagan, Kell, Metcalf, Crowther, Durkells, Berrington, Lamb, Woodford, Whiteley, Barras, Parker, Stableford, Cocking, Hart, Holmes, Burnett, Donaldson, Rymes, Front row, R.P. Dodsworth - Chief Draughtsman. photo credit J.H. Kell.

Photo 95. Type XIX:TX223, one of the last Anson's built at Yeadon to enter service with the RAF-with which it served until 14th October 1963-photographed summer 1946 outside 'Civvy' hanger. Note 'Club House' / Flying Control Building; M.A.P. van and pre-war Riley car; also Fire - Watchers tower on top of hangar.   photo credit R. Scatchard.

Photo 92. AVRO Nineteen's:G-AGZT (which went to Minister of Civil Aviation, Gatwick) and G-AGUD (one of those sold to RAS), seen here in the flight sheds at Yeadon prior to flight testing. Note other Anson under construction. photo credit R. Marshall.

Photo 100. A group of Flight Sheds employees. W Hyde, Senior Foreman, seated centre of front row with glasses, arms crossed. credit A Marland.

Photo 97. Anson Flight Sheds Inspectors 1945/6.   photo via Mrs. D. Foster.

Photo 105. 'Pilot Officer' (later Wing Commander) A.B. Walker who flew 28 of the Lancasters built at Yeadon. credit A.B. Walker

106. The last Lancaster built at Yeadon: TX273 seen here when converted to MR.3 and serving as 'U' (Uncle) with No. 38 Squadron, at Luqa, Malta in ...ber 1950. Note: below rear turret the rear facing F.24 camera for assessing ...g accuracy. credit Wing Commander A.B. Walker RAF(Ret'd)

Photo 104. York: G-ANTK, formerly MW 232. credit Ken Ellis Collection.

Photo 107. left, Anson C.19: VL349 of Southern Communications Squadron RAF. Built in the last batch of aircraft produced at Yeadon. This aircraft is preserved by the Norfolk and Suffolk Aviation Museum, Flixton. credit M.O.D.

Photo 90. right, Passenger cabin of the Anson Nineteen. It had seven seats and a fuselage provided with a modicum of soundproofing. Note, curtained off, toilet at rear of cabin ! credit A.V.Roe/MAP.

Photo 99. Staff and apprentices employed in the Pattern Shop. L to R. Wilks Richardson, Eddie -, Jack Dewhirst, - Fletcher, Frank Colling (Shop Steward from Sunderland), ?,?,?, Lewis Howarth (in Trilby) The Chargehand, ?, Cyril Neild (member of factory dance orchestra), Harry Illingworth. credit R. Scatchard.

Photo 98. Vera Marland (4th from right) and colleages from the factory Tax Office pictured with unidentified York. photo via Mrs V Marland (Nee Addison). Photo 29. right, one of the many thousands of descriptive drawings produced to aid 'Green' unskilled workers in assimilating the procedure for a specific job. This one refers to 7th operation in the construction of the Bomb Carrier. Note: every item was given an ID no. credit J.H.Kell

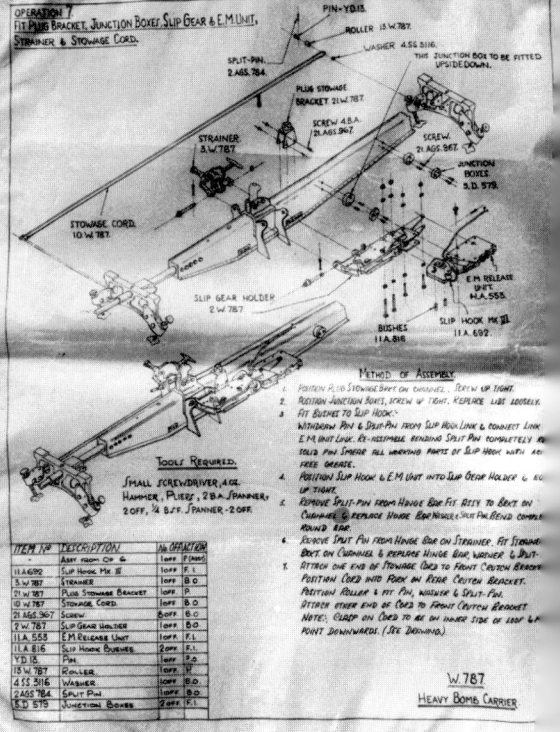

Photo 103. Yorks at Gatow during Berlin airlift. The aircraft centre is Yeadon built example MK.C.1:MW267, KY-N of No. 242 Squadron, almost certainly some of the other Yorks were similarly, ex Yeadon. credit via Bruce Robertson.

Photo 108. Destruction of the original Gatehouse No. 1 during 1990, to make w a new improved version. credit G Lanvin

Visits from the Luftwaffe - and Further Development at the Factory

Surprisingly, the number of air-attacks, locally, proved far less than anticipated; the conviction held, however, that "they" - the enemy - knew of the factory and would try to bomb it out of existence. Relative thereto it is, perhaps, pertinent here to take a closer look at the *actual* activities of the GAF, from 1940.

Between August, 1940 and the end of April, 1941, Bradford and Leeds were attacked by the Luftwaffe on four and seven occasions respectively. Thereafter, Bradford was not raided again although, at 12.50a.m. on Monday, 5th May, 1941, a Junkers Ju88 crashed on fire into houses in High Street, Idle: a suburb of the city, killing three civilians and seriously injuring five more. As there was no other Luftwaffe activity in the area that night and, as Idle is but four miles from the factory, the incident inspired a local belief that the enemy aircraft had come to attack it. This seemed confirmed when it became known that German 'parachutists' had landed, not far away, in Farnley, Otley and Guiseley. The reality, as is often the case in wartime, was quite different for, as a result of lengthy research, it can now be confirmed that the aircraft: Ju88A - 5 (Werke No.0656) 'M2-DK' of 2 Staffel, Kustenfliegergruppe 106 (2/106): a specialist unit, then based at Caen, primarily engaged in maritime-reconnaissance, mine-laying and anti-shipping activities, was miles off-course from its intended target at Barrow-in-Furness, having been chased and, ultimately, attacked above Nidderdale by an AI radar-equipped Beaufighter: R.2156 of No.25 Squadron, crewed by Sergeant Ken Hollowell and his radar-operator, Sergeant Crossman. **(Photo 45 - centre pages)**

They had taken-off from their base at Wittering at 23.15 hours, returning at 01.25 claiming '...one E/A probably destroyed and one damaged...' (north of Bradford). The German pilot: naval officer Oblt. zur See R. Metzger, stayed with his stricken aircraft until shortly before it went out of control, descending by parachute onto the roof of the Ings Hotel, Guiseley, breaking an ankle. The other mysterious 'parachutists' were the three members of his crew; the last mentioned being only eighteen-years of age: Oblt.E. Jürgens, Ober Fw.H. Beeck and Fw.H. Jänicken. Among those involved in their capture were Police Constable 'Tim' Heeley (later Superintendent) who would gain fame, in retirement, broadcasting on Radio Leeds; Frank Pawson of the A.F.S.; Fire-Watcher W.A. Bishop and Air-Raid Wardens' Arthur Broady and E.L. Whitewick.

It was reported that his captors considered Metzger to be a 'real Nazi', but his arrogance would surely have been dampened had he but known what type of aircraft had attacked his own! The four 20mm cannon of a Beaufighter were usually lethal at short range and he and his crew were extremely fortunate to have survived.

A drogue parachute from the Ju88, collected by a local policeman, is now on display in the 'After The Battle Collection', at Plaistow, London.

No.25 Squadron is still active, being based, currently, at RAF Leeming, North Yorkshire from where, coincidently, present aircrew require only minutes in their Tornado F.3's to overfly the exact location where, on that night in May 1941, two of their predecessors were called upon to take such dramatic action in defence of their country.

From the Spring of 1941 the Luftwaffe was never again able to mount a sustained bombing offensive against Britain; this being due, in the main, to the demands placed upon it by the campaigns in North Africa, the Balkans and, principally, the Russian Front. By the late summer of 1942, the German bomber force available in the West had been reduced to 10% of that available two years before. This is not to say, however, that its activities over Britain came to an end but, ignoring some notable exceptions outside the scope of this book, most of its raids were carried out by small numbers of, or even individual, aircraft.

Two such forays occurred locally on the nights of Saturday, 8th August, 1942, when bombs were dropped in the Cardigan Road area of Leeds and, on the following Wednesday, 12th August when, barely three miles from the factory (and less than a quarter of that distance from where this is being written), the 18th green of Bradford (Hawksworth) golf-course became the recipient of a load released by a lone raider. Enemy aircraft returned on Thursday 27th/Friday 28th: a visit which could have proved dire for the factory.

Visits from the Luftwaffe - and Further Development at the Factory

Nancy Blezard, who had commenced work riveting Lancaster bomb-bay doors on 26th May, having first spent some time at the Kirkstall Training Centre stated: "I was on night duty when Guiseley (Hawksworth) and Carlton were bombed and, as usual, everyone believed AVRO was the target. When a fire broke out in the machine shop at the same time, sabotage was suspected and no one would go into the shelters until the Fire Brigade arrived."

Leslie Briggs who, readers will recall, was seconded from the R.A.F. to work at the factory, stated that his memories of one raid had been made more vivid by an unexpected sequel.

"A week or two before my secondment ended and I went back to the R.A.F., the red air-raid warning lights flashed on in the factory (the system was: Yellow when enemy aircraft crossed the East Coast, Purple when they reached the West Riding and Red when aircraft were nearby) and, at this juncture, we were required to dash into our shelters. I state 'our' shelter for each one was given a specific letter: A, B, C and so on, and every worker was allocated a place in one or other of them, so that there would be no panic rush or overcrowding. Initially the shelters were very rudimentary with no mechanical or electrically operated ventilation system, and even though this was installed later it made little difference to me as I still felt claustrophobic. During the alert I made my way to my shelter but, once inside, the close proximity of warm bodies and the stale breath of those who had called before shift at a pub, brought back that feeling of nausea and memories of that night, two years before, in the shelter of Sunbridge Road (Bradford: see appendices). I just had to get out as quickly as possible and I lay down on the grass outside.

Overhead I could hear the drone of planes, and they were undoubtedly German (easily identified when twin-engines due to their not being synchronised) and, as it was a clear moonlit night, it wasn't long before I picked them out - the first I had *seen* in the war although I had, of course, previously been on the receiving end of their bombs. As I expected them to be flying roughly from east to west it came as a surprise to find them travelling in the opposite direction. As one of them droned away towards Leeds, another followed a bit nearer this time but, after a few minutes, it too flew off in the direction of Leeds where, by now, searchlights were plying the sky. Then a third enemy plane came over, and he was quite near us, less than a mile away I would say, and he slowly began to orbit round, as if looking for something. He kept at it for quite a while and, at the time there seemed no other activity but, eventually, he flew off eastwards, the all clear was sounded and we trooped back into work."[1]

Some forty-five years later, Leslie met up with a former Luftwaffe pilot and, from this chance encounter, astonishingly, they were able to establish that it had been the German, Gerhardt, who was flying the third aircraft(!); that the 'raid' had taken place sometime in August/September 1942 and that the factory *was* the intended target! From research it appears almost certain the date was the night of 27th/28th August 1942, when the Luftwaffe made the last of its attacks on the Leeds/Bradford area; damage to property being sustained in the Armley, Stanningley, Bramley and Kirkstall areas although, fortunately, without loss of life. During their chance meeting Leslie took Gerhardt to the factory ("to show him what he had missed!") and pointed out the very spot where he had lain all those years ago looking up at the German aircraft overhead....." we looked at each other and, to be honest, it would be impossible to say which of us was most amazed at the turn of events..."

It is interesting to note that the German crews were attempting to locate their target by visual methods: a situation which had been forced upon them by very effective British 'jamming' of their sophisticated navigational aids (so successful in 1940) as is confirmed by Robert Götz who flew with 1/KG55 "..... there is total interference with the radio navigation system. Since last December, the precision of our target finding has suffered extremely from the British radio-jamming ....."
(Photo 46 - centre pages)

Equally obvious is the effectiveness of the camouflage given to the factory for, despite the fact that the Luftwaffe knew of its existence, and its general

---

1   Despite making extensive enquiries, the author has been unable to ascertain the reason why the enemy aircraft were not engaged by the heavy anti-aircraft batteries, situated on Plane Tree Hill and Otley Old Road (Carlton). The suggestion that this was to avoid attention being drawn to the factory is a non-starter for an aircraft required only seconds to release its bomb-load, thus it is far too dangerous to allow one to 'slowly orbit' with impunity; and, in any case, there were so many gun-sites around the area that, at night, from several thousand feet it would have been impossible for the enemy airmen to identify which were adjacent to the factory.

location, they were unable to pinpoint it on a 'bright, moonlit night.' **(Photo 47 - centre pages)**

To complete the story of this remarkable episode it would have been satisfying to be able to confirm the identity of the Luftwaffe unit involved and, indeed, that of Gerhardt whose surname Leslie Briggs cannot recall [2] but, regrettably, many Luftwaffe records from this period of the war have not survived. The Bundesarchiv at Freiburg has, however, confirmed that only two units of the GAF were operating over North-East England that night: KG2, which lost two of its Dornier Do217's destroyed off the east coast, and KG77 from which a Ju88A-4 of Stab.1 was shot down into the sea off Sunderland. Dr. Alfred Price and Ken Wakefield, two noted historians with a special and detailed knowledge of Luftwaffe activities, agree that KG2 was the most likely participant.

On 1st September, 1942, a reporter from a local newspaper wrote in his notebook "shortly before midnight an enemy plane flew up Wharfe Valley and dropped flares in the Pool and Ilkley districts. Tracer bullets were seen, and the whole district was illuminated. A few minutes later (11.45p.m.) the sirens sounded but the plane did not return and there was no further activity. 'Raiders passed' sounded at 12.20a.m."

The last two sentences of this unpublished reported proved to be prophetic for, never again, did an enemy aircraft come within striking distance of the factory.

Virtually all recorded information pertaining to the involvement of AVRO at Yeadon was destroyed in a fire at its Chadderton factory during 1959. Twenty-one years later, Flt.Lt. G.R. Sunderland, R.A.F. (Ret'd.) having, meanwhile, gained access to some contemporary data, compiled an excellent short history of the Yeadon factory which remains of inestimable value to the serious researcher.

One short extract from this work refers, briefly, to the enlargement of flying facilities on the airfield: "..... as the factory's output grew, extra hangars were added on the airfield, and runways had to be extended at the expense of six nearby houses and several holes of the local golf course. The main runways are now at their maximum possible length - East/West 1,250 yards and North/South 1,100 yards ....." (Maximum length was based on the boundaries of the airfield existing at that time. The East/West runway became 10/28 and the North/South 01/19: the figures indicating their magnetic heading minus the last digit.)

The wartime originator of this piece, reporting on improvements carried out during 1942, surprisingly makes no reference to the fact that, to accommodate the Lancaster, the hitherto grassed runways had been provided with a hard, asphalt, surface. This work, although not considered worthy of comment in the report would, postwar, have a profound influence on the destiny of the place for, had its runways remained grassed then, almost certainly, the development of a regional airport would have been more viable elsewhere.

Perversely, the first Lancaster officially listed as having been built at Yeadon: B.Mk 1: LM301, which was completed in October, 1942, left the ground on its first test flight *without* using the new runways. Leslie Stott remembered the occasion. "It was around ten-thirty or eleven o'clock one Saturday morning, I can't recall the date but the weather was good: a lovely clear morning. Captain Worrall was doing the test and he took off diagonally across the grass between the two runways, just to prove it could be done with a Lanc', I suppose, and he flew off towards the 'Peacock'." (A popular establishment, well frequented by AVRO personnel, situated a half-mile south-west of the airfield).

According to some published work, LM301 left the factory during October to join No.12 Squadron at Wickenby, where it served as 'PH-O' but, in fact, the Lancaster was not ferried there from Yeadon until 10th November. As has been stated earlier, albeit that the King and Queen appended their names to two Lancasters, these aircraft were not LM301 nor LM302, officially the second of the type to be completed at Yeadon. The Royal signatures were placed on R5489 (named George) and R5548 (named Elizabeth) the eighth and forty-eighth, respectively, from a batch of 200 Mk.1 Lancasters officially listed as having been built at Chadderton (initially ordered as Manchesters).

In researching aircraft production it is soon evident that due to various factors (human error being one) there are, inevitably, some 'grey' areas, where apparent truth cannot be confirmed as being absolute. This is certainly manifest where completed contracts, officially designated to one factory, are found to contain a number of aircraft

---

2   Leslie said that Gerhardt was so ill when they were together he probably did not survive long afterwards.

Visits from the Luftwaffe - and Further Development at the Factory

which, in reality, were 'finished' elsewhere. It might, therefore, have been the case that R5489 was the original 'type sample' Lancaster sent (along with 5 other 'sets' to Yeadon in January, 1942 but, if not, how did it and R5548 - supposedly forty places behind it in the production line at Chadderton - come to be together at Yeadon on that auspicious day? Was one, or both, built at Yeadon? If so, production records are incorrect; or was one, or other or, indeed, both transported there by road, partially completed? Alternatively, as none of the Lancasters officially listed as being under construction at Yeadon would be ready for another six months, were they simply flown in that morning to take part in the naming ceremony?

It is known that R5489 was not ferried from Yeadon to No.44 (Rhodesia) Squadron at Waddington until 10th May - more than six weeks after Their Majesties visited the factory - so can this be taken to indicate that, on 26th March, the aircraft was not fully completed? Intriguing as these questions might be, it is now more than likely that the answers to them will never be revealed.

Regrettably, the Royal blessing did not prevent either aircraft from suffering an early demise. On 16th August, R5489 crashed at Brampton on approach to Waddington, having flown a total 115 operational hours thereto and R5548, which served as 'OF-A' with No.97 Squadron at Woodhall Spa, met its nemesis there on 28th December, when it burned out after a photoflash exploded on board, having completed 261 hours service. Fortunately, in neither incident were there any crew casualties.

J.A. "Séamus" Stuart served as a ferry-pilot with No.7 FPP, ATA, at Lennerton Farm, Sherburn-in-Elmet and, in correspondence with the author, he wrote: "The King and Queen came to Yeadon to sign their names on two Lancasters. I had the privilege of flying George VI to 44 Squadron at Waddington. In later years I heard that it had never flown successfully over Germany as it had four engines changes in as many months." (The original engines were Merlin type 20's replaced by type 22's) [3] **(Photo 48 - centre pages)**

In his Log Book, Séamus erroneously recorded 'George VI' as being R8549 (there was no such serial number), and it was the Lancaster not the King which he ferried to Waddington!

Six months later, on 10th November, he again arrived at Yeadon to collect a Lancaster: B.Mk.1: LM301 which, as has been mentioned, was officially the first of the type to be built there. His task was to ferry the aircraft, via Sherburn-in-Elmet to its operational station at R.A.F. Wickenby but, unbeknown to him on the day, the event would have two consequences: Firstly, it would prove to be the last aircraft, of any type, which he would ferry from Yeadon (he was posted elsewhere shortly afterwards) and, secondly, his actions would, subsequently, appear in print - twice!

Forty-two years later, in an effort to raise money for St. Dunstan's, Yorkshireman John Booth wrote and published 'The Day War Broke Out'; a book in which he recalls his boyhood during the war, when he lived at Cawood on the River Ouse, where his father, following a family tradition, was Bridgemaster. In one hilarious chapter entitled 'The Wager' mention is made of a Lancaster being flown by a ferry-pilot, for a wager, at nought feet over Cawood Bridge; much to the consternation of John's father. Most regrettably, limitations of space do not allow the reproduction of the full story here but, suffice it to say, it is now known that the pilot was Séamus Stuart and the Lancaster: LM301! Sadly, Séamus died in December 1990.

Although the large presence of the Lancaster would dominate the scene at the factory until the end of the war, it should not be forgotten that, concurrently, production of the Anson continued unabated. By the end of May, 1942, the number of Mark 1's built at Yeadon had risen to more than 500 and, from that month, when in excess of 100 were completed, this monthly figure was maintained for the next two years, despite a sizeable increase in the output of the Lancaster.

The majority of Ansons built at the factory during its first year of operations, were sent overseas to be used in the various flying training schools. By the end of 1942, however, the situation had changed, with double the number being retained in the U.K.**(Photo 50 - centre pages)**

In January, 1943, the first of the type to be fitted with a Bristol power-operated gun turret emerged from the factory, and LT290 was despatched to No.3 Air Gunnery School (3 AGS) at Mona on the Isle of Anglesey; as were several others in its pro-

---

[3] R.5489 did, in fact, take part in three raids on German targets and, unusually, for an aircraft of Bomber Command, went on Atlantic patrol, operating out of Nutts Corner (N. Ireland). On 15th/16th June 1942 when, under the command of Fl.Lt.T.P.C. Barlow DFC, the Lancaster was involved in an attack on a U-Boat which was claimed sunk !

duction batch: the first of a substantial number of similar aircraft ultimately to serve in a variety of gunnery-schools.

Largely taken for granted and, as far as the media is concerned, almost universally overshadowed by the more 'attractive' fighter and bomber types, the importance of the Anson to Britain's war effort has been grossly undervalued. It is, however, hard to conceive of another aircraft, available at that time, which could have performed safely such a multitude of tasks, in many parts of the world and in such a variety of climatic conditions, yet give so little trouble. Although the Anson was not an aircraft which attracted a glamour and mystique, its multi-rôle function, in such large numbers, was paramount to the effective operation of the R.A.F.; and denied it, who can say what might have been the outcome?

An interesting, and slightly amusing anecdote in respect of the Anson, concerned Turkish Air Force Officers who, up to December, 1942, were still receiving flying training on the type at No.12(P) Advanced Flying Unit (12(P) AFU) at Grantham (Spittalgate) while, concurrently, a number of their countrymen were undergoing not dissimilar training with the Luftwaffe in Germany! (Turkey was, at the time, a neutral country).

As production at Yeadon developed so did the organisation of the factory. During 1942 a Joint Production Committee was formed, consisting of ten representatives elected by the workers, and a similar number from management, which discussed and acted upon all aspects of the day to day running of the works. As an adjunct to this body, an Accident Prevention Committee also came into being which, by investigating accidents and illnesses, was able to initiate preventative measures which reduced the numbers being absent from work. In fact, so successful were its policies, monthly 'lost time' soon averaged a mere 5%.

The Company also established a Sickness and Benevolent Fund and, generally, 'Welfare; was very much to the forefront of the struggle to maintain successful production. Every effort was made to ensure that the workers task was not aggravated by any stress or illness which could be avoided by forethought and planning.

A Surgery was opened at the northern end of the works (so far from the Flight Sheds that those employed there joked that they would have been dead before they could have reached it!) with Dr. Outhwaite, who also had a Practice in Yeadon, in charge.

He was ably supported by a Matron and eleven Nurses who not only treated multifarious accidents and illness cases, but also dispensed a variety of vitamins and injections which helped prevent the spread of minor epidemics.

AVRO COMMITTEES

Photo 51.

This banner which is made from aeroplane fabric (well doped) was produced by the aid of a spray gun, and is something of an enigma.

We are at a loss to see anything significant to committees in this design.

A gentleman, riding on a donkey round a circular path, the while holding out a carrot, simply has us at a loss. We can give no explanation.

Even the inscriptions on the ribbons do not convey any sense. One reads 'For further consideration' the other 'And everything of the sort' copyright J. Bruce.

To further reduce their possible absence from duties, workers were allowed a period of rest - when deemed appropriate - in a purpose built 'sunny' rest room, run by Mrs. Holdsworth, "a charming lady", rather than being sent home.

Visits from the Luftwaffe - and Further Development at the Factory

In the case of employees suffering an illness or injury of a more serious nature, the patient was despatched to home or hospital; and, on such journeys, any female workers was always accompanied by trained medical staff or a companion.

On the occasions when husbands were home on special leave from the Services, their wives were allowed time off to be with them; and once it was realised that in this, any many other welfare matters, they were being treated fairly, absenteeism dropped considerably. It is of interest to note, however, that this was at its lowest among those required to travel the longest distances to and from the factory!

The Surgery was also utilised on three days each week by a local Dentist and an Optician who, in those pre-Welfare State days, somewhat surprisingly, tested workers' eyes and repaired their damaged glasses free of charge.

Protective clothing, including clogs and overalls, were provided where necessary, as was milk for personnel working in the Dope House.

From the foregoing it could be misconstrued that the factory was a veritable Utopia and, indeed, compared with working conditions extant in Britain before the outbreak of war, its employees enjoyed many privileges. To balance against this, however, by January, 1943, when more than 680 new employees were taken on, many of the several thousand workforce had been engaged in this seemingly relentless task for more than three years; and some were beginning to feel the strain.

The situation was not improved by the paucity of that often underestimated commodity in any successful enterprise - middle management: the skilled and experienced men of whom a substantial number were engaged with the armed forces. To further exacerbate matters, certain intransigent attitudes of some trade unionists came to the fore not, necessarily in disputes with Management but, quite often, in rivalries with other Unions - which were legion - and one has only to look at the number and variety involved at Yeadon to realise that such a development was inevitable.

The organisations ranged from the Amalgamated Engineering Union (AEU); Electrical Trades Union (ETU); The National Union of General and Municipal Workers Union (NUGMW); The Transport and General Workers Union (TGWU) through a host of medium sized unions to the small, specialist, and more romantic sounding, Amalgamated Union of Upholsterers and the National Union of Musical Instrument Makers!

WEELY STAFF EMPLYEES - WAR ALLOWANCE

The company has decided to pay until further notice, as from 29Th May, 1944, an additional War Allowance on the following scale:-

Age	Males Increase	Total War Allowance	Females Increase	Total War Allowance
14	1/-	5/6	1/-	5/6
15	1/-	5/6	1/-	5/6
16	1/3	6/3	1/3	6/3
17	1/6	8/-	1/6	8/-
18	2/-	10/-	2/-	10/-
19	2/6	12/6	2/3	11/6
20	3/-	15/6	2/6	13/-
21 & over	4/-	23/6	3/-	16/6

It is clearly understood that this is a War Time Allowance and is subject to modification or withdrawal at any time at the option of the Company. In view of this the War Allowance will not be part of the emplyee's fixed rate of salery.

The War Allowance will, however, rank as part of the employee's renumeration for Income Tax purposes.

A.V. Roe & CO.LTD

K.B.CREWE
Accountant,
Yeadon Factory

Union activities were controlled by more than 70 shop stewards, of whom the Chairman and the Convenor of the Shop Stewards Committee worked full-time on Union matters. AVRO (Yeadon) was not, however, a 'closed shop' for, although the majority of its employees owned a 'Union Card', a substantial number had no affiliation.

Compared with some industries, notably coal mining and ship building, the aircraft industry was largely spared major disputes during the war, but industrial action was not avoided totally, as Miss Nancy Blezard recalled. "Part of the factory was on strike on Tuesday, 18th November, 1942, and a complete strike on Thursday, 20th November. We were not allowed on the shop floor and had to spend the time in the large corridor which went down the length of the factory alongside Harrogate Road (the A658). I cannot remember what it was all about, and I am not certain that, even then, we were all that clear as to the reason for it."

That there were industrial disputes whilst Britain was at war has remained a topic of considerable disagreement. On the one hand there are those who have argued that, in a democracy, even in wartime, workers should retain the right to withdraw their labour. Others have taken the opposite view: some going as far as to say such action was treasonable. It is beyond the scope of this book to discuss such matters in depth but, during more than five years involved in its research, the author has become convinced that, as far as Yeadon was concerned, its recipe for occasional disruption was concocted from a modicum of inexperienced and ineffectual management, a slice or two of political opportunism and more than a soupçon of sheer bloody-mindedness.

It would be inaccurate and misleading, however, to create an impression that all workers were pre-occupied with such disharmony. On the contrary, most of them were more concerned with less strategic matters. Mrs. Lyndis Winterbottom remembered: "I had a lovely lady, Annie Carriss, who helped me at AVRO. She lived at Horsforth near the Railway Station and, one day, we had to flatten ourselves against the factory wall and, literally, hold our breath for one of the great wheels had come loose from the trolley taking it for fitting to a Lancaster. It crashed through the doors and out into the field."

Mrs. M. Wright also recalled that she was finding the Lancaster to be a very different proposition to the Anson. "I remember when they were taking a Lancaster out to go across to the flight sheds, one of its huge tyres burst - we all ran for cover very quickly, I can tell you. Then, on another occasion, I was going by a Lancaster on the tarmac near the flight sheds, and I didn't realise there was someone in it doing tests. As I came around the corner the engines were run-up and, as I couldn't dodge out of the way quickly enough, the blast knocked me off my feet and blew me quite a distance."

Sometimes, problems were of a self-inflicted nature, as Terry Carter recalled (in the 1950's he became a ground-control officer at LBA). "I saw little of Dad during the war years, for he worked at AVRO as a senior foreman electrician and left for work around 7a.m. and, usually, didn't get back until I was in bed. Alternatively, he was on nights so the same applied, but in reverse. One event I *can* remember him being involved in, concerned the catapult he gave me for my birthday in 1943. He had made it from duralumin scrap, with shock cord elastic - a very modern commodity at the time - with a sling of soft leather, and I was the envy of all my pals (most youngsters then owned, or wished to own, a catapult). Before bringing the catapult home Dad just had to try it out - he was still a lad at heart - but he made the mistake of doing it *inside* the factory. I suppose the shock cord must have been a bit stronger than he anticipated for, when he let go of the missile - probably a small nut - it flew unerringly, straight as an arrow towards the mercury vapour lights which, in that section of the works were, I was given to understand, like the Christmas tree lights of old, fused in multiple banks. There was a loud bang, and the sound of breaking glass, followed by equally loud cries and curses as a large section of final assembly was plunged into darkness in a spectacular fashion. Not surprisingly Dad, for an hour or so, became persona non grata, not least of all among those who were working on Lancasters' wings some twenty feet above the ground!"

Amusing as the foregoing incidents might appear it is, similarly, obvious that injury to someone was avoided only by good fortune. This was not always the case as Mrs. Winterbottom confirmed:

"There were places in the factory where, for our own safety we were not supposed to go but, one day, a worker insisted on taking a short cut and he slipped and fell into a vat containing scalding hot liquid. When he was pulled out, screaming, he looked like a boiled rabbit."

The advent of the Lancaster also posed problems for those engaged in the fitting or servicing of its engines; as was succinctly demonstrated in a little ditty composed by ground crew 'erks' at an Operational Station in East Anglia:

"On a Stirling, props a-whirling will miss your head,
but on a Lanc you'll get a spank -
and then you're dead!"

John Holroyd remembered that, at Yeadon, to extract a partially completed Lancaster from the main factory, prior to it being moved across to 'finals', caused some headaches: "As the main doors of the works had been intended for the Anson, or other planes of smaller wingspan, that of the Lanc made it necessary for them to be taken out with main wheels locked, and lifted off the ground by the tractor which then pulled them through slightly sideways, castoring on their rear wheel ....."

Difficulties experienced with immovable objects such as the structure of the building were, however, as nothing compared with those brought about on occasions by the sheer stupidity of some of its workers. Alf Harris remembered: "There was one chap who always fancied himself and, one dinner time to 'show-off' he had taken a girl from another department up into a Lancaster. Not content with a kiss and cuddle he had to take her into the cockpit and, no doubt, trying to give her the impression he knew how to fly the thing, it wasn't long before he pulled the wrong lever. You could hear the crash of the collapsing undercarriage, above the sound of machinery. There was hell to pay!

He wasn't the only lever-puller who got himself into trouble though. There was another who couldn't tell right from wrong whose action emptied a Lancaster of the contents of its fuel tanks. It took ages to get rid of the smell for it had seeped through the floor. We were not allowed to smoke for ages, and we were most careful not to make a spark with our tools or equipment. The chap who caused the trouble found there were plenty of verbal sparks going his way though."

Bernard Hepton added to this diary of misdemeanours: "I remember the time when the factory shook because somebody had forgotten to put the supports under the centre section to test the undercarriage retraction. A complete Lancaster, except for port and starboard outer engines and wing tips - three quarters of the way up the production line - hit the concrete. A write-off!"

Carelessness could, and did, have more serious and tragic consequences. On 13th July, 1943, on its return from an attack on Turin, Lancaster B.111: LM311 'PO-L' of No.467 Squadron Royal Australian Air Force (RAAF) - the first B.111 to be built at Yeadon - dived out of control into a cornfield on approach to its based at Bottesford, killing all its seven crew. F/Sgt. S.A. Chapman RAAF, its pilot, had named the Lancaster 'LIZ'BETH' after his WAAF driver girl friend who, most regrettably, was a witness to the accident as she sat in the cab of her R.A.F. lorry waiting to collect the crew from dispersal. Later. the cause of the crash was found to have been due to faulty riveting in the tail section of the Lancaster and, for a while, all Lancasters in its production batch, and others subsequently completed at Yeadon, were grounded until thorough checks were carried out.

The others who died with F/Sgt Chapman were: Sgt. J. Greenwood, Sgt. N.C. Smith RAAF, Sgt. A.E. Michaels RAAF, Sgt. P. Donlevy RAAF, F/Sgt. W. Bruce and Sgt. W.S. Buchanan.

LM311 was not the only aircraft, or crew, to be lost through bad workmanship, carelessness or even sabotage - wartime necessity was no guarantee of absolute efficiency - but, considering the vast numbers produced, such incidents were comparatively few.

Aluminium alloy fuel tanks, up to 500lb/600lb (2373 litres/2727 litres) capacity, were produced at the factory in quantity; each being tested for the strength of its welding. On occasions a fault could only be rectified by some unfortunate individual being required to crawl inside a deficient tank to effect a repair and, not surprisingly, this led to embarrassing difficulties when inexperienced workers attempted to extricate themselves.

Fuel for flight-testing, and the ferrying of completed aircraft: 100 octane for a Lancaster's Merlins, and 87 octane for the Armstrong-Siddeley Cheetas of the Anson, was delivered to the factory by road tankers and, thereafter, stored in large, underground, tanks. On receipt *each* consignment was tested; the 'sample' being kept in a small brass can, measuring 5" x 9" (12.7cm x 22.86cm), until all the contents of its batch had been used.

This system allowed for a speedy analysis of any specific delivery of fuel, if such was subsequently suspected of being the source of a problem found with an engine. For reasons never clear to a certain ex-Inspector of the AID, the small brass containers assumed an unexpected attraction (for somebody) as they kept disappearing! He now wonders if they have since become a collectors item?

Gun turrets for the Anson and the Lancaster (and later the Lincoln) were supplied, ready made, by sub-contractors, and this applied to the ammunition channels which were produced by 'Meccano'.

During the Second World War, the use of sub-contractors reached a peak of activity which has never been surpassed; the number and diversity of those involved being quite astonishing. By the time production got under way at Yeadon many local firms had already become contracted to other war factories and thus, with a few exceptions,[4] a majority of those which eventually became involved were firms many miles distant from the factory. B. & T. Air-

---

4   Among local sub-contractors were Hustlers of Yeadon who made ailerons, and the Silver Cross Pram Works and White Cross Garage, both at Guiseley, which made a variety of small components.

craft of Mansfield made wing trailing edges, Northern Coachbuilders of Newcastle-upon-Tyne did similar work and the L.N.E.R. workshops at York produced wooden parts for the Anson. In addition, a veritable army of other firms were contracted to Yeadon; these being as widely dispersed as London (28 firms), Liverpool, Bristol, South Wales, Glasgow and Airdrie - to name but a few. From time to time it was found necessary for an AVRO or AID specialist to visit one of the suppliers to check on work being done, or to correct known errors, but this was far from being the pleasant diversion it might have been in peacetime.

With petrol in desperately short supply, most journeys were required to be made by rail; a diabolical prospect for those involved, as trains were slow and often considerably delayed. Railway carriages were dirty, with compartments, corridors, guards-vans and even toilets packed with a mass of humanity: most of whom were Service personnel encumbered with kit-bags, webbing-equipment and, regularly, their rifles. There were few, very few, trains with any catering facilities and station buffets were either vastly overcrowded or closed. During night journeys, seating compartments (if one could find a seat!) were cold and illuminated only by a dim, blue bulb to obviate any problems should passengers forget the blackout restrictions.

Eric Dean recalled a trip he was required to make to a sub-contractor at Pontypridd, in mid-Glamorgan. "I set off one Monday morning by the 6.45a.m. train from Leeds but, because of wartime exigencies (possibly because bombs had fallen on the line somewhere), we had to detour and did not arrive at Cardiff until almost 8.00p.m. By the time I reached my hotel the restaurant was closed for the night (the Government urged people to eat early to save electricity) so I got nothing to eat until next morning, when I received some fried dried-egg on toast, and one cup of tea. Then I set off by public transport up the Rhondda Valley to the suppliers, after which I returned to Cardiff a couple of hours later. There I caught a train at 1.30p.m. for the trip back to Leeds but, again, it was terribly delayed - and it had no restaurant car or buffet - and I did not arrive in City Station, Leeds, until 7.30a.m. on Wednesday morning, having had nothing to eat or drink, except for the fried dried-egg and a cup of tea, for more than forty-eight hours."

Remarkable as it may seem to younger readers, such journeys in wartime were the norm rather than the exception. The never to be forgotten slogan: 'Is Your Journey Really Necessary' was not intended as the Music Hall joke it became, but as a very serious attempt to get all but essential users off Britains considerably overcrowded rail network. Even the most direct journeys became tedious and frustrating. "..... I often had to travel to London and it seldom took less than twelve hours from Leeds. On one trip the train was so overcrowded I travelled in the bellows connection between two carriages, standing the whole way for thirteen and a half hours, almost face to face with a Wren Officer, and we could barely move! ....." Eric Dean also remembered "..... travelling back from a sub-contractor in London during August. The train was packed, as usual, and it was stifling hot. Eventually, after much pushing and shoving, I succeeded in getting into a toilet where, in addition to assuaging a call of nature I had a really good wash. When I struggled out, a lady in the throng in the corridor outside asked if she could borrow my soap and towel (experienced wartime travellers never journeyed anywhere without them), as her young daughter was distressed with the heat and the crush. I quickly agreed to her request and when she returned, some minutes later, she admitted having been tempted to use the soap and towel herself. Of course, I didn't object but, on reaching home, it was a bit embarrassing trying to explain to my wife why there was lipstick on my towel!"

As far as the Lancaster was concerned, all sub-contractors first supplied AVRO factories in the Manchester area. This system, coupled with the questionable practice of 're-allocating' (a convenient euphemism for 'getting rid of') doubtful components therefrom to group factories elsewhere, led workers involved at the latter, not surprisingly, into a belief that they were being short-changed.

One who was in a privileged position to corroborate this assertion stated: "Nobody should be in any doubt that Yeadon got what Manchester didn't want. At least half the components they sent to us were faulty. Not, necessarily, seriously so, but it was often obvious that attempts had been made, unsuccessfully, to install them. As this had failed they sent them to us. The sort of thing I recall were bolt holes wrongly positioned - somebody had got the jig wrong - metal damaged as if someone had run a trolley over the end; that kind of thing and, as interchangeability man, I was regularly called in to give advice. Quite often the only remedy meant putting the offending component into our jigs to repair them, or replace parts and all this, of course, reduced our production norms and earned us the usual taunts from Manchester. Make no mistake, any kudos or praise was always absorbed by Manchester; Yeadon was treated as a poor relation, with every opportunity, and I mean *every* opportunity, being taken by them to lower the value of Yeadon in comparison to Manchester."

Visits from the Luftwaffe - and Further Development at the Factory

Strong words indeed and not, it must be said unique, for a number of ex-Yeadon employees have given voice to such opinions. Perhaps, as has been mentioned earlier, there were a number of Manchester staff who considered themselves superior and, more than likely, some who felt apprehensive about possible post-war developments. Whatever the reasons for the rivalry, however, there seems little doubt that, on occasions, it went beyond acceptable inter-factory competitiveness.

Despite all the activity created by the factory, the presence of Leeds University Air Squadron at Yeadon was maintained: its Tiger Moth having been repaired after resident instructor, Flight Sergeant Hulme, had 'turned it over' when landing at York on 8th October 1942.

By mid-1943 a substantial number of students had flown in the aircraft; many going on to join RAF squadron's. One of their number, Arthur Aaron (one of the original ninety-three entrants), being awarded a posthumous Victoria Cross for saving his crew, despite being mortally wounded, flying his Stirling of No.218 Squadron to North Africa after a raid on the Fiat works at Turin, during the night of 12/13th August 1943.

On 15th September of that year, the squadron acquired its third Commanding Officer: Squadron Leader W.J. Harper (ex-Middle East) who replaced Wing Commander S.C. Gretton CB. who, in turn, had taken-over from Wing Commander Ridley in October 1941. Flying training at Yeadon was not all it should have been, however, as is evidenced by a report in the squadron diary:

".....Owing to the distance of the aerodrome from the University (8 miles), the poor bus service and the inclement weather of this industrial area, not a great deal of flying has been done, but it can be said that no opportunity has been missed....It is noticeable that some cadets names feature more frequently on the notice-board for flights.....Whenever cadets from the University are not forthcoming, the School of Architecture is telephoned and it is usually possible for F/Sgt. Hulme to get some customers from there...."

Not the kind of report to put fear into the ranks of the Luftwaffe (had they obtained access to it), but the remarks belie a keen esprit de corps engendered within the squadron; a substantial number of its recruits going on to play a distinguished rôle in the air-war: many making the ultimate sacrifice in doing so. During the post-war years, L.U.A.S. students continued to make their mark; two, at least, rising to very senior Air-rank within the R.A.F.: but that is another story!

"Lighter Moments"

Hitherto, only brief mention has been made of the huge works canteen at Yeadon, but it played such an important rôle in the life of the place that it is important to elaborate on its wider function.

Leslie Stott recalled: "Originally, all workers ate in the same canteen but, as our numbers grew, then class gradually exerted itself, and it was not long before extra rooms were added to accommodate the different stratas of the workforce ....."

Agnes Ludlam (nee McNally) who, as a member of the canteen staff, had a direct involvement remembered: "When I went to work in the canteen it was divided up into several dining rooms, the biggest one being for the ordinary workers, with some smaller rooms alongside for the inspectors, junior executives and top management. The Manageress in charge of everything, was Miss Chisholm, who had under her two supervisors, Winnie Nairne (see signature on photograph of canteen pass) and Winnie Bell. We called Miss Nairne 'Big Winnie', but never to her face. She didn't allow any informality and we were forbidden to talk to executives unless they spoke to us first. Her code was 'familiarity breeds contempt'

Leslie Stott added that on one occasion he, and two other inspectors, plucked up courage to confront Miss Chisholm about the monotonous regularity of Lancashire Hot Pot, Harricot Beans and Semolina Pudding ....." She replied that due to shortages she found it very difficult to provide a more varied menu, but she would try and acquire some rabbit, and she did!" (Might it have been the very same which put Eric Dean in hospital?)

Agnes Ludlam continued: "The two chefs were called Richard and I can't remember their sur-

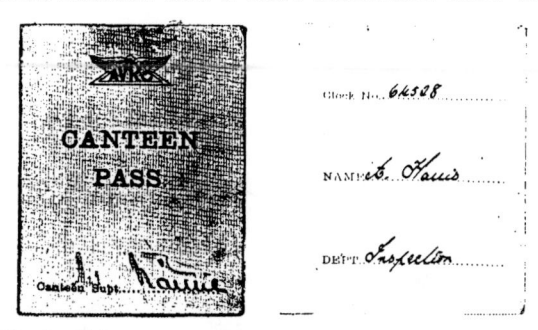

CANTEEN

Photo 54.

Canteen pass showing both sides. Coloured blue and signed Winnie Nairne

Photo 53. Left

The design takes the form of a shield with quarterings.

Emblazoned on the first quarter are three recumbent sausages, placed here by the right of long usage

The second quarter shows three fishes 'passant' of a species which frequently find their way into the menu, Viz-90% bone and 10% skin and greif.

The third quarter depicts two Depth Charges. These probably refer to a certain stolid kind of pudding, concocted by the chef, which is sometimes apt to cause violent disturbance in the entrails. Further reference to pudding is given on the flying ribbon. This is really bill posters paste, which during war time, is of course not used for its original purpose.

The symbolic characters £.S.D. give the key as to why the canteen is run, and the whole is mounted on a basal ribbon bearing the insigna in German, -I SERVE. copyright Joe Bruce.

- 79 -

"Lighter Moments"

names. One of them had been employed at the posh Royal Hotel at Scarborough before the war. They compiled the menus but Miss Chisholm had to approve them. Food being in such short supply it was mostly very plain fare, and I remember we used sack upon sack of powdered potato (a relatively new commodity them) and semolina which the workers called 'Wallpaper paste' and 'glue' ....."

Fred Ryner who worked in the drawing office, recalled: "There was the occasion when I was delighted to see 'Braised Beef' on the menu, it being a favourite of mine, but I was dismayed to find that what we had served up was corned beef with gravy poured over it. There was a great deal of grumbling, but when I suggested getting a petition about the deception few seemed keen on the idea. I suppose, with 5,000 or so people sitting down each meal time, mistakes were bound to be made, and I particularly remember the time when onions were over ordered, with disastrous results .....!"

Agnes Ludlam continued: "..... with so many workers to be fed our turnover in food was simply enormous, and so was our workload. As soon as we clocked-in we would begin cleaning cutlery, laying tables, counting out crockery, etc., and the pastry-room people would start their mixing and baking, and the chefs would commence cutting, chopping and then cooking the meat and veg. When those of us who were also waitresses were not on the table rota, we were expected to work as canteen assistants, so off came the frilly cap and apron and on went the old green overall, and many times we had to deck-scrub the concrete floor of that huge canteen, which seemed to stretch for miles! ....."

Keeping clean a canteen and kitchen of such enormous size by purely manual methods (there were few 'mod cons' available then) must, indeed, have been a daunting task. That it was not entirely successful is confirmed by the recollections of Ada Walker, who worked at one or other time on both Anson and Lancaster assembly: "Once, when I was on night shift, I went into the canteen to make myself some tea - it was long after 'dinner' time - and the floor was just a carpet of cockroaches. After that I took a flask, I can tell you!"

Agnes Ludlam added: "One of our worst jobs was in the kitchen washing-up area where we had to stack seemingly endless piles of dirty crockery, plates, cutlery and so on, from the collecting trolleys, into a machine which steamed them clean. When that was finished we took them all out again, polished them with clean cloths, re-stacked them onto trolleys which we then wheeled out into the canteen, where the whole process began again. I used to have nightmares about that job long after the war, and I am sure it was partly responsible for my nervous breakdown. Altogether, on day and night shifts, I suppose there was somewhere between 100 and 125 canteen staff, which seems a lot now but, I can assure you, it never seemed anywhere near enough to cope with the work at the time. For a twelve hour shift, six days a week, I was paid about £2.16.0d (£2.77½p), and I never got much more than that even though I was at AVRO for four years. I used to get so tired that, sometimes, I slept-in and then I was late for work. One day, five of us were late and we were summoned to appear before the Absentee Committee in the hut in the woods (Novia Plantation). We were all severely told-off and given a permit to purchase an Alarm Clock!

These recollections have brought to mind others I knew well in those days: Mary Wilkinson, Helen Duffy (Union Representative), Kitty and Mary Warden, Vera Sunderland, Joyce Hanlon, Joyce Horner, Dorris Cadman, Rene Hainsworth, Peggy Storey, my sister Nora, of course, (who worked in the machine shop), Nancy Sibbons, Kathleen Stevens, Helen Quinland, the Hardman twins, Nellie Slingsby, 'Treasure' Johnson (the pastry-cook supervisor), Edna Walker with the 'big blue eyes', Amy (known as Amarylis), supervisor in the inspectors' canteen, Mr. Wood a 'boss' and Jimmy Rooney, the Union Convenor ....."

In the opinion of another ex-employee, the main canteen "..... was as big as a football pitch and, when celebrities came, it resembled one as well ....."

Joe Walton recalled that: "..... girls from the canteen went around the factory during the morning and the evening, selling dinner tickets but, to get into the canteen, we also needed a canteen pass. These were blue, and our works passes were orange, - this reminds me of the time a chap lost his and for weeks he used the top of a 'Gold Flake' cigarette packet to get past the police at the gate, - and, at meal breaks, there were several thousand of us all milling and trying to be first in the queue. It go so bad that Mr. Harper, the Works Manager, one day tried to stem the tide to get some order. He was just bodily carried along in the crush and, although not seriously hurt, he was taken away on a stretcher ....."

The primary function of the canteen was, of course, to provide food for the workforce, but is also became the centre for 'dinner-time' entertainment. Allen Modley, the comedian and pantomime dame (and brother of comedian Albert), was put in charge as Entertainments Manager. He also worked as an Inspector in the Bought-in Store and served as a Sergeant in the Works Home Guard Unit but,

"Lighter Moments"

Photo 55.

This is purely a symbolic crest.

The first quarter depicts the comedians (some unintentional)

The second quarter - the musicians. From superb to Hells Bells.

The third quarter, the singers, (as above). and the fourth, -all other entertainments.

Surrounding the whole is a series of famous names whose excellence some of our Avro artists can easily match, (in some peoples immagination)

The ribbon gives the clue to the reason for all the effort of the entertainers and the committee.

Translated it reads ;- *To Please the Rabble.*
copyright Joe Bruce.

somehow, found time to organise, and often take part in, a considerable number of shows which were performed on the canteen stage; and, as the war progressed, also promoted works concert parties at other venues. Modley was the ideal choice for the job as, in addition to being a natural comedian and accomplished 'drummer', ... "he used to travel with us on the bus as far as Apperley Bridge, and he had us in stitches with a seemingly endless fund of funny stories ....." He also had many contacts within the entertainment industry which, from 4th September, 1939, was very much involved with ENSA - the Entertainment National Service Association - in taking to the armed forces and the war factories 'music, variety and drama'.

In Allen Modley, "..... a professional in every sense of the word ....." and in several other excellent performers, the factory possessed an abundance of highly gifted 'home grown' talent. Allen Modley in addition to his duties elsewhere in the factory, was its entertainment manager.

One of them was Mrs. Eileen Southgate who, in addition to being employed in a senior position in the aerodrome facility, was a very accomplished pianist, often involved with both resident and visiting artistes.

Photo 56. Allen Modley

Another pianist and a local man to appear on the canteen stage, although not employed at the factory, was Burt Rhodes who, post-war, made his name as an instrumentalist and conductor in radio and television. He visited the factory when an eighteen years old member of the Regimental Band of the York and Lancaster Regiment. "..... I was playing Gershwin's 'Rhapsody in Blue' when, half way through, the bandmaster stopped us to allow an AVRO official to make an announce-ment over the microphone. I was so annoyed at being broken off that, like some prima-donna, I stalked off the stage and refused to go back. Later, after we had returned to the depot at Pontefract, I was summoned before the C.O., Major Derby and, in mitigation, I told him it was just not cricket for an artiste to be interrupted in such a way. He tersely reminded me that there was a war on, and that I was in the Army now, not the Yorkshire County Cricket Club, and he gave me fourteen days C.B.!"

"Lighter Moments"

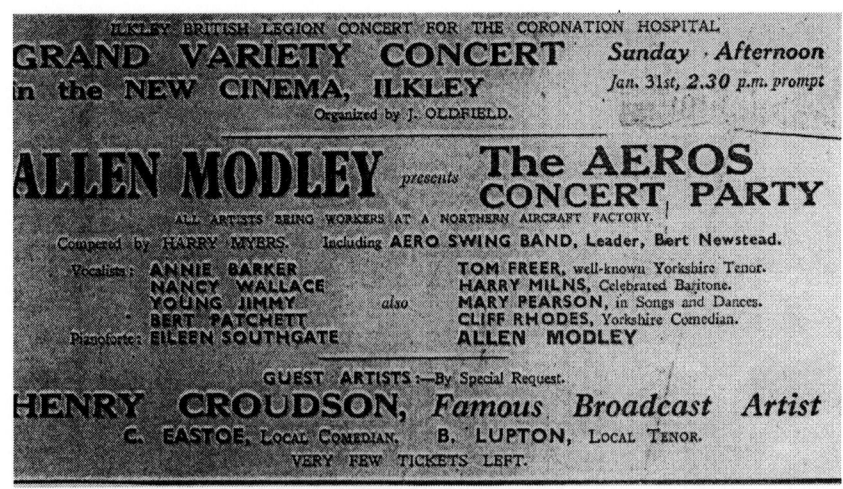

Photo 57. The concert party was, not surprisingly, made up of personnel from the factory.

Jack Kell remembered that: "..... very often artistes who were appearing at the theatres in Leeds or Bradford would come to entertain us. I well recall the visit by the D'Oyly Carte Opera Company, who did excerpts from the Mikado, which they were performing nightly at the Princess Theatre, Bradford; the singing of Helen Roberts being particularly notable.

Joe Walton recalled: "ENSA concerts were usually on Mondays, when we had the AVRO Dance Orchestra or Light Orchestra with Eileen Southgate, to play for the performers. At other times we had talent days (!) from the workforce, and even religious services in the main canteen when we worked Sundays. I remember some of the dance-bands that came. There was Billy Cotton, The Squadronaires, York and Lancaster Regiment, and other military bands and, of course, Joe Loss. One lunch-time all the tables were piled up round the edges of the canteen and a full Highland Pipe Band, complete with drums, marched up and down for a full half-hour. I remember, too, when Vera Lynn came and Christopher Stone of the BBC who played records (the first British broadcaster to do so over the BBC: thus the first native 'disc-jockey',) and, almost every day, we were entertained by comedians, singers, jugglers, dancers, and instrumentalists; not forgetting the visits of many non-theatre personalities such as Lord Beaverbrook, Sir Stafford Cripps (who succeeded Lord Beaverbrook as Minister of Aircraft Production), J.B. Priestley and General Sikorski (Prime Minister and Commander-in-Chief Polish Forces in exile; killed later when shot down flying from Gibraltar to England). Then there was the visit of Guy Gibson and his crew just after the Dams raid. It was a very big event for us when they spoke from the stage, for we thought them national heroes."

Several ex-employees have made mention of the dance bands which visited the factory, and, overall, the war produced an extra-ordinary boom in dance music and a surge in popularity for the bands which provided it. This was certainly the case of that under the baton of Joe Loss which, during a period of war-time residency at Green's Playhouse Ballroom in Glasgow, 'packed them in' at a rate of 10,000 per week!

Fred White, who was employed at Yeadon as a pattern maker (drafted in from Manchester) always maintained to his workmates that, pre-war, he had played the double-bass with Joe's band. This, they firmly refused to accept, albeit that they realised he was an accomplished performer on the instrument; until the day when Joe first brought his band to play in the canteen.

Fred took the opportunity and made his way to the stage where he was greeted like a long lost friend; being invited to sit-in with the band during the remainder of its performance.

Geraldo who, with his orchestra, was as well known and respected as Joe Loss, was put in charge of the dance band section of ENSA; thus it became the practice, rather than the exception, for the orchestras and bands visiting the factories to be of a high quality - despite their being denuded of many outstanding performers due to the exigencies of war.

In addition to those already mentioned, the following dance bands are known to have performed at Yeadon: Ambrose, Eric Winstone, Sidney Lipton, Harry Kaye, Ivy Benson (the first all woman band to become, in December, 1942, resident BBC dance band), Henry Hall, Lew Stone, Harry Roy, Nat Gonella, The Skyrockets and, of course, Geraldo's own orchestra: each a top-flight 'outfit', quite capable of filling the leading dance halls and theatres of the day. (The phenomenon of Glen Miller did not - contrary to current belief - arrive on the British scene until late in the war.) Thus war workers were provided with the best music available; and this was also the case when it came to the leading variety performers of the theatre and radio. Flanagan and Allen, Nosmo King, Jack Warner, Elsie and Doris Waters - 'Gert and Daisy', (in real life Jack Warner's sisters), Cicely Courtnidge, Claude Hulbert, Florence Desmond, Wee Gorgie Wood, Arthur Askey - who sang his song about the munitions girl who produced 'Thingumy-bob's' - were just a few of the many top British performers who graced the stage in the canteen.

Of them all, however, there is one to whom virtually all ex-Yeadon employees refer, when discussing the subject of factory entertainment: Gracie Fields who, at the time of her visit on Monday, 30th August, 1943 was, through her films, radio performances and recordings, a huge, internationally known 'Star', whose popularity in Britain was rivalled only by that of George Formby. **(Photo 58 - centre pages)**

Despite her stardom, Gracie Fields never lost her common touch, being fondly known as 'Our Gracie' or, more simply, 'Gracie', and her reception at Yeadon was in keeping with that today accorded to 'Pop Stars': "..... I can't remember the cast of many 'Workers' Playtimes' we had at AVRO, but I will never forget Gracie coming. She sang, and made us laugh as only she knew how, and she came over as one of us - just an ordinary North Country lass - even though she was wearing a beautiful mink coat, expensive jewellery and a lovely red, white and blue dress. Its only now when I think back that I realise, most likely, that dress was deliberately chosen to be patriotic. I know she nearly brought the roof down, with our cheers and applause after she sang 'Sally' and the 'Biggest Aspidistra in the World'. I remember, afterwards, going back to work as if I had just come back off holiday." [1]

'Workers' Playtime', 'Music While You Work' and 'Break for Music' were among several radio programmes developed by the BBC primarily for the benefit of war workers; the shows being broadcast daily (or nightly) 'from a factory somewhere in Britain'. On four occasions the canteen at Yeadon was the venue:

<u>7th August, 1942:</u>
An ENSA concert party performed a 'Break for Music'.

<u>1st/2nd January, 1943:</u>

'Workers' Playtime' was broadcast live to North America at midnight dinner-break. A transmission which, in a period when live trans-Atlantic broadcasting was still a novelty - and of dubious sound quality - was a very special event indeed.

<u>25th August, 1943:</u>
'Work Wonders'

<u>25th November, 1945:</u>

'Workers' Playtime' (peacetime broadcast). (For details of the schedules of programmes see Appendices.)

These, and other radio programmes were "..... an excellent antidote to the monotony and boredom, bringing cheer to the gloomiest surroundings and helping to relieve the stress and strain of wartime production .....", so said the BBC Year Book for 1941. That its pronouncement was accurate is confirmed not only by former war workers but also by official reports; one of which quoted a factory "..... where the radio was shut down for a week there was a 20% drop in output ....."

By the end of the war 'Music While You Work' was being broadcast three times each day - morning, afternoon and at 10.30p.m., - to a regular audience of more than 4,500,000 workers in 8,000 large factories, and a similar number in smaller factories, workshops, forces canteens and private homes. There being no television it was through the medium of radio (then called 'the wireless'), the dance halls and the cinema, which a war weary public gained some respite.

Ballroom dancing was, similarly, a highly popular form of relaxation from ones war work. Jack Rowbotham recalled its benefits, and some of the dance halls patronised by himself and many of his colleagues: "We used to frequent the Broadway Hall at Horsforth and the Mechanics Institute (now the Civic Centre) at Otley - we always tried to get tickets for the Farmers Ball there for, even though it was wartime, they still managed to provide a good table - and we attended the AVRO Ball and, on occasions, we went to the Coconut Grove at the Parkway Hotel near Bramhope or the Capitol at Meanwood, or the Astoria in Roundhay and the Mecca in Leeds. We were never short of somewhere to go dancing but now, when I recall the long hours we worked, I don't know how we did it. I suppose the place we danced at most was the Town Hall at Yeadon. The bands were always pretty good, and the unattached could always find a partner ....."

Jack certainly did so during his days at the factory, for it was when he was working there he met

---

1   Not everyone was so enamoured: a number of workers reputedly walked out on Gracie's performance...'To let her know we hadn't forgotten her going off to America in the early dark days of 1940.'

"Lighter Moments"

Monica Nolan, his future wife, and they have remained partners ever since!

He went on "..... interestingly, we had a chap at AVRO called Simonette who worked as a tester of welders - on the tubular frame of the Anson - and he had a real penchant for dancing. Many of the best welders - and dancers - were girls because they had a lighter touch, so he was never short of partners; and I have often wondered if the two went together: welding and dancing, that is? ....."

As an aside to the world of the ballroom, Jack had as a colleague at the factory, one Albert Waterman who, on an occasion, invited Jack to his home in Leeds: ".... when we got inside I was astonished to find not one, but *two* Grand pianos. 'Do you play' I asked, and Albert replied 'No, but my sister does, very well.' I never met the young lady, but I have often wondered since if she was the one and only Fanny Waterman, who has been so involved with the Leeds International Piano Competition?"

War workers (and Service personnel) did not, of course, solely restrict their off-duty hours to visits to the cinema or the dance halls, for Britains' pubs also enjoyed a boom in business - despite the restrictions and poor quality of the beer on offer.

As Yeadon was endowed with a huge munitions factory and several Service Camps nearby, its dozen or so pubs were seldom short of customers; thus it is somewhat surprising to find that many ex-factory employees, when reminiscing on the subject, have referred to favourite hostelries located *outside* the town: The Stone Trough at Rawdon, The Hare and Hounds at Menston and the Stanhope Arms at Horsforth - where Allen Modley entertained when not similarly involved elsewhere - being just three.

The notable exception (notorious, according to some) was the Peacock Hotel situated, until 1992, near The Fountain, alongside the A658. Thousands of workers from the factory travelled by it every day, and many were tempted to 'tarry there awhile', even during their hours' dinner-break, to enjoy its oak-panelled ambience. **(Photo 59 - centre pages)**

Throughout the war years its clientele, and reputation, grew and some locals were scandalised by reports of 'goings-on' there and, without doubt, The Peacock attracted - among others - many who could euphemistically be described as 'enjoying a good time.' One former apprentice who, for reasons which will become obvious, wishes to remain anonymous, recalled being "..... sorely tried by some girls; young women I should say, who had been to the Peacock one dinner-time. I had gone to work at AVRO straight from school as a fourteen year old, and I had only been working there about a fortnight when they came back 'merry' from the Peacock. Three of them grabbed me and took my trousers down, and the more I shouted for them to give up, the more they laughed and played around, threatening what they would do with a compressed-air hose if I didn't conform. I dread to think what might have happened if the foreman had not arrived back from his dinner. I learned more about the facts of life in my first fourteen days in that place than I had done in my previous fourteen years!"

Many of the stories associated with the Peacock are, to say the least, highly colourful; and some have, undoubtedly, grown in the telling. Others relate to incidents which, for a number of onlookers, were simply amusing. One such was recalled by Mrs. Renée Calloway: "I remember an occasion when my late father, 'Bill' Pittam, who worked as a Progress Chaser at AVRO, was asked by some of his colleagues to join them for a drink - I think it was around Christmas time - at that big hotel just down the road from the factory. He was not a drinking man, just taking an occasional one, but that day he must have been tempted to have more than usual. How he travelled back to Bradford we never found out, only that he arrived home literally on all fours through the doorway, and he had a huge feather stuck in his trilby. He immediately started singing to the cat, telling it what a lovely animal it was, which was strange as he normally treated it with contempt. We children were sent upstairs but, having never seen him, or anyone else, in that state we left the door ajar so as not to miss the excitement. Father was despatched to our Grandparents, who lived two streets away, and ordered to stay there until sober - and we noticed he drank a lot more tea thereafter, and he never again 'celebrated' Christmas on his way home from work!"

To obviate the possibility of readers beginning to think that it was only those employed on the shop floor who were, occasionally, tempted from the straight and narrow path when off-duty it is, perhaps, pertinent to quote further comments made by Eric Dean: ..... "Low Hall, in Ghyll Lane, Nether Yeadon (since the 17th century the home of, firstly, the Marshall and then the Barwick families) was taken over by AVRO as its staff house, where key personnel without their own local accommodation, or visiting V.I.P.'s could stay overnight. The Stewards were a Mr. & Mrs. Croon, and they supplied food which was superb. Top V.I.P.'s from the Ministries and senior executives from Rolls-Royce, Hawkers or Glosters, among others, stayed in a separate part of the house from the lesser mortals temporarily accommodated there but, as there was only the one Billiard room, and as drinks were provided free-of-charge to the top brass, when invited to join them you did so with alacrity; at first, that is, for it soon became evident that some of the itinerant V.I.P.'s knew their way around a snooker table and a bottle, and for us lower ranks it proved costly in lost wagers and bad heads! **(Photo 60 - centre pages)**

Neither were things improved when those of us who knew the area were asked by the visitors, most of whom came for one night only, to act as navigators aboard their cars (always provided for V.I.P.'s) as they made nocturnal excursions to the more lively hostelries thereabouts. Many of those journeys dragged on into the wee small hours, and we who were required to start work at 7a.m. paid a heavy price for a brief taste of the high life. Imagine our thoughts when we realised that those who were responsible for our discomfort could lie a-bed and make a later start to the day. Ultimately, however, the situation got out of hand and the practice was stopped ....."

Eric was most impressed with Low Hall and spoke in glowing terms about its ambience and comforts. He also recalled an incident concerning one of its expensive artifacts: ....."Just outside the billiard room was a huge, six-foot tall, Chinese vase. It must, I suppose, have been worth quite a lot of money, yet it was carelessly used by all and sundry as a receptacle for used toffee papers, cigarette packets and cigarette ends. Once, one of the latter cannot have been extinguished before being discarded and subsequently, during the night, its contents caught fire. There was smoke everywhere, and the Croons' were far from being pleased but, amazingly, the vase remained intact. I have often wondered since if it is still there?....."

Nineteen Forty-three was the year when it began to look as if the Allies would win the war, yet people were still blacked-out and browned-off. Rationing had become a way of life, with 'coupons' being required for almost everything. The nation was, however, fully employed and working people had more money in their pockets than ever before: a situation which gave rise to the development of the 'Black Market' by means of which luxuries, by then almost unobtainable in the shops, might be acquired - at a price!

The vast majority of people did not get involved in the Black Market - well, not to any large degree - but a substantial number were not averse to the friendly persuasion of their local shopkeeper with hopes of obtaining a little extra from 'under the counter'. Such unofficial dealing was not restricted to the High Street, however, as Joe Munns remembered: "Some of those who worked at AVRO always seemed to have 'connections' who could get you a suit length, or a jumper or silk stockings - no coupons required, of course. I didn't mind because such things were almost impossible to get hold of and, to be honest, I made a few bob getting stuff for people outside ....."

In war, as in peace, there are those who have an eye for the making of a 'quick buck', as Joe Walton confirmed: "One chap at AVRO started a fixed-odds football coupon, and another became an agent for a tool firm. There was also a worker who ran a de-greasing service, in which he cleaned your dirty overalls - in a Trico bath - over the weekend; all unofficial, of course, and at a price. Black Market chocolates: a 5lb box (virtually a forgotten commodity in the shops) were raffled each week by somebody, and you could get shirts, ties and shoes and, if you wanted one, a suit could be measured, made and delivered within two days!

I remember a chap organising a raffle for a camera his brother was supposed to have taken from a German soldier. He sold tickets all over the factory, but when it came to the time for the draw it was discovered he had left AVRO. Later, someone saw him in Leeds and said he had better pay up, or else! He said he was sorry, it had happened through a misunderstanding and proferred £50 which was brought back with the intention of making refunds of 2/-d (10p) per ticket. It was soon discovered, however, that even if he had handed over £200 it would not have been enough ....."

Joe added that there were always individuals at the factory who were 'up to something sharp' and he recalled one particular occasion when "..... there was a collection for a girl who had lost her wage packet containing just over £5. The collection raised around £12 so, the week afterwards, several others 'lost' their wage packets too!

Another girl had a collection organised for her wedding present - she conned others into doing it - before it was discovered she had been married for quite some time ....."

Bernard Hepton added to the catalogue of dubious activities when he recalled "..... the time when a whole lathe went missing from the machine shop: stolen was the talk. How anyone could steal such an object remains a mystery?....."

Alf Harris remembered another criminal act: "It was around Christmas time when one worker fancied 'acquiring' an AVRO vice. He somehow got hold of a chicken or a goose, I can't remember which, and wrapped it with the vice in a brown

"Lighter Moments"

paper parcel. with the head and neck of the fowl hanging out. When questioned by the AVRO police at the gate he said that the bird had been a present from a farmer friend and the policeman congratulated him on his good fortune! ....."

Only a minority of workers were involved in such doubtful activities, but many others were engaged in the 'unofficial' production of innumerable items found difficult to come by in war time. Notable among them was the ubiquitous AVRO cigarette lighter of which, it has been claimed, more than 10,000 were made at Yeadon from duralumin 'scrap'. One former worker laughingly stated: "We built about half the number of planes we did lighters, and at one time or another everyone (including many with no direct connection with the factory) seemed to own one."

Photo 61. The AVRO lighter. £1 coin for scale 10,000 believed to have been made at Yeadon

In addition, there came into being by various means, a plethora of ashtrays, figures, book-ends, models and toys - the two latter being an extra-mural activity for the pattern makers; at which they were wonderfully adept - constructed from scrap metal, perspex and wood; and, during the 'forties, it was a rare event to find a local household which did not have on display some item produced unofficially within 'AVRO'.

From the foregoing it could be misconstrued that all its workers were 'on the fiddle', and cared little for the war effort. Such was not the case, however for, apart from several notable exceptions, the vast majority were mindful of the purpose imposed upon the factory and of their part in it.

In July, 1943, the factory achieved its peak production figures on the Anson, when 130 were produced, and for the next eight months this figure was maintained. During the year, 887 Ansons - 3/5ths of the years production on the type - were fitted with Bristol power-operated gun-turrets but, thereafter, on the directive of the M.A.P., production of all Anson types was steadily reduced.

Photo 62. Objet d'art

One of the considerable number (and variety) of unofficial objet d'art produced at the factory.

Here Britannia, modelled from a shilling, sits astride a burnished convex podium - constructed from an old penny-holding aloft a 'Lancaster' filed to shape from a three penny bit. The whole being seated on a cap from an aircrafts fuel tank !

Concurrently, Lancaster production had grown to 7 per month by April, 1943, and to 12 per month by October, with new workers arriving at the factory in excess of 170 per month. The place had become a veritable hive of industry; but the activity was not a means unto itself: the whole purpose of its product being to play a part in dealing the enemy a devastating blow. That this was achieved is now common knowledge, but not necessarily so the price paid by the machines built at Yeadon; nor by the men who flew them.

Ad Extremum - Press on Regardless

(The unofficial motto of the R.A.F. during the Second World War)

By mid 1943, heavy day bombing of enemy targets in Europe had become an almost exclusive prerogative of the United States Army Air Force through its 8th A.F. units based in the east of England. Concurrently, night bombing by the R.A.F. had been stopped up to a point where 5,000 sorties per month were being made and, within a year, this figure had doubled yet again. Such increased intensity of Operations was not achieved, however, without a commensurate loss in men and machines, and, by the cessation of hostilities, from a total of 7,377 Lancasters built, including 3 prototypes, 3,349 had been destroyed; the majority as a result of enemy action.

Statistics are, of course, notoriously obliging witnesses but nothing is contrived in the stark historical details concerning the Lancasters built at Yeadon. Of those completed before mid-1944 few survived the war: only one doing so from the first 50; 13 from the first 150; 24 from the first 250 and just 31, or ten per cent, of the first 300. The average life expectancy of *all* operational Lancasters was a mere 40 hours (similar for a Halifax, but even less for a Stirling); an incredibly small reimbursement, it would seem, for the time and resources required to build each one; and this was only part of the story.

As this book is concerned with one of the factories which built the Lancaster the author is, perforce, constrained to concentrate on its product, but would ask readers to bear in mind that *all* bomber aircrew, irrespective of the type of aircraft in which they flew, were subjected to similar fears, dangers and privations as those mentioned in actions relating to the Lancaster.

A 'tour' of Operations with Bomber Command was officially designated as being 30 bombing sorties (45 if serving with a Pathfinder Squadron) which, due to a number of factors, could occupy a period of six or seven months, throughout which the young aircrew lived on a veritable knife-edge in the full knowledge of the inherent dangers posed by a ruthless and cunning enemy; the ever present threat of bad weather, and the discomfort of the aircraft in which they flew for four, eight, ten or even more hours at a stretch. It is little wonder that many who returned from an Op. unscathed, did so near to mental and physical exhaustion yet aware that, in all probability they would be expected to repeat the process the next night, or the one after that !.

For every 100 aircrew who undertook training at an Operational Training Unit (OTU) and then began a two 'tour' cycle of service with Bomber Command, the following statistics indicate their chances of survival: [1]

Killed on operations 51
Killed in crashes in Britain 9
Seriously injured in crashes 3
Prisoners of war 12
Shot down and evaded capture 1
Survived unharmed 24

In all, 55,539 personnel of Bomber Command 'Failed to Return' and only those serving in Torpedo Bombers or as U-Boat crewmen had a smaller chance of survival. Of the 120,000 or so who flew Operationally with Bomber Command, a sizeable number, probably several thousand, did so in a Lancaster built at Yeadon albeit that, at the time, they were unaware of the fact.

Of the thousands of young men who saw action over occupied Europe (where the activities of Bomber Command were concentrated) many remain unsung for their exploits; thus the stories which follow, although exclusively describing Operations concerning men who won awards for gallantry when flying in aircraft built at Yeadon are, nevertheless, intended as an acknowledgement of the bravery and determination required of all who served with Bomber Command. For it was one of their number who, postwar, recalled "No matter how many (Ops.) you had been on, or how experienced others thought you to be, when you climbed out over the North Sea you were always aware of that eighth passenger-fear."

---

[1] As quoted in "The Bomber Command War Diaries", (see Bibliography).

Ad Extremum - Press on Regardless

During the 1939-1945 conflict, the Victoria Cross - Britains supreme award for gallantry - was awarded just 182 times. Thirty-two of the recipients were from the Royal Air Force, of whom 19 were serving in Bomber Command. Only 7 of them survived the war.

One member of this very exclusive group was William Reid; born at Baillieston, Glasgow on 21st December, 1921, the son of a blacksmith. He was educated at Coatbridge Secondary School, before going on to study metallurgy and, on 28th April, 1941, joining the Royal Air Force Volunteer Reserve (RAFVR). Subsequently, after undergoing training in Britain, Canada and the U.S.A., he gained his 'wings' and was commissioned. On return to England he was kept back from operational flying to serve as an Instructor with No.29 OTU at North Luffenham; but, in July, 1943, he converted to the Lancaster and was posted to No.61 Squadron at Syerston. There he was allocated a Mk III. Lancaster:LM360 (fitted with Merlin type 38 engines) built at Yeadon earlier in the year, and allocated the Squadron code 'OR-O ('O' for Orange). His crew comprised Flt. Sgt. J.A. Jeffries, RAAF (Navigator), Flt. Sgt. L. Rolton (Bomb Aimer), Flt. Sgt. J.W. Norris (Flight Engineer), Flt. Sgt. J.J. Mann (Wireless Operator), Flt. Sgt. D. Baldwin, DFM (Mid-Upper Gunner) and Flt. Sgt. 'Joe' Emerson (Rear Gunner), who was on his second 'tour' of Ops.

On 3rd November, 1943, Flt. Lt. Reid's crew, along with others of his Squadron, were briefed for attack on Dusseldorf. It was to be his 10th Op. and what follows is his account of the action which followed:

'We were over Holland at around 20,000 feet on our way to Dusseldorf when I received an almighty thump on my left shoulder. At the same time there was a blast of cold air and fragments of perspex peppered my face as the windscreen panels shattered. The night fighter didn't attack again - he was either driven off by the gunners or lost us when the kite started skidding around. The elevator trim had obviously been hit, but I could not get any information from the rest of the crew as the intercom was out. Eventually Jim Norris, the flight engineer, came up to me and indicated that everyone else was all right. To protect my eyes from the grains of perspex coming off the shattered windscreen I put on a pair of flying-goggles. The silky gloves I usually wore were no longer sufficient to keep my hands warm and the heavy leather pair kept in the cockpit were used to lessen the effects of the icy blast. The compass was u/s but as I could remember the briefed course changes there was no reason not to go on to the target. My shoulder was a bit sore but I wasn't really aware of any injuries at that busy time. Then,

crash, we were riddled with cannon-shells and bullets gain. I dived the Lancaster in an effort to evade, but the enemy fighter gave us a second burst before he lost us. My hands had been hit by shell fragments and the oxygen supply was failing. After a minute or two the flight engineer came back from the navigator's cabin and spread his arms out, meaning that Jeff was out; I didn't realize he was dead and that the wireless operator was wounded. I made signs for Norris to get me a portable oxygen bottle which I connected to my mask.

Despite the mauling the Lancaster had received, all engines were operating satisfactorily and although we had no port elevator it was possible to keep the plane straight and level by holding the stick back hard. So I decided to continue to the target, an estimated 45 minutes' away. To turn back now and fly a reciprocal course in the midst of the bomber stream presented a high risk of collision, while without communications or compass, guessing a new course away from the bomber stream might get us hopelessly lost and make us even more vulnerable to night fighters. In my mind, continuing to the target was the right action to take. I was now becoming conscious of my wounds; blood kept trickling down my face from under my helmet. My memory of course changes was proved correct and there was no difficulty in finding the target. After Les Rolton, the bomb-aimer, released our load I used the Pole Star and moon as direction guides to help in getting home.

As the flight progressed I began to lose my concentration and felt I might lapse into unconsciousness. Norris and Rolton had been helping with the controls all along and now that the bombs had gone Les stayed at a position where he could help hold the stick back. As the intercom had been out the bomb-aimer had been unaware that there were casualties among the crew. We received the attention of the Flak batteries before leaving the Dutch coast. After crossing the North Sea, landfall was made over Norfolk and we prepared to land at the first airfield we saw that was big enough for us to get down on. Morning mist shrouded the runway making it difficult to see the lights, and what with the blood still getting in my eyes and my own weakened state, it required both the flight engineer and bomb-aimer to put all their strength on the control column to counter the lack of an elevator on the approach. We made it, but one leg of the undercart started to fold and we ended up on our belly about fifty yards along the runway. Only after being removed from the aircraft did I learn that our navigator had died of his wounds.

I was carted off to hospital to have metal and perspex removed from wounds that I had not real-

ized were so extensive. There was a hole in the left shoulder and my hands were skinned on the surface like a gravel rash. My head had a bad cut just above the hairline and my face had been peppered with perspex fragments. Minute pieces of perspex appeared on my skin for weeks afterwards whenever I shaved. While in hospital I received a visit from AVM Cochrane who commanded No.5 Group. He was full of praise for my determination to carry on to the target and said this would be an example to others. I think they felt there were too many turn-backs on raids, and that some were not for genuine reasons. I got the impression that was why they made such a big fuss about my experience. It was not for me to say so at that time, but had I known the navigator was badly wounded - which I did not - and that there had been any hope of saving him, or if I had not felt the aircraft was still capable of reaching the target and bringing us home, then I would have turned back without hesitation. There was no intended act of bravado on my part; I did what I thought the right thing to do in the situation.'

For his incredible courage and determination he was subsequently awarded the Victoria Cross, while Jim Norris deservedly received the Conspicuous Gallantry Medal, and 'Joe' Emerson the Distinguished Flying Medal. Sadly, Flt. Sgt. J.J. Mann, their wireless operator, died from his injuries the next day. **(Photo 62a - page 92)**

Bill Reid brought LM360 back to earth at Shipdham, the wartime home of the 44th Bombardment Group U.S. 8th Air Force (the first American heavy bomber base in Norfolk), and remarkably, after undergoing repairs the Lancaster returned to operational service with No.50 Squadron at Skellingthorpe and No.9 Squadron at Bardney before, ultimately, being Struck-Off-Charge (SOC) on 11th November, 1944. **(Photo 63 - centre pages)**

Flt. Lt. Bill Reid was the only man to be awarded the Victoria Cross while in action in an aircraft built at Yeadon. Interestingly, however, he was one of four recipients of the medal, from Bomber Command, who are known to have been presented with a silver replica of a Lancaster when they made visits to the factory. Wing Commander Guy Gibson was one and, not long before he died, Group Captain Lord Leonard Cheshire, V.C., O.M., D.S.O., D.F.C., R.A.F. (Ret'd), kindly confirmed that he had been a third; but as to the identity of the fourth member of this unique quartet, the author remains in frustrating ignorance! **(Photo 64 - centre pages)**

During the war 20,000 Distinguished Flying Crosses (D.F.C.'s), 3,500 Distinguished Flying Medals (D.F.M.'s) and 1,087 Distinguished Service Orders (D.S.O.'s) were awarded and, undoubtedly, some were won for actions involving a Lancaster built at Yeadon. It is not practicable, however, to list them here but, in the case of the Conspicuous Gallantry Medal (C.G.M.), no such difficulty arises; there being so few awarded.

The C.G.M. ranks second only to the V.C. for acts of conspicuous gallantry displayed by non-commissioned officers and other ranks, being roughly equivalent to the D.S.O.; the latter being awarded only to officers holding the Sovereign's Commission or Warrant Officers.

During the Second World War only 109 men won the C.G.M. thus, after the V.C., it became a very rare distinction. All but 20 of the recipients came from Bomber Command; 59 of them being Lancaster crewmen of whom, at the time of their specific act of heroism or subsequent death, 6 were operating in a Lancaster built at Yeadon. In addition to F/Sgt. Norris the others were:

Warrant Officer Richard Jack Meek, R.C.A.F., was a Canadian navigator serving with No.626 Squadron (Wickenby) who, despite having received serious injuries during an attack on Berlin, on 30th/31st January 1944, successfully guided his pilot back across Germany and the North Sea in their badly damaged Lancaster:LM584 'UM-Y2'

Just short of three weeks later, on the night of 19th February, flight-engineer Sergeant Barry Wright stayed at his post, although badly injured from an enemy attack, throughout a hazardous journey back from a raid on Leipzig in Lancaster: LM382 'AS-Q' of No.166 Squadron (Kirmington).

On the night of 30th/31st March 1944, Flt. Sergeant Arthur Jeffries of No.550 Squadron (North Killingholme), was killed along with three others of his crew, when taking part in the calamitous attack on Nuremberg (details follow), in which their Lancaster: LM425 'BQ-M' was shot down near Liege. He had received the award of the C.G.M. (for bravery during 25 Operations) only two weeks earlier.

On 1st November 1944, Lancaster: LM650 of No.44 (Rhodesia) Squadron, Dunholme Lodge, was attacked and its pilot killed when involved in an attack on Homberg. Bomb-Aimer Flt. Sergeant Stanley Walters who, previously, had not handled a heavy aircraft, somehow succeeded in flying the badly damaged bomber back across Germany and the North Sea to the English Coast, where he allowed his crew-mates to exit by parachute before doing so himself.

Ad Extremum - Press on Regardless

<u>Sergeant Dennis R. Bowers</u>, flight-engineer of Lancaster: <u>ME378</u> 'GT-Q' of No.156 Squadron (PFF), Upwood, despite having his left leg almost severed when the aircraft was attacked, continued to fulfil his duties throughout a dangerous return journey from Harpenerweg, on 24th March 1945. Later, Bowers' leg was amputated.

The 'Battle of Berlin' which began on 18th/19th December, 1943, was the longest and costliest of the 'air-battles' fought in the skies over Europe and, during the seventeen weeks of its duration, the 'Big City', as Berlin was known to Allied aircrew, was attacked sixteen times by Bomber Command[*2]. The statistics speak for themselves: 9112 sorties flown for the loss of 497 aircraft (381 Lancasters - 25 of them built at Yeadon, 110 Halifaxes, 4 Stirlings and 2 Mosquitos) and 2,938 men, with a further 92 being wounded. 716 others became P.O.W.'s and 36 more evaded capture. Additionally, 60 Lancasters and 12 Halifaxes crashed on return to England, due to damage sustained during the attacks. **(Photo 65 - centre pages)**

Some readers might, perhaps, feel that this résumé of a limited number of Bomber Command Operations is extraneous to the history of a former factory? If so, they are surely mistaken for the place was not an end unto itself; its sole raison d'être being that of a cog in an enormous wheel of enterprise which culminated, at the 'sharp end', in the attempted aerial destruction of the enemy's war machine. Thus the author makes no apology for continuing in this vein, at least until the end of the chapter, for its content is fundamental to the very existence of the factory, and all others similarly engaged in aircraft production; and, moreover, it serves as a reminder that the price of freedom - our freedom - came high!

The 'Battle of Berlin' was called to a halt after the attack of 24th/25th March. The men of Bomber Command, notoriously scruffy on the ground but so determinedly efficient in the air, had given the 'Big City' a terrible pounding; but they, too, had suffered grievously. The war, however, went on; no early victory had been achieved - as Harris had hoped - and worse was to come.

"Eastward they climb, black shapes against the grey
Of falling dusk, gone with the nodding day
From English fields.
Not theirs the sudden glow
Of triumph that their fighter-brothers know;
Only to fly through cloud, through storm, through night
Unerring, and to keep their purpose bright,
Nor turn until, their dreadful duty done,
Westward they climb to race the awakening sun."
Anon. (first pub. in Punch).

On the night of 30th/31st March, 1944, 779 aircraft of Bomber Command flew from their English bases to attack Nuremberg in southern Germany. Twelve hours later 108 of them lay destroyed in a wide path stretching across northern Europe; with 545 of their aircrew dead, and a further 178 wounded or taken prisoner. The enemy, operating in an unforecast, cloudless and moonlit sky, enjoyed a veritable field-day, shooting down bomber after bomber virtually unmolested; losing just 10 night fighters. It was and, hopefully, will remain the worst disaster in the history of the Royal Air Force which, that night, suffered a heavier number of casualties than it experienced throughout the whole of the Battle of Britain!

Nuremberg, coming immediately after the cumulative losses of the Battle of Berlin, and the additional destruction of 78 of its aircraft in an attack on Leipzig six weeks earlier, proved a watershed for Bomber Command. Never again was such a large number of its aircraft to be seen en-route to a single German target (it was two weeks before *any* in Germany were visited) it being deemed more propitious, thereafter, to attack several simultaneously. This is not to say, of course, that Bomber Command was finished: far from it, for its attacks - and losses - against the enemy continued until the very final days of the war (and the number of young men volunteering for aircrew duties, similarly, continued unabated to the end) but, after Nuremberg it was accepted, at the highest level, that Germany could not be defeated solely by aerial attack.

At this time it is little wonder that, with the average loss rate being sustained by Bomber Command hovering around the 5% mark, many of its young aircrew measured their life expectancy in hours if

---

2   These were night attacks complemented, on occasions, by daylight 'follow-up' attacks by units of the U.S. 8th Air-Force.

not days. Others tried, usually unsuccessfully, to mitigate their fear of the future by involvement in wild 'bashes' in the Station Messes, and in excesses of forced humour.

Aircrew songs tended to be downright bawdy, or pertinent to the mens wartime experiences, and were many and varied. The following were just two of the more respectable ones - to spare our lady reader's blushes - but neither can hide the inherent concern which always lurked just behind the humour.

<u>Sung at the beginning of 'Bless 'em All':</u>

'They say there's a Lancaster leaving Berlin
Bound for old Blighty's shore,
Heavily laden with terrified men
Bound for the land they adore .....'

<u>Sung to the tune accompanying 'Abdul The Bulbul Amir':</u>

'Just an old fashioned AVRO with old fashioned wings,
And fabric all tattered and torn,
She's got old fashioned Merlins all tied up with string
And a heater that never gets warm.
But she's quite safe and sound, 'cos she won't leave the ground
And the crew are afraid of The Chop,
One day we will try to see if she'll fly
While Mother looks after the shop.'

Such songs, and many, many, more sung with gusto and tankard in hand, were part and parcel of the deliberately overt Mess get-togethers attended by the tired, largely fearful, and over-stressed young men of Bomber Command. The outcome was often riotous, but the 'bashes' could never completely hide the fear which stalked the corridors of an Operational Station like a phantom. Not that this was too obvious. Oh no as, for the majority of the young men involved, the fear of being seen to be afraid was the greatest fear of all.

"..... Despite the appalling losses the spirit of Bomber Command was fantastically high....I think this was partly a consequent of youth....partly the feeling that nothing nasty would ever happen to you (as distinct from other people), and partly a fear of showing fear to one's comrades...." [3] *

* Fl/Off W.W. Burke, navigator, No's 207 & 627 Squadron's

The number of sorties flown by all Lancasters (not to mention those flown by other aircraft) during the war was in excess of 152,000; and this excludes the 3,191 supply drops made to the starving people of Holland during 'Operation Manna': which took place between 29th April and 8th May, 1945.

The author is unable to provide details of the total number of Op's flown by aircraft built at Yeadon, nor the total number of men who crewed and were killed or injured in them. In each case, however, the figure must have been substantial for, from November, 1942, when LM301 began its service with No.12 Squadron, Lancasters bearing 'RY' as a symbol of their place of origin were operating over enemy territory until the final week of the war in Europe. **(Photo 66 - centre pages)**

That this was possible was due, in no small measure, to the enterprise shown by the workers at Yeadon (and, of course, in respect of other aircraft, by workers at similar establishments elsewhere) for, irrespective of the bravery and determination displayed by the young men of Bomber Command, their task would have been impossible without a ready supply of new aircraft. That this was consistently maintained is one of the unsung achievements of the Second World War.

"There was complete belief throughout all ranks that even in the darkest moments we were superior to the enemy in equipment and skills, and that we could not possibly lose the war" [4] Flt/Lt. J. Waterhouse DFM, navigator, No. 9 Squadron.

---

3   Quoted in "The Hardest Victory" by Denis Richards (see Bibliography).
4   Refer to footnote 3

Ad Extremum - Press on Regardless

SECRET

DETAIL OF WORK CARRIED OUT
By No. 61 SQUADRON
For the Month of NOVEMBER, 1943

Page No. ONE

Date	Aircraft Type & Number	Crew	Duty	Time Up	Time Down	Details of Sortie or Flight	References
3/4th	LANCASTER JB.138.	W/G. R.N. STIDOLPH. SGT. E.J. ANTHONY. P/O. J.H. DYER. P/O. G.F. ALEX. SGT. J.D. BARNES-MOSS. SGT. E.A. GARDENER. P/O. J.H. PULLMAN.	CAPTAIN. FLT. ENG. NAV. A.B. WT/AG. A.G. 1. A.G. 2.	17.00	21.31	ATTACK ON DUSSELDORF. Weather clear, thin layer of stratus cloud below and cirrus above, and excellent horizontal visibility. W/C. STIDOLPH reported a very good attack. Reported spoof attack on COLOGNE to be dead on time. Opposition was rather aimless, little heavy flak and searchlights in large numbers. attacked centre of four Red T.I's from 21,500 ft. Photos : Fires, incendiaries and searchlights on (No.4 frame)	A1335
	LANCASTER EE.176.	P/O. R.A. WALKER. SGT. H.E. HOULDSWORTH. P/O. N.J. CORNELL. P/O. J. WELLS. SGT. E.C. BAILEY. SGT. C.R. TAYLOR. SGT. D.R. KELLY. SGT. G.L. WARD.	CAPTAIN. FLT. ENG. NAV. A.B. WT/AG. A.G. 1. A.G. 2. 2nd NAV.	17.17	21.56	Fires, incendiaries, ground detail and searchlights on (No. 8 frame) P/O. WALKER attacked Green T.I. from 20,700 ft. Fires were observed with a great deal of smoke. Photo, fires and incendiaries.	
	LANCASTER W.4198.	P/O. A.J. EAVES. SGT. G. WHITLEY. P/O. D.G. WHITE. SGT. R.C. CANVIN. SGT. J.A. WESTON. P/S. F.K. FULLER. F/S. H.L. SWEET.	CAPTAIN. FLT. ENG. NAV. A.B. WT/AG. A.G. 1. A.G. 2.	17.20	22.04	P/O. EAVES bombed three Red T.I's from 18,500 ft. Good fires were observed. His aircraft was coned for 15 minutes and subjected to accurate heavy flak and attacked simultaneously by a JU.88 which M.U. Gunner observed as damaged after a short burst. Photo. fires and incendiaries.	
	LANCASTER W.294.	F/S. F.W. BURGESS. SGT. R. CANN. SGT. G.W. FRANKLIN. SGT. C.P. STEEDSMAN. SGT. V. DACRE. SGT. C. WICK. SGT. J.T. MCQUILLAN.	CAPTAIN. FLT. ENG. NAV. A.B. WT/AG. A.G. 1. A.G. 2.	17.09	21.59	F/S. BURGESS bombed M.P.I. of cluster of Red and Green T.I's from 20,000 ft. Many fires were observed in target area, though somewhat scattered. Searchlights and flak ineffective though smoke bursts seemed heavy around 15,000 ft. Photo. fires and incendiaries.	
	LANCASTER DV.311.	F/L. J.D. WOODS. SGT. W.A. IKE. SGT. D.R. TREVETHICK. F/S. P.J. LYNCH. F/S. W.E. GREEN. SGT. L.A. PURCELL. SGT. E. PARRY.	CAPTAIN. FLT. ENG. NAV. A.B. WT/AG. A.G. 1. A.G. 2.	17.16	21.30	F/L. WOODS attacked two Green T.I's from 20,000 ft. Little flak was encountered and a few fighters were seen over Target. Photo. searchlights and fires.	
VC →	LANCASTER LM.360.	F/L. W. REID. SGT. J.W. NORRIS. W/S. J.S. JEFFRIES. SGT. L.G. ROLTON. F/S. J.J. MANN. P/S. C. BALDWIN. F/S. A.F. EMERSON.	CAPTAIN. FLT. ENG. NAV. A.B. WT/AG. A.G. 1. A.G. 2.	16.59	22.01	F/L. REID was attacked by enemy night fighters on the way out but although he and Flight Engineer were wounded and the Navigator killed outright he proceeded on to bomb the target. On returning aircraft landing was made at SHIPDHAM.	

Photo 62a. Extract from the ORB of No. 61 Squadron for 3rd/4th November 1943. source Public Records Office.

Onto Victory

'Skylark' was one of the biggest hit songs of the war, but there was very little skylarking in the business of building aeroplanes. From 1942 this steadily became the largest industry in Britain employing directly, or indirectly through a host of sub-contractors, more than 2,000,000 men and women who, by the summer of 1944 when production reached its peak, were producing 26,000, of various types, a year.

Throughout the war the factories were constantly hard pressed to keep up with a seemingly insatiable demand: in 1940 only 40 four-engined bombers were built; in 1941 the total rose to 498; 1,796 in 1942; 4,615 in 1943 and 5,507 by the end of 1944; in addition to many other types built in their thousands.

AVRO Yeadon played its part, continually escalating its output and, in 1944, its machine shop was averaging 2,000,000 operations per week - peak production being reached during April with a figure of 2,118,0002 operations - an average of 5 being required to make each component.

This huge output was achieved by a workforce of which only 16.4% were skilled and, overall, of whom almost 60% were women (at its peak in April, 1944, the factory employed 11,075 people) and they became so proficient that the level of scrap metal produced dropped below 2½%: a remarkable achievement for a so-called 'green' labour force; the majority of whom, pre-war, would not have known the difference between a centre-lathe and a centre-forward!

By 1944 the pressure on the factories was such that, despite their already considerable working week, employees were often required to put in extra shifts to cope with the work load, and it was not unusual on one's day off to receive a telegram (only a small minority of the population then owned a telephone) urging them to return to the factory immediately.

Necessity is indeed the creator of invention and throughout the munitions industries prodigious efforts were made to overcome apparently insuperable obstacles. Before the war Britain barely had a light metal industry and yet, within months of the commencement of hostilities, a host of new factories came into being for the production of aluminium from bauxite (for engines and the 'skin' of aircraft) and, as the requirement for aircraft rose so, similarly, did the need for an increasing quantity of aluminium: 15,000 tons (15,241 tonnes) per *year* in 1935 rising to 26,000 tons (26,418 tonnes) per *month* by 1944!

Photo 67.

This medal, the premier award of the Scrap Metal Dealers Assoc. has been struck in L40.

The design has been adopted as the seal of the scrap graveyard, and may soon be seen impressed on every consignment of scrap leaving the works.

In June of that year, the AVRO Group was averaging 260 new Lancasters each month: yet this was barely enough to keep pace with the losses: 9,000 British bombers of all types being destroyed during the war. The daily average strength of Bomber Command in mid-1944 stood at 616 Lancasters, 354 Halifaxes, 58 Stirlings and 72 Mosquitos, yet between 1st January and 8th June, 848 were lost to enemy action and a further 24 were written-off in crashes.

Thus, by force of circumstance, manufacturers were compelled to take on any new method or invention which might make difficult, and/or time consuming, jobs more simple and, one such innovation which AVRO evolved was a machine known as a 'Manipulator': a device which could bend to shape a heavy, extruded former in just two minutes rather than the many hours it had taken two fitters to do the job previously.

Photo 68.

Telegram sent to Alf Harris by his section manager. It reads: Can you report for work tomorrow Sunday morning. Will arrange Chadderton conveyance.

The conveyance was a 60' long "Queen Mary" low loader which was taking a fuselage to Yeadon!

In March, 1944, an order was received for an Ambulance type of aircraft - considered necessary for the planned invasion of Europe - and AVRO Yeadon converted Anson Mk.1, NK753 to meet the specification. Powered by Armstrong-Siddeley Cheetah XIX engines, and fitted with hydraulically operated undercarriage and flaps, the type became the Anson Mk.X, Series 2. Twenty-one were built at Yeadon within the first month following Air Ministry approval but, within weeks, a development of the Mk.X, having a deepened fuselage, came on the scene, and known as the Mk.XI. Its prototype: NK870 first flew at Yeadon on 30th July, 1944, and, eventually, this was delivered on 19th January, 1945, to the Balkan Air Force for use by Marshal Tito. **(Photo 69 & 70 - centre pages)**

Further modifications of the type, including the addition of variable pitch propellers, Cheetah XV engines and a reinforced wing, produced the Mk.XII: the ultimate Communications/Ambulance variant, of which: NL153 was the first to fly (at Yeadon) on 27th October, 1944. Three months later, on 30th January, 1945, this Anson was delivered to the Royal Australian Air Force. **(Photo 71 - centre pages)**

When production came to an end at Yeadon in 1946, the factory had produced 103 Mk.X's (series 1 and 2), 90 Mk.XI's and 264 Mk.XII's in addition to more than 4,000 Mk.I's with, or without, Bristol turrets. To detail the history of each one is unnecessary here, for this has already been done to a standard far beyond the capabilities of this author.[1] Suffice it to say, therefore, that examples built at the factory flew in a multiplicity of rôles; from that of serving Royalty to the most humble of passengers; and being on the strength, at one or other time, of almost every Air Force of any note. If ever an aeroplane justly (and affectionately) earned the title 'ubiquitous' it has to be the 'Faithful Annie'.

At Yeadon, monthly production of the Lancaster increased from 12 in October, 1943, to 32 in March, 1944, and, thereafter, continued at a rate of between 30 and 40 per month up to the end of the war. The design of an aircraft and its components is, however, constantly evolving and even the Lancaster, which was not forced to undergo the radical changes found necessary on some other types, required 800 modifications (Mods.) by early 1944. Each Lancaster was 'factory fitted' with a type T.1154 radio transmitter, R.1155 receiver and an R.1196 intercommunications set (Intercom) for crew contact within the aircraft, from aircraft to aircraft and for communication with the ground. From time to time this equipment was also subject to mods.

From, and including, LM522 which was built at Yeadon during the late winter of 1944, all Lancasters were fitted with H2S: this being the first airborne radar set to provide navigators with an image, albeit a shadowy one, of the ground over which they flew, and thus enabling bomb-aimers (by this time more usually termed air-bombers) to more accurately bomb 'blind' through cloud. H2S was not the ultimate blind bombing device, and it had many teething troubles but, from its inception, bombing became far more accurate.

The sets were issued, initially, in the main to aircraft serving with Pathfinder Squadrons - although not so in the case of LM522 for it flew as DX-G with

---

[1] 'The Anson File' compiled by R.C. Sturtivant, published by Air Britain, 1988.

a Main Force Squadron: No.57, out of East Kirkby from March, 1944. Sadly, the Lancaster went 'Missing' with all crew on 8th July during an attack on St. Leu d'Esserent.

Eventually, H2S became standard equipment in all Bomber Command 'heavies'; its presence therein being easily detectable by the 'bulge' protruding beneath the rear fuselage. Although the device more than proved its worth, it was found to have one considerable disadvantage in that its signals could be used by enemy aircraft, operating a system known as NAXOS, to 'home-in' on the bombers from a distance of more than 30 miles. Not surprisingly, once this became known to the navigators of Bomber Command their H2S sets were used only in very short 'bursts'!

Contrary to some opinion H2S sets were not fitted to an aircraft during its construction but, later, by specialists at MU's or at Operational Stations.

With the Axis forces defeated in North Africa and Sicily; the British and Americans advancing through Italy, and the Russians making headway across a broad Front in the East, the scene was set for the long awaited liberation of Europe, and this began on 6th June: 'D-Day', when a mighty Armada of more than 4,000 ships carried a huge force of men and material to the beaches of Normandy. Although, thereafter, it was some weeks before the bridgehead was firmly established, once this was achieved there was a new optimism in the air.

On the night of 5th/6th June 1944 - the eve of 'D-Day' - two, eight aircraft, flights of Lancasters of No.617 Squadron flew from their base at Woodhall Spa to take part in 'Operation Taxable'. This involved overflying the English Channel some sixty miles east of the intended invasion area, at a specified height and speed and, with an eighty mile gap between the two groups, the Lancasters were required to fly a *precision* course - backwards and forwards - for a period of *eight hours*; at *stop-watch timed* intervals therein dropping bundles of thin strips of metal-backed paper (code named 'Window'), to create an impression on the enemy's radar screens of an approaching invasion fleet! This remarkable piece of airmanship resulted in the complete deception of the enemy for a critical period prior to the actual seaborne landings further west!

Three Yeadon built Lancasters are known to have taken part in the Operation; led by the Squadron's C/O, Wing Commander G.L. Cheshire DSO, DFC., who flew (as second pilot) in **LM482**:' AJ-W', captained by Sqn. Ldr. J.L. Munro RNZAF[*]., along with eleven others (each aircraft carried two pilots,

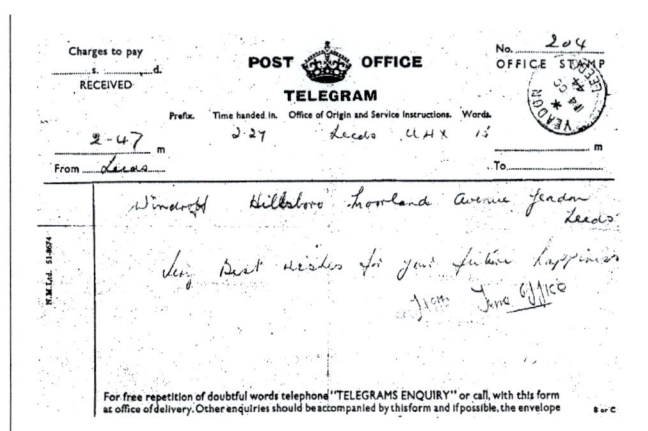

Photo 73.

The telegram received by Marie & William Windross, from her colleages in the Time Office on the occasion of their marriage. 14th October 1944. via Mrs Windross

and two navigators, plus additional crew members to deal with the distribution of the bundles of 'Window'); they were: Fl/Off. P. Kelly., Fl.Lt. C.K. Astbury., Fl.Lt. F.G. Rumbles.,F/Sgt F.E. Appleby*.,Fl. /Off. P.E. Pigeon* RCAF., P/O. W. Howarth*., Fl./Off. H A Weekes* RCAF, F/Sgt. H Johnson*., Fl./Off. F.C. Atkinson RCAF, F/Sgt. J.E. Baker., F/Sgt D. Wilson-Williams. **LM492**: 'AJ-Q', captained by Sqd/Ldr. J.C. McCarthy DSO, DFC., RCAF* with Sqd.Ldr. D.J. Shannon DSO., DFC., RAAF* as second pilot, led the second echelon but, unfortunately, no further crew details are to hand:this applies, similarly, to the third 'Yeadon' Lanc' involved: **LM485**, AJ-N; the former having

Photo 74. AVRO police.

This well balanced shield requires practically no explanation, the arm of the law is there and one should be careful of poking fun at policemen. It may be interesting to note the supporting rifles, these being relics of the early days of the force. The motto refers to the patron saint of the force. copyright J. Bruce.

12 men aboard, the second 14! The asterisks denote those who took part in the Dams raid, on 16th May 1943. Fifty years later, 'Joe' McCarthy and 'Dave' Shannon, among others, were back in England to attend special events to mark the anniversary of that epic attack.

On 12th August, Allied forces landed in the South of France and, on the 23rd Paris was liberated as were Brussels and Antwerp by 3rd September. Five days later the first V2 German rocket fell on English soil at Chiswick, creating a huge explosion. This 45ft (13.71 metres) long, steel canister, with a one ton (1.01 tonne) warhead flew at supersonic speed, and gave no warning of its coming until the sound of its approaching screech could be heard *after* it had exploded! Ultimately, more than 1,000 V2's were launched from sites in Holland, the last one falling in England on 27th March, 1945; with the last V1 following two days later. In the short period they were in use the two deadly weapons killed and injured 31,500 people and damaged 1.5 million houses. Given such grim statistics it requires little imagination to foresee the probable outcome if, on the night of 17th/18th August, 1943, Bomber Command had not successfully attacked the German rocket research establishment at Peenemunde on the Baltic Coast, thus delaying development of the weapons by several months, or had the invasion of Europe, which facilitated the capture of their launching sites, been postponed? A relative of author, Sgt. C.C. Smith (later Flg. Off. D.F.C.) to whom this book is jointly dedicated, took part in the attack; as did several Lancasters built at Yeadon. On the Home Front there was no relaxation of rationing but certain other restrictions were abandoned. In September the total 'Black-Out' was replaced by the 'Dim-Out', through which a light could be shown after dark - but it had to be dimmed. In the same month the Home Guard was stood down, though not without *considerable* opposition (!), and there were some who dared to believe that, at long last, they could see a light at the end of a very dark tunnel. **(Photo 72 - centre pages)**

William and Marie Windross were married at St. John's Church, Queensbury, a suburb of Bradford, on 14th October, 1944. Marie recalled: "We felt that we could start to look forward, which might sound silly now but, for years, we had got out of the habit of doing so ....." Earlier, during the summer of 1942 she had gone to work at the factory at Yeadon, travelling from her home in Bradford by public transport, "..... as I stood up to get out of the bus, quite unexpectedly, an unknown lady gave me a kind of blessing for the future and , remarkably, it seemed to change things for me......".

Marie was employed in the Time Office, where Arthur Dobson, aided by his second-in-command Mr. Fergie, was in charge. "I made friends with Audrey Lilley" recalled Marie, "she now lives in Felixstowe and we are still good friends. We worked permanent nights for over a year which had an advantage in that it gave us a full weekend off every month ....." Part of Marie's job was to collect pass-out cards (issued to workers who had been given permission to leave the factory before the end of their shift) and time-clock cards from the AVRO police who manned the gate offices. "A welcome task," continued Marie, "for it gave us a chance to get out and breathe some fresh air. In those days you couldn't take a walk outside just if and when you wished, you know ....." Although simply welcomed as a means of taking a breather, on one such excursion Marie met William, a member of the AVRO police, who would be her future husband. "He had served in the Royal Artillery during the First World War but he had experienced such dreadful things he never spoke about it. In civilian life William was a professional gardener, in fact he was a Fellow of the Royal Horticultural Society, and he worked for a time at Messrs. Mansel and Hatcher of Rawdon, the noted orchid growers. There can't have been many girls in wartime England who were lucky enough to have a spray of orchids in their Wedding Dress, as I did!? I recall some of William's police colleagues: there was George Dennison, Leonard Prentice, Graham ? from Hull, another fellow from Hull called Garland and a Mr. Walmsley."

On 12th September, Anson Mk.1, NK826, built at Yeadon earlier in the summer, became the first aircraft of the ATA to land on the continent of Europe; the incident being recalled, subsequently, by Hugh Bergel in his book 'Fly and Deliver' (Airlife 1982):

"..... the C.O. (of ATA, Gerard d'Erlanger) very much wanted to go to Paris to try and make contact with his sister and brother-in-law there. Watkins (Wing Commander and C.O. of No.84 GSU) didn't think he could lay on an Anson but, by chance, Jim Mollison with one of White Waltham's Ansons (NK826) was actually on the aerodrome at Thruxton ..... the C.O. commandeered this Anson and instructed me to take it over ..... after landing at Le Bourget the group persuaded a taxi driver - with 20 Players cigarettes - to drive them into the city ..... we rode into Paris ten days after it had been liberated ....."Postwar, NK826 became G-AJFX and had a varied civilian career which ended, sadly, after colliding with a donkey when making a forced landing near Cairo on 10th July, 1951. What became of the unfortunate animal thereafter is unknown!

Why d'Erlanger needed to commandeer NK826 remains unclear, for he had as his personal aircraft another Yeadon built Mk.1: NK270 which, postwar, he retained when he became Director-in-Charge of British European Airways Corporation (BEAC) in 1946. The aircraft became the first Anson. 1 on the civil register: G-AHBN on 28th February, 1946, registered to BOAC White Waltham and, subsequently, was used by Sir Harold Hartley, KCVO, CBE, Chairman of BEA, and then by the BEA Flying Club, prior to being sold to an Italian purchaser.

The first 'civil' Anson of any type was Mk.XI: G-AGLM (constructors No.1204), a conversion of ML246, which first flew as a non-military aircraft (at Yeadon) on 9th November 1944, thereafter obtaining its Certificate of Airworthiness (COFA), on the 24th. Delivered to the Ministry of Civil Aviation, at Croydon, in July 1945, the Anson returned to the RAF - again as NL246 - in February 1946; ultimately being broken up at Woodford on 19th August 1948.

The giant German battleship Tirpitz, sister ship to the Bismarck, remained a constant threat in northern waters throughout five years of war. Many attempts were made to put her out of action and, after a series of attacks by Lancasters of No's 617 and 9 Squadron's, made during the autumn of 1944, the menace was finally removed when she was sunk on 12th November, while at anchor in Tromsö Fiord. The following are the Lancasters, built at Yeadon, which were involved!

15th September: LM485 'AJ-N'; LM489 'AJ-A' LM492 'AJ-W' of No.619 Sqn., LM715 'WS-O' of No.9 Sqn., and LM587 'JO-L' of No.463 Sqn., RAAF. of the Bomber Command Film Unit: the aircraft from which the action was filmed.

29th October: LM 489 and LM 492 (carrying the same codes as on 15th September) and LM 695 'AJ-N'; all of No.617 Sqn.

12th November: LM 489 and LM 492 (again same codes) and LM 485, this time coded 'AJ-N', all of No.617 Sqn., plus LM 448 'WS-M' of No.9 Sqn. Thus, possibly, one of these aircraft was that which effected the coup de grâce!

On 16th December, in the Ardennes, German forces aided by bad weather which kept Allied aircraft on the ground, began what proved to be their last offensive in the West. Nine days later, thousands of people in many parts of Europe celebrated Christmas free from the harsh brutality of occupation, for the first time in five years.

At AVRO Yeadon the festival was marked by a special Dance, of three hours duration, organised on the shop floor of the Finals, and made possible by the departure therefrom of three Lancaster's. Alf Harris remembered: "..... the booze 'materialised' from the wings of another, incomplete, Lancaster, brought in on a Queen Mary!"

Other festive visitors included a B24 Liberator of the U.S. 8th Air Force from which, after landing, came its crew requesting help to unload a consignment of fruit destined for an address in Bradford - reasons not given. The flight sheds and aerodrome personnel, for so long denied the sight of anything other than home grown produce, were astonished to find the big aircraft filled with bananas, melons, oranges, grapes and other foreign grown fruit which had not been seen, let alone eaten, in the area for many a long day. Although most of the consignment was despatched to its destination, several local families benefitted from an unexpected Christmas present; and included among them were two young ladies in Bacon Street, Guiseley, to whom Father Christmas provided fruit they had never seen before!

Another American visitor was a Curtiss C46 'Commando', of the United States IXth Air Force; a very unusual sight at that time north of the Lincolnshire border or east of Burtonwood, which arrived unannounced and began to disgorge two jeeps and several occupants, who then drove off without a 'bye your leave', leaving their aircraft 'camped' at the side of the apron. Two days later, a bunch of laughing airmen returned accompanied by several 'ladies' who were shown around the C46 before emerging clutching various gifts. The whole party then climbed aboard the jeeps once more and drove off at high speed - all screams and giggles. Several hours later the jeeps returned with now sober-faced servicemen, minus their female companions. When questioned, the Americans stated, in effect, that it had been no big deal, they had just been visiting some friends in Leeds for Christmas and, after handing around candy and gum to the astounded aerodrome staff, they trundled the jeeps back on board the C46 and, with no further ado, proceeded to fly back whence they came!

Thousands of others viewed Christmas in a more subdued fashion: praying and hoping that it would be the last they would experience under the duress of war. Everyone longed for peace and a return to normality although, after five years of war, that in itself had become difficult to define: "..... it seemed there had always been a war, and always would be," said ex-WAAF Joan Beech, and another poignantly remembered, "..... one viewed permanence as going

Onto Victory

through a week without hearing of someone you knew being killed."

New Years Day 1945 heralded no break in the bombing campaign and, on 5th January, a large force was despatched to attack Hannover. The next evening, Saturday, the author was present when members of the family were informed that Clifford (Flg.Off. C.C. Smith, DFC) was reported 'Missing'. Seven months were to pass before it was officially confirmed that he, and four others of his crew, had been killed during the raid. **(Photo 75 - centre pages)**

The Allied leaders met at Yalta, in the Ukraine, on 4th February and, on 6th March, Cologne was captured. On 12th of April Franklin D. Rooseveldt, President of the United States of America, who had been ill for some time, died within virtual sight of the victory for which he had so earnestly worked.

By the 25th Russian troops surrounded Berlin and two days later they, and American units, linked-up further West. The same day Benito Mussolini, for twenty-one years Fascist Dictator of Italy, and his mistress, were shot by partisans - who then hung their bodies on a lamp post for all to see - and on the 30th, in his Berlin bunker, Adolph Hitler killed himself along with his mistress Eva Braun.

Two days later the city was captured by units of the Russian Army and, on the same day, German forces in Italy surrendered, followed by those in North-West Germany, Holland and Denmark on the 4th. Full, unconditional, surrender of the remaining German forces was agreed, and the war in Europe was officially declared to be over at 'One Minute past Midnight on Tuesday, 8th May.'

That evening, despite inclement weather, on the high ground of Otley Chevin, a mere mile from the AVRO factory, a huge beacon fire, containing 100 tons of wood and other waste material, was lit by the Vice-Chairman of Otley Town Council, Mr.G. Lambert. "..... at this moment," commented the Airedale and Wharfedale Observer, "the crowd of more than 7,000 people (of whom the author was one) broke into the spontaneous singing of 'There'll always be an England'." What the newspaper did not report, however, was that burning fiercely on the bonfire was an effigy of Adolph Hitler: feelings still ran high.

The rejoicing on the Chevin, and elsewhere was, however, tempered by the knowledge that Japan remained undefeated and, in the event, would remain so for three more months.

The end of the war in Europe saw the completion of 'Operation Manna', during which the men of Bomber Command dropped huge quantities of food to the starving people of Holland. This was followed, almost immediately, by 'Operation Exodus'; under the terms of which released British Prisoners of War were flown home by men who, only days before, remained conditioned to expect a hostile reception when flying through the same skies!

Bob Pierson, then an 18 years old Air Gunner with No.100 Squadron at Elsham Wolds took part in both 'Manna' and 'Exodus' and recalled: "It seems I flew in 'N2' to Pomigliano in Italy, a trip of some six and a half hours, bringing back ex-POW's, some of whom you can see in the second picture enclosed ..... and the last trip I made in 'N2' was from Scampton, on 25th March, 1946, that being for just 35 minutes on air-test; probably the shortest flight I ever made in a Lanc ....." **(Photo 76&77 - centre pages)**

'N2' was Lancaster RE118: HW-N2, more usually referred to as 'N Squared', completed at Yeadon in March and delivered to No.100 Squadron soon after it moved to Elsham from Grimsby (Waltham) early in April, Bob Pierson continued, "..... it is some comfort to us ex-aircrew to know that there are those who record history for future generations. For our part we are proud of that episode in our lives ....."

Right up to the end of the war in Europe production at Yeadon and elsewhere was fully maintained for, even as late as the month of April, Bomber Command lost 58 Lancasters; and who could predict what might be required, or how long it would take, to defeat Japan?

The majority of aircraft were ferried from the factories to various MU's rather than direct to operational (or other) units; and, moreover, not in strict rotation. Thus it should not be presumed that a serial sequence confirms that a specific aircraft reached its first deployment ahead of one which followed it along the production line!

In view of this (and some other factors) it is virtually impossible to be certain which of the Yeadon built Lancasters was last to leave the factory, and yet still be engaged with the enemy. As far as it has been possible to ascertain, however, the last of the type *newly* built there to reach an Operational unit prior to the end of the war in Europe, was Mk.III: RE176, which was taken on strength by No.103 Squadron, at Elsham Wolds, during the first days of May; but it was not involved in Bomber Command's last Operation (of an aggressive nature) on 3rd/4th.

Mk.III: ME424, which joined No.153 Squadron at Scampton, during February, earned the very dubious distinction of being the last of Yeadon's 695 Lancasters to be lost in action, when it was shot down during a daylight attack on Bremen, on 22nd April.

Interestingly, six Lancasters from the final batch delivered from Yeadon to Bomber Command: RE138; RE154; RE157; RE161; RE162 and RE163, all Mk.III's, were received by No.101 (RCM) Squadron, at Ludford Magna, high on the Lincolnshire Wolds, during April; thus maintaining to the end of the war a consistent (and substantial) connection between the factory and this specialist unit.

As to the longevity of Yeadon built Lancs', MkIII: LM346 survived in *active* service for the greatest period. It commenced duties in August, 1943, with the Navigation Training Unit, alternatively known as No.8 (Pathfinder) Group NTU, at Upwood, and continued in No.8 Group service as OF-U with No.97 Squadron at Bourn (during the period when WAAF, Joan Beech, served there), then became TL-Q with No.35 Squadron at Graveley; F2-? with No.635 Squadron at Downham Market, back to No.97 Squadron, by then at Coningsby, as OF-O and, finally, to No.100 Squadron, in No.1 Group, at Elsham Wolds, prior to being Struck-off-Charge (SOC) on 7th May, 1947, when residing at No.22 M.U. at Silloth. Although the author cannot confirm the total number of hours flown by LM346, it can safely be assumed that this was substantial - certainly several hundred: a very rare achievement if compared with the 40 hour average life-span of a Lancaster and, particularly so, when viewed against the mere 4 hours completed by another built at Yeadon: LM330, when it was shot down on 22nd/23rd June, 1943!

LM426, which began life at Yeadon as a Mk.III, saw no operational service, being delivered to Rolls-Royce at Hucknall, on 20th December, 1943, but, nevertheless, by 17th August, 1945, had flown almost 700 hours on Merlin type 38 and 24/2 engine development trials, ending its days as a Mk.I. It was scrapped in February, 1947.

With the exception of those used by No.6 Group (RCAF) Bomber Command, which flew the Mk.II (Bristol Hercules powered) and the Mk.X (Canadian built), and the mainly war-weary examples which saw services with a number of training units deployed, at various times, at Finningley, Lindholme and Sandtoft, the Lancaster was conspicuous by its absence from the 28 bomber stations in Yorkshire until late in the war;[*2] and, even then, No.4 Group, which operated from airfields situated, roughly, south a line Harrogate-York-Bridlington remained, exclusively, equipped with the Halifax. From 4th January, 1945, however, four of the Canadian Squadrons of No.6 Group in the north of the County, began replacing their Mk.X's (which were being flown back to Canada by 'tour-expired' crews) with new Mk.I's and Mk.III's; the following being those produced at Yeadon. Aircraft marked with an asterisk were Mk.I's, the remainder being Mk.III's.

No.424 (Tiger) Squadron, RCAF. Skipton-on-Swale (near Thirsk) was the first unit to convert to the new Lancasters on 4th January, taking On Strength: ME456[*] (QB-K) and ME458 (QB-T), which undertook their first operational sorties in an attack on Ludwigshafen on 1st February.

No.427 (Lion) Squadron, RCAF, Leeming, converted on 15th March, receiving: ME485 (ZL-A), ME426 (ZL-C), ME393 (ZL-D), ME498 (ZL-K), ME501 (ZL-T) and RE160 (ZL-G).

No.429 (Bison) Squadron, RCAF, also based at Leeming, converted during the same month and operated the following; beginning with an attack on Hamburg on 31st. ME539 (AL-A), ME543 (AL-B), ME538 (AL-E), ME537 (AL-N), ME534 (AL-O), ME540 (AL-P), ME536 (AL-Q), RE153 (AL-V) and RE155 (AL-X).

No.433 (Porcupine) Squadron, RCAF, was based at Skipton-on-Swale and commanded by Wing Commander G.A. Tambling when, on 17th January, it received ME375[*] (BM-D) and ME457[*] (BM-U) which, almost certainly, became the first Yeadon built Lancasters to operate against the enemy from a Yorkshire airfield when, on the 29th, they took part in an attack on Krefeld.

From a total of 695 Lancasters built at Yeadon, only the 19 listed above were involved in attacks on

---

2   No.101 Squadron flew the Lancaster for eight months, when operating from Holme-on-Spalding Moor (September 1942 until 15th June, 1943), but its first Yeadon built examples, Mk.III's: LM367 and LM369 were not taken on strength until October, 1943, by which time the Squadron was at Ludford Magna in Lincolnshire. Similarly, No.460 Squadron, RAAF, did not receive its first Yeadon built Lancasters, Mk.III's: LM315 and LM316 until 15th and 16th April, 1943, the day and day after the unit departed Breighton for residence at Binbrook; also on the Lincolnshire Wolds.

targets in occupied Europe when flying from bases in Yorkshire, and just one: ME456 (QB-K) of No.424 (Tiger) Squadron, RCAF, which went 'Missing' during a raid on Dortmund on 21st February, 1945, was lost when operating from the county of its birth.

Throughout the early summer of 1945 production of the Anson and the Lancaster continued at Yeadon unabated but the types had, by then, been joined on the assembly lines by the eventual successor to the Lancaster: the Lincoln, and a chunky, slab-sided, derivative of the Lancaster intended for a transport role: the York.

The Lincoln B.1 evolved from Air Ministry Specification B14/43 for a bomber able to operate at an all up weight of 70,000lbs (31,751Kgs) up to 35,000ft (10,667 metres) and, initially, the project was known as the Lancaster Mark IV. The design incorporated an increased wing-span and a fuselage correspondingly lengthened, with a re-designed nose and bomb-bay, but the basic configuration remained similar - although, arguably, somewhat less attractive - than its progenitor, from which many components were inherited. Although planned crew positions remained virtually unchanged the armament specified was of heavier calibre, involving .50mm machine-guns and 20mm cannon.

Ultimately, 532 Lincolns were built by the AVRO Group for service with the R.A.F., plus 18 for the Argentine Air Force; with 74 others being produced in Australia and Canada. Contrary to some local opinion (to which, until very recently, the author subscribed) only 6 Lincolns: 2 - B.Mk.I's and 4 - B.Mk.II's, were built at Yeadon, against Contract No.3858/C4(a) of 15th May, 1944.

The York, however, played a significantly more prominent role in the history of the factory; approximately 113 examples of the type being produced there [3], and this is examined in more detail in the Appendices.

On 26th July, the Labour Party, led by Clement Attlee, achieved a remarkable victory in the first General Election since the outbreak of hostilities. The result clearly showed that, in addition to being desperately weary of war, many people longed for the much promised 'New Society': a *genuine* 'land fit for heroes' their fathers had been denied after the First World War.

All this was overshadowed, however, when on 6th August, Hiroshima was laid waste by the first atomic bomb, to be followed, three days later, by the similar devastation of Nagasaki. On the 14th, Japan surrendered unconditionally and victory was celebrated next day - 'VJ Day' - ..... 'with rejoicing throughout the land, and street parties went on into the night .....'

Mrs. M. Wright recalled, "..... we, Doreen, Sam, Jack and I, left the factory and went into town (Bradford) and everybody was dancing in Broadway, and some fireworks were let off. We were so happy it was all over and that, after six years, the lights were coming on again but, most of all, because no more of our boys were going to get killed ....."

Twelve days later, Mrs. Anie Smith learned, officially, that the youngest of her four sons, twenty-one years old Clifford, would not be coming home.

---

[3] Sources vary as to the definitive total!

Peace

"The day Peace broke out I told my missus she wasn't looking too cheerful, and she said, 'there's nothing to look forward to now - Before, there was always the ALL CLEAR'!"

Many a true word is spoken in jest and that jester par-excellence, Robb Wilton, well understood the mood of the British people.

The war had been a long, disturbing and often frightening experience but, when peace came, and the initial rejoicing and euphoria had subsided, reverting to a normal way of life proved, for many, to be a great deal more difficult than anticipated. Six years is a very long time to live under almost constant fear and stress and, for some, the process of rehabilitation was a slow and painful one.

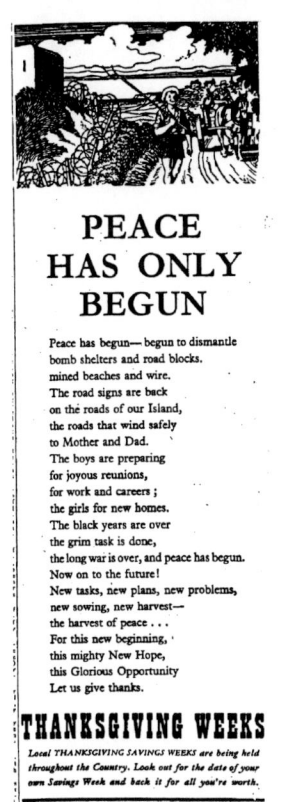

PEACE HAS ONLY BEGUN

Peace has begun— begun to dismantle
bomb shelters and road blocks,
mined beaches and wire.
The road signs are back
on the roads of our Island,
the roads that wind safely
to Mother and Dad.
The boys are preparing
for joyous reunions,
for work and careers ;
the girls for new homes.
The black years are over
the grim task is done,
the long war is over, and peace has begun.
Now on to the future !
New tasks, new plans, new problems,
new sowing, new harvest—
the harvest of peace . . .
For this new beginning,
this mighty New Hope,
this Glorious Opportunity
Let us give thanks.

THANKSGIVING WEEKS

Local THANKSGIVING SAVINGS WEEKS are being held throughout the Country. Look out for the date of your own Savings Week and back it for all you're worth.

Issued by the National Savings Committee

Yes, there was Thanksgiving; quite rightly so, and sadness too - much of it - but there were some, civilians and Service personnel alike, for whom the dangers and excitement of the war had acted as a kind of drug and, now, denied it they found the first weeks of peace dreary indeed.

A degree of anti-climax seemed to pervade the air, and even an important event such as that held at the factory on 18th October failed to inspire much enthusiasm. H.W. Harper, its Chief Executive and Works Manager, flanked by a representative from the Royal Air Force [1], Senior Works Staff and Union executives, spoke to several thousand of his employees as they stood outside the 'Finals' alongside the last Lancaster built at Yeadon: Mk.III: TX273; Anson Mk.XII: PH815 (which, subsequently, flew until 1966) and a York - identity unknown. **(Photo 80 front cover, 81 rear cover)**

In thanking the workers for their tremendous endeavour he remarked "..... our efforts represent one twenty-fifth of the total number of aircraft built in the British Isles in the course of war. In just four and a half years we have built, in addition to 700 Lancasters, 3,920 Ansons - 'Faithful Annies' as they have become affectionately known to the R.A.F. - plus spares for a thousand more ....." **(Photo 82 - centre pages)**

The event was intended to be a very high-key affair but, in fact, spontaneous rejoicing was conspicuous by its absence. Perhaps this was due to general war-weariness among the workers or to their concern about the future, but it is very evident from photographs taken on the day that many of them seemed less than inspired by the occasion. Roland Scatchard recalled "..... there was no bands playing, or anything special like that and, after we had heard the speeches, we simply walked back to the Canteen where we were given a cup of tea and a bun, and then we went back to work!"

The next day's edition of the Wharfedale and Airdale Observer reacted rather differently, giving over half a page to report the event, and to eulogise on the achievements of the factory: written under a banner headline which ran: "VEIL LIFTED ON HUSH-HUSH AIRCRAFT WORKS". The detail which followed has, very largely, already been covered in the narrative, but some comments referred to current and anticipated developments.

---

1   Group Captain B. D. Sellick DSO, DFC - see front cover.

Peace

"..... The change over from wartime to peacetime production has been gradual and for a time there has been overlapping. Already five giant York transport aircraft have left the factory for delivery to the R.A.F. for transport duties - chiefly the bringing home quickly of troops from overseas - work that has up to now been carried out by bombers. There is a big civilian demand for the machine which has a wing span of 102 feet, is 78 feet long and is capable of carrying 78 passengers.

Air Ministry contracts for Ansons alone will keep the factory busy for many months and inquiries are coming in from all parts of the world for civilian passenger and freight machines. The civilian version of the Anson trainer is a twin-engined nine seater airliner and has a range of 600 miles. At present experimental work is going on in connection with a quite new type of aircraft. It will be a 14 seater passenger liner of all metal construction with a range of 1,500 miles, and a cruising speed of 168 m.p.h.

It is hoped that the first machine will be completed by the New Year. A name for it has not been found (it was AVRO type 700: not developed) .... There are splendid opportunities at the factory for men with an engineering background, not necessarily in industry, but ex-R.A.F. personnel and ex-Servicemen who have had mechanical and technical experience in the Navy or Army, and already many R.A.F. trained mechanics are finding their way into the works for whom, of course, aircraft production has particular appeal.

Girls are wanted for upholstery work, electrical installation and similar light jobs. It is hoped to stabilise employment at the factory at around 6,000 people ....."

Thus, even though it would be necessary to reduce the workforce to anticipated peacetime requirements, there was NO intimation from A.V. Roe & Co. Ltd. - obviously, the source of this information - that it did not intend to keep the factory in operation. Within six months, however, confidence in its future would be shattered and the words of optimism which, during the Autumn of 1945, were so glibly issued, would sound very hollow indeed.

At the time of the change over to peacetime operations, however, such considerations were some way ahead. The workforce at Yeadon - those who hoped to stay on, that is - felt that the tough, but vital, job they had carried out so earnestly during the preceding four and a half years, had earned them a bright future; and, when a study is made of their production achievements, it has to be admitted that their case was not without justification.**(Photo 83 - centre pages)**

Of the 3,881 Ansons (a figure compiled up to the end of July, 1945) 2,368 were completed aircraft flown from Yeadon to various locations throughout the U.K.; the remaining 1,513 being packed, partially assembled, for shipment overseas.

In addition, the factory was responsible for the production of a substantial quantity of Anson 'spares' and, from February, 1943, until the end of July, 1945, 36,000 individual items - made up of 6,500,000 parts, valued at £4,500,000, were completed and despatched. This figure represented enough components for a further 900 Ansons, resulting in a total output on the type (to that date) of 4,800 aircraft: a truly remarkable achievement in just 50 months!

SUMMARY OF AIRCRAFT PRODUCTION AT YEADON

JUNE 1941 TO V-J DAY 1945

YEAR	TORNADO	ANSON	LANCASTER	LINCOLN	TOTAL
1941	5	96			101
	(four of which were completed but not flown)				
1942		1217	24		1241
1943		1459	103		1562
1944		917	354		1271
1945		192	207	2	401
Total	5	3881	688	2	4576
(to 15th August)					

In the case of the Lancaster, the factory was, similarly, responsible for the additional production of a huge quantity of spares; this work including the construction of a very substantial number of bomb-bay doors - the most vulnerable part of a bomber - and also bomb carriers, in a special department known, most appropriately, as "Basher Bates Madhouse": the 'Bates' being its foreman! **(Photo 84 - centre pages)**

The quantity of bomb-bay doors produced at the factory (they were constructed in pairs) was:

1942	507
1943	1789
1944	1865
1945	850 (to end of July)
Total	5011

The bomb-carriers, made of aluminium pressings and duralumin castings, were of an AVRO design and, being suitable for use in a variety of aircraft, were known as the 'Universal' type.

They were of two specifications: one of 2,000lb (907Kg) capacity: 'Heavies' and the other of 500lb (226.80Kg): 'Lights' and, approximately, 150 to 200 of the former and 500 to 600 of the latter were produced *each week* from 1941 up to the cessation of hostilities, resulting in a grand total of 7,331 'heavies' and 30,895 'lights'.

Before being sanctioned, each carrier was 'equipped' with a bomb - minus its explosive contents - which was filled with sand and then released from six or eight feet (2 or 3 metres), to check the correctness of its mechanism. On one such test, possibly as a result of repeated use, the plug at the end of the bomb dropped out to reveal a brass cover marked 'FUSED'. Not surprisingly, some panic quickly ensued among those recently employed!

The responsibilities of its staff to the aircraft built there did not stop at the factory gates, however, for AVRO ran a repair service, which employed squads of skilled personnel who visited R.A.F. Stations and crash sites to inspect and, where possible, repair any damaged aircraft. **(Photo 85 - centre pages)**

The Anson repair service operated out of Yeadon from 1941 and, by the end of the war, had dealt with 663 damaged aircraft of which 626 were repaired 'in situ'; some, many miles distant from the factory, and often in locations where access was difficult.

On completion of repairs all aircraft were required to be inspected by an appropriately qualified AVRO employee and, thereafter, by an Inspector of the AID who, if all was as it should be, would then issue the '1090' allowing the aircraft to be flown off. Eric Dean recalled one such event concerning an Anson which had come down in a field near Grassington, in Wharfedale:

"It was one of the earlier Marks of Anson with the one piece, wooden, wing and it had been force-landed in a field full of cows. Having arrived on the scene and decided that it was causing no immediate danger to anyone, the repair crew, no doubt enamoured with the loveliness of the surroundings, departed to enjoy the charms of a local hostelry. Some time later, in joyful mood, they returned to the Anson to find impaled thereto the horns of two of the more obviously inquisitive bovines which, on spying unfamiliar humans, panicked and began charging around dragging a now creaking Anson with them. As the repair crew tried to release the bellowing animals, the latter succeeded in impaling themselves even further and, when finally freed, the aircraft looked more like a colander than something intended to fly!....."

As mentioned earlier, it was the York which dominated the scene at the factory during its last months of existence (as an aircraft factory), albeit that the jigs for the type did not arrive from Ringway until August 1945.

Photo 86. Early example of the York.
Credit AVRO

The York was a high-wing monoplane, which incorporated the same wings, tail-planes, fins, rudders and engines as the Lancaster, but with a deeper, slab-sided fuselage which provided double the cubic capacity of its illustrious forebear. The York came on the scene at Ringway, on 4th July, 1942, with the first flight of prototype: LV626, then known as the AVRO type 685, built to fill a requirement for a large transport aircraft capable of flying long distances. All went well with this, and several subsequent, test flights but an additional, third, fin was added centrally to the third prototype: LV633 to give extra stability. Just before Christmas 1942, the Air Ministry issued Contract 2429/C4A for 200 of the aircraft, by then known as the York, to specification C1/42.

The emergence of the York facilitated the formation of R.A.F. Transport Command on 25th March, 1943, but, as the AVRO Group factories were then fully committed to existing contracts, and as the new aircraft was given no official priority, production of it proved a slow process. All but a handful of York's built before the end of the war served on V.I.P. duties: LV633, for instance, after modification became 'Ascalon' the personal aircraft of Prime Minister, Winston Churchill, and it is interesting to conjecture which of those early York's was that photographed with Flt.Lt. 'Bill' Reid, V.C., and members of his crew, when they visited Yeadon? One thing is certain, however, it was not built there. **(Photo 87 - centre pages)**

Ultimately, 257 Yorks were produced: 4 prototypes plus 208 for the R.A.F. and 45 for civil use (one other in Canada) of which half were built at Yeadon; two thirds of these going to the RAF, the remainder to civilian operators. One, MW295, named 'Ascalon II', went on to earn the distinction of being the last operational York in the R.A.F., staying in service until March, 1957.**(Photo 88 - centre pages)**

Eric Dean recalled his first flight in a York as being "..... like travelling in a very large open room .....". Another thought it distinctive in another way, "..... it was comparatively slow, docile and reliable and was notable, from the pilot's point of view, chiefly for the fact that the throttle, propeller, undercarriage and flap operating levers, were in the roof of the cabin to the right of his head ....."

Bernard Hepton was less complimentary when, after perusing a photograph of his former colleagues at Yeadon, he wrote, "..... I can see them all, the way they walked, the way they spoke, and that dreadful hybrid monster behind them .... the York, trying to make a Lancaster into something it wasn't ....." **(Photo 89 - centre pages)**

The 'monster' image might be a little contentious - although the author once had a young contemporary who thought the York resembled a frog with wings! - but not so the description: 'hybrid Lancaster' for, in essence, that is what the York was.

From its conception on the drawing board, to its first flight, occupied barely six months: an achievement made possible only through the clever utilisation of Lancaster components. Irrespective of some criticism, the York went on to play a vital rôle as, at the time, Britain possessed no other large, transport/passenger aircraft - extant or in the immediate process of development - as, for more than three years, production of aircraft within the country had, predominantly, been of types more necessary to its very survival!

The U.S.A. on the other hand, with greater resources and manpower, and some very clever perception of post-war aviation requirements, was not similarly constrained. Thus, in the immediate post-war years, was able to gain an ascendency over its British rivals through the ready availability of the Lockheed Constellation, which made its first civil trans-Atlantic flight, in the service of Pan American Airways, on 19th January, 1946, and, later, the Douglas DC6.

Late in 1945, however, the men and women employed on the shop floor of AVRO Yeadon were unaware of such developments, seeing in the York (then still on the secret list), which could carry up to 70 passengers, and the new 'civilianised' derivatives of the Anson [2], possibilities for their ongoing employment in an industry where the pay was good.

Not that they could, immediately, have chosen to do otherwise for, although the war was over, all National Service conscripts, be they Service personnel or civilians, were not allowed to return to pre-war employment at will. The massive upheaval of men and women made necessary by the war was not reversed overnight; many months were to elapse - in some cases up to two years - before all were free agents again.

As the weeks went by, gradually small numbers of workers were released but, initially, they were replaced by ex-servicemen or civilian conscripts transferred from war establishments which had ceased to exist. One such was Fred Ryner ..... "I was an engineer officer in the ATA at No.7FPP at Sherburn-in-Elmet, but when the ATA ceased to exist I went to work in the drawing office at the

---

[2] The Mk. C.XIX, Alternatively known as the AVRO Nineteen or, later, C.19. The series I. had a one piece wooden wing and tail-planes, whereas the series II. was fitted with metal wings and tail-plane. Both were powered by Armstrong Siddeley Cheetah XV engines, giving an all-up weight of 10,400lbs (4717Kg). 100 C.XIX's were ordered on Contract 5037/C.B.6(a) on 26th January, 1945, and a further 60 as C.19's (same contract number) on 7th August, 1945. Some Mk.XII's were converted to C.XIX's before completion.

AVRO works at Yeadon ..... which was where the new all metal wing and tail-plane of the Anson was designed. I lodged with the Shaw family in Rawdon - where it was so windy we had to tie the cabbages down! - and I remember walking to and from the factory, a couple of miles or so each way, through soon deep snow ..... the Shaw's were a fine family, especially Alec the son, who had been a proof reader and reporter with the Yorkshire Post. He had also been a member of the Yorkshire Aero Club at Yeadon and, later, during the war, he became a bomber pilot doing two tours of Operations in Europe and one in Burma ..... in due course he became a pilot with BOAC and the last I heard of him he was flying Yorks - what else!?

During my time at Yeadon, Stuart Davies [3] took over as Chief Designer, concurrent to his working on the AVRO Athena' [4] and he was quite a character. He had previously been assistant to Camm (Sidney Camm, Chief Designer at Hawker Aircraft) the designer of the Hurricane, and he modelled his very abrasive Cockney manner on that of Camm. He was nicknamed 'Cock' Davies because of his habit of saying , 'now see here, Cock .....', and I remember the time Don 'Pathfinder' Bennett [5] came to order some Yorks for British South American Airways, indicating his specific requirements to Davies: 'I want the navigator's position here, and the toilets there' etc., to which he received the blunt reply, 'you can't ..... well have 'em.' (The author suspects many ex-No.8 Group personnel would have loved to have been a fly on the wall at this juncture but, regrettably, no record exists of Bennett's reposte!)

Another well known for his colourful use of language was the chief draughtsman, a fellow called Smith - his assistant I recall was named Grinrod - and, not being a draughtsman myself, I kept a low profile in Smith's presence. One time, however, I reported to him a complaint of inaccessibility to one of the fuel tanks in the wing of a York, and he replied, 'You can get your ..... arm in there.' So I took him down onto the shop floor and got him to look up into the fuel tank bay and, as he did so, I asked him if he could get *his* ..... arm in there; to which he gave me a very funny look!

Later he acquired another assistant and he and I, and some others, came together with a view to starting a gliding club, but none of us knew how to start and, moreover, none of us had any money. (Sometime during 1945 No.23 Elementary Gliding School (No.23EGS) became involved with the A.T.C. at Yeadon, but its length of residence and whether or not this was a detachment from the units known presence at Rufforth, has not been established). **(Photo 90 - centre pages)**

I remember an amusing episode concerning an Anson to be supplied to the Abyssinian Royal Family. Its specification stated: 'This will be a Mark XIX with a toilet. It will be a seven-seater.' Somebody in the drawing office then produced a sketch of an Anson with seven bearded gentlemen seated on a toilet! In fact, although an Anson could be fitted with a loo (single-seater!), nobody could find a way to fit in a door, so the passengers had to be satisfied with a curtain ....."

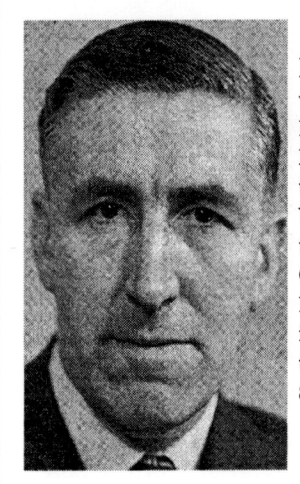

Photo 89a. Stuart Davies was responsible for spearheading the conversion of the Manchester into the Lancaster, and chief designer at Yeadon from 1944-1946. After the untimely death of Roy Chadwick in 1947 he became his successor. Awarded CBE in 1968. President of Aeronautical Soc. 1971-72. Died aged 88 during February 1995.

This very special Anson was, almost certainly, type Nineteen: VL358, delivered to the Imperial Ethiopian Air Force as No.120, for the express use of Emperor Haile Selasse, who had spent the war years in Britain. Two years later the aircraft returned, to be re-registered as G-AGUH, and continued a very varied career which culminated with Bristol Siddeley Motors at Filton, where it

---

3   S.D. Davies, A.F.R.Ae.S., B.Sc., was 38 years of age in December, 1945, when he succeeded Roy Chadwick, who had become AVRO's Technical Director.

4   Originally designated AVRO Type 701, the Athena was a low-wing monoplane of 40ft span.

5   Air Vice-marshal D.C.T. Bennett, C.B., C.B.E., D.S.O., A.O.C. of No.8 (Pathfinder) Group, Bomber Command, became the Liberal Member of Parliament for Middlesbrough West, and was also appointed to head British South American Airways (B.S.A.A.)

ended its days - still very much centre stage - on the Guy Fawkes bonfire in 1960!

On 19th October, 1945, Douglas Broom, a R.A.F. fitter, recorded in his diary: "..... I left Gilze (Gilze Rijen) for Brussels - Melsbroeck aerodrome. My last recollections of Gilze (on 5th October) was of an Anson which veered off the runway and wrapped itself around a lorry. The 'Annie' suffered the loss of both u/c legs and one engine ripped off. The crew clambered out shaken but unhurt and my last job was to clear up the mess [6] ....."

The Anson was Mk.XII: NL251 built at Yeadon, from where it was ferried to join the 2nd Tactical Air Force (2/TAF) in November, 1944, for forward light ambulance duties; eventually being absorbed onto the strength of the British Air Forces of Occupation (BAFO), with which it was serving at the time of its demise.

Thus the finale of just two Ansons, drawn at random from the histories of the thousands built at Yeadon, demonstrates the widely differing type, and length, of service which could be their lot. One was involved in a long and quite illustrious career before ending its days, literally, in the glare of a public display; the other, fulfilling a very basic function, operated barely a year before being despatched for scrap; unsung except by a single airman. Alexander Pope was indeed correct when he wrote: "Heaven from all creatures hides the book of fate."

In November, AVRO Nineteen: G-AGNI (converted from Anson Mk. XII: MG159), was loaned by MAP/Associated Joint Committee from the Anson's Yeadon base to Railway Air Services (RAS) which, in keeping with several other civil operators, was gradually getting back to running scheduled air services, for suitability trials. During the trials G-AGNI flew 60 hours for the West Coast Air Services division of R.A.S. on its London (Croydon) - Liverpool - Belfast (Sydenham) route. **(Photo 91 - centre pages)**

Although the 'Nineteen' was not considered ideal for commercial airline use it, nevertheless, proved superior in several ways to the DH89 Dragon Rapide then in service and, on completion of the trials, R.A.S. placed an order for 14 Nineteens, all of which were subsequently built or converted to type at Yeadon. Four of the aircraft: G-AGUD (converted from VL360), G-AGUE (converted from VL361), G-AGUX and G-AGVA were delivered almost immediately, with the remaining ten following during the Spring and Summer of 1946, for operations on the London - Belfast; London - Dublin and, later, the London - Glasgow (Renfrew) routes. **(Photo 92&93&94 - centre pages)**

Meanwhile, on 1st January, 1946, the prohibition on private flying, which had existed since the outbreak of war, was lifted and the Yorkshire Aeroplane Club was re-formed, as a joint proprietary club, wholly owned by Ronald H. Braime and Arnold G. Wilson. The airfield at Yeadon was, however, still under requisition by the Ministry of Aircraft Production and, as it appeared likely to remain so for the foreseeable future, it was decided to recommence activities at Sherburn-in-Elmet (which was no longer under similar restrictions), where, in the event, the Club would remain until 22nd February, 1958.

Given the order for the Mark XIX's and the substantial contract for Yorks; with hopes of further contracts to supplement the number of Lincolns under construction; and, moreover, having heard and read the optimistic statements issued by management that prospects were indeed bright, understandably, many workers at Yeadon believed that the factory was where their future lay.

Thus it came as a veritable bombshell when, on Thursday, 18th April, S.G. Joy, Secretary of the Company, announced that aircraft production would cease there by the end of the year! Never has a man been gifted with a more inappropriate name to be the bearer of such tidings; concluding his dramatic statement by indicating that the wind down would be gradual, and that it was not known what plans the Government had in mind for the factory thereafter.

Addressing a meeting of 5,000 stunned and angry workers, packed into the canteen, the Chairman of the Works Committee, Sidney Elias, outlined what had been done to try to keep the factory open:

"We have made representations to the Government and other agencies, including Aireborough Urban District Council but nothing specific has materialised ....." He then asked the workers to note that local communities were directly involved in the future of the factory, and that it was thought, if it closed, there would be little difficulty in placing the women and girls in other jobs, although "..... parity

---

[6] Quoted in his article in an edition of Fly Past magazine.

with AVRO rates of pay could not be guaranteed ....." He went on "..... scores of families living in the MAP bungalows would wish to remain and find other work in the neighbourhood where they had come to make their home and many friends. Of particular concern are the ex-R.A.F. men who had come to work at the factory on demob and brought families with them from other parts of the country. What would happen to them if the factory was to close?....."

A statement by the Joint Shop Stewards Committee suggested that the factory could be used for other purposes, such as the production of agricultural equipment or other engineering products, and that the Board of Trade was endeavouring to find new tenants for a proposed trading estate to be established within the factory complex. One official told the workers that the factory would not be allowed to become derelict, as the site was too valuable.

The Wharfedale and Airedale Observer greeted the news as "..... a great disappointment of hopes bringing about a sense of frustration and loss. It would be a scandal (stated the leader writer) if the sheds, tools and other equipment should be allowed to become derelict. Yeadon, if it cannot go on producing aircraft, should be allowed to go onto producing products of value to the community at large. Here is a case of 'We have got the tools; find a job for them to do!' It is the threat of closing down factories such as that at Yeadon which causes the dread spectre of unemployment to appear again .... The establishment of AVRO has brought considerable prosperity to Aireborough and surrounding areas and it is feared that closure would mean a corresponding decline. Every effort must be made to keep the factory working as a great production centre ....."

Lord Calverley who, with the impending closure of the factory, had taken an interest in its future, quoted a letter he had received from the Minister of Supply and Aircraft Production which pointed out that the aircraft industry was re-concentrating its production, and A.V. Roe did not have sufficient orders to enable it to keep in production at Yeadon as well as at its Manchester based factories.

Thus the die was well and truly cast, but when A.D. Jenkins, the Regional Director of the West Riding Group of the Engineering and Allied Employers stated that many engineering firms in the West Riding were desperately short of labour of the sort available at Yeadon - and that the textile industry could easily absorb the rest - his comments were greeted with derision by the AVRO Joint Shop Stewards Committee, "..... this is not the case and Mr. Jenkins, along with other employers, is hoping to use the closure of the Yeadon factory to return to pre-1939 conditions, where labour outnumbered jobs ....."

The Committee went on to reiterate its belief that the factory could, and should, be turned over to the production of agricultural machinery, plus other commodities such as bus bodies, housing components and many other engineering products in short supply. The Committee even suggested that the factory, with all its modern, up-to-date equipment and facilities, should not only be kept open but form the nucleus of a new satellite town ..... "better a thriving production concern," the statement continued, "..... than a derelict storehouse ultimately to become a playground of rats and vermin ....."

There were, of course, others who had suggestions for the future of the factory. One such was Alderman Alan Bretherick of Bramhope, who proposed that it could easily be adapted into a permanent exhibition ground, similar to the one at Leipzig which, before the war, had attracted potential buyers from all parts of the world. "The AVRO buildings are large enough to display almost every type of machinery, and offer plenty of room for development. Yeadon is also well situated being near the main railway, adjacent aerodrome and main arterial roads, and nearby Ilkley and Harrogate could provide the class of hotel accommodation desired by foreign visitors."

With the exception of interest shown by various trade unions, his proposals received scant support but, when subsequent developments at Harrogate and Birmingham are considered, it is clear that Alderman Bretherick was a man of vision - albeit twenty or thirty years ahead of his time - and it could well be the case that, in ignoring his suggestions, the local community missed a considerable opportunity!?

A letter to a local newspaper by a group of textile workers reminded their colleagues who had left, or had been directed, to work in the modern munitions factories, of the lower wages and "..... slum conditions pertaining in the mills ....." but, nevertheless, by the end of May, AVRO workers were requesting permission to leave at the rate of more than 100 per week. Others had no say in the matter, as Eric Dean recalled, "..... on 6th May, 1946, I received three months notice and, although I had been expecting it, things happened so quickly it still came as a shock ....."

An even greater surprise came to Harry Rowan, as was recalled by Fred Ryner, "Harry was a little, dark-haired, chap from Leeds, who worked as an Inspector on Lincoln assembly. He and his wife were very much attached to each other; they hadn't been married very long, so they were devastated when he received his call-up papers. The last time I saw him he was feverishly rushing about trying to find someone who could suggest a means of escape ....."

Harry Rowan, as did Albert Marland and numerous others, found himself trapped by a piece of legislation through which employees who volunteered for work in munitions could, subsequently, be required to serve in the Armed Services if their employment in the war factories was terminated before their obligations under the National Service Act had lapsed.

As is sometimes the case, under this Order, the innocent were treated rather worse than the guilty, for a substantial number who, earlier, had *genuinely* volunteered to work in munitions rather than simply await their call-up elsewhere were, thereafter, compelled to serve in the uniformed Services; whereas many of those who, quite deliberately, had connived in using the war factories as a means of avoiding something, possibly, much worse also succeeded in avoiding the second 'call-up'!

Donald Winn [7] remembered "..... there was some 'super specialists' employed at the factory who were paid over the odds for doing vital and complicated work. I never minded them, for I could appreciate the need of them, but I couldn't stand the others who had no skills at all, and were only there because they had influence in high places to keep them out of the Forces, where they might have got shot at. They were cowards, but they didn't fool us; we knew who they were, and we despised them ....."

On 10th May, under the Command of Squadron Leader P.A. Womersley, D.F.C. and Bar, one of the last Auxiliary Officers to have joined it before the outbreak of war, with the Rt. Hon. The Earl of Harewood, K.G., G.C.V.O., D.S.O., T.D., [8] as its Honorary Air Commodore, No.609 (West Riding) Squadron reformed, at Church Fenton, as a Night Fighter unit in the Auxiliary Air Force; being equipped with Mosquito NF 30's; but, on 31st July, after an absence of seven years, the Squadron returned to its birthplace at Yeadon. Concurrently, Leeds University Air Squadron departed to Church Fenton.

Meanwhile, between April and July, the remaining ten AVRO Nineteen's on order for RAS were completed, and left the factory to commence operations on its summer schedules. The aircraft were finished silver overall, with red and green markings and bearing the distinctive RAS insignia on their fins; a colour scheme which, no doubt, made a nice change for the painters involved who, for more than five years, had been required to apply dull, wartime, camouflage. The ten aircraft were: G-AHIB, 'IC, 'ID, 'IE, 'IF, 'IG, 'IH, 'II, ''IJ, 'IK.

The 'Nineteen' made possible the first direct, non-stop, London-Glasgow (Renfrew) service, operated on behalf of RAS by Scottish Airways, cutting the time flown by the DH Dragon Rapide - required to make a refuelling stop at Liverpool - from 3 hours 40 minutes to 2 hours 45 minutes. Unfortunately, as the aircraft were not allocated to one route, the author has been unable to positively identify which of the Nineteens was that involved in this historic flight; but it was certainly one of the following: G-AGNI, G-AGUD, G-AGUE, G-AGUX or G-AGVA. Similarly, one or other of these aircraft flew the first non-stop London - Belfast (Sydenham) and London - Dublin services, operated by West Coast Air Services (RAS), which were inaugurated on 3rd December 1945.

Concurrently at Yeadon, "..... once the ball started rolling the run down of the factory was quite dramatic, and by the end of the summer, people were leaving at the rate of 500 a week .....", recalled Alf Harris.

There was a simultaneous diminution in sports and social activities, although AVRO maintained its 1st XI cricket team in the Airedale and Wharfedale Senior League, and its 2nd XI in the Wharfedale Cricket League, until the close of the 1946 season.

The last game played by the First XI in the Airedale and Wharfedale Senior Cricket League, was brought to a disappointing end (not unlike the factory) on 13th September, 1946, when 'rain stopped play':see next page.

---

[7] On 31st December, 1989, Donald Winn died aged 94: the last surviving member of the original No.24 Squadron and, incidentally, quite a character!

[8] In May, 1947, the Earl died and was replaced as Honorary Air Commodore, most fittingly, by Air Vice-Marshal G.H. Ambler, C.B., C.B.E., A.F.C., D.L., LL.D.

Alf Harris added, "..... during the last summer - I can't remember exactly whether it was 1945 or 1946 - there was a Sports Day at Green lane, and it was revelation to see all those workers who were, supposedly, unfit for military service leaping about all over the place like two year olds. Some of them even won prizes! ....."

From AW Observer 20.9.46 details of last game played by the AVRO (Yeadon) 1st XI 13.9.46 Airedale and Wharfedale Senior Cricket League.

BURLEY v AVRO, 13th September 1946.

AVRO - H. Bolton not out 29; H. Farmer not out 4; Extras 2; Total (for no wkts.) 35. Rain stopped play. Bowling - L. Lambert 3-0-6-0; W. Harrison 5-1-11-0; A. Maston 4-1-14-0; H. Driver 2-0-2-0.

FINAL LEAGUE POSITIONS: 1946 SEASON

AVRO 1st XI   AVRO Second XI

FINAL LEAGUE TABLES

AVRO Ist XI

	P	W	D	L	P
Ilkely	24	13	9	2	48
Guiseley	24	11	10	3	43
Hall Park	24	7	11	6	32
Burley	24	5	16	3	31
Skipton	24	7	10	7	31
North Leeds	24	4	18	2	30
Earby	24	5	13	6	28
Avro	24	5	11	8	26
Menston	24	5	11	8	26
Rawdon	24	5	11	8	26
Addingham	24	4	12	8	24
Horsforth	24	4	11	9	23
Otley	24	3	13	8	22

AVRO Second XI

	P	W	L	D	Pts.
Otley West	20	12	1	7	43
Butterfields	20	9	1	10	37
*Rawdon Bapt.	20	10	4	6	37
Calverley	20	9	2	9	36
*Esholt A	20	8	4	8	33
*D.P. & E	20	7	4	9	31
Avro	20	7	5	8	29
Otley Mills	20	6	3	11	29
Guiseley	20	6	6	8	26
Rawdon	20	6	6	8	26
*Esholt B	20	5	7	8	24
Hall Park	20	5	7	8	23
Horsforth	20	5	5	8	23
Arrow Sp	20	5	7	8	20
Lecra Sports	20	4	8	8	20
Turner T.S.	20	4	10	6	18
Booth Bros.	20	2	13	5	11
Ross Mills	20	0	12	8	8

* Teams marked thus receive two points each for a tie.

Production came to an end at the factory with the completion of 'civil' York: LV-XIX (c/n 1366), on order for Flota Aerea Mercante Argentina (FAMA), for which an application for a 'C of A' was made on 24th October; officially the last Anson being type XIX:G-AHYO (c/n 1366) which was flown to Croydon to join Westminster Airways on 16th August (it crashed N. Rhodesia 31st October) [9]. Within a few weeks the remaining incomplete aircraft, and partially completed wings, fuselages and tail units, along with engines, myriad fittings and a host of other paraphernalia associated with the production of aircraft had been transferred to AVRO factories in the Manchester area. Test flying of completed aircraft continued for a little while thereafter, as did their onward despatch. **(Photo 95 - centre pages)**

On 6th September, the Wharfedale and Airedale Observer announced: "YEADON AIRCRAFT WORKS PRODUCTION CEASES" and went on "..... the W. & A. reporter who spoke yesterday to a representative of the Works was told that all production had now ceased. A year ago the factory was a busy hive of Industry with 10,000 people employed. Today it has the sad desolation of a mausoleum. It is possible to walk the corridors and shops in ghostly quietude, the few people about emphasising the solitude and emptiness of the huge buildings."

'I feel like one
Who treads alone
Some banquet hall deserted,
Whose lights are fled,
Whose garlands dead,
And all but he departed!'

These words of Thomas Moore, penned at least a hundred years earlier, might well have been written for the occasion.

---

9   This is somewhat confusing as others with lower constructors numbers were not flown away until much later: G-AHKX, for instance, not doing so until November! Others partially constructed, were completed elsewhere.

Peace

The rapid metamorphosis was dramatic and remarkable, but no more so than the comparative ease with which its ten thousand workforce was, speedily, re-employed. "..... Nearly all workers have been found other jobs and the only real difficulties have been with placing the unskilled, although (locally) not more than 40 people are still signing-

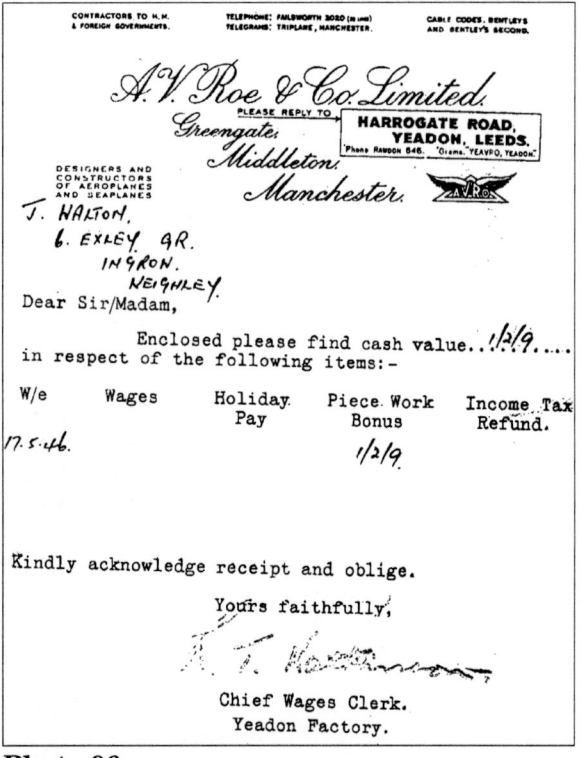

Photo 96.

The last 'Piece-work' Bonus issued to Joe Walton (£1.2.9 or £1.14p), 17th May 1946.

on at the Employment Exchange ....." commented a local newspaper.

It was an extraordinary end to an equally extraordinary era. From first days until its closure: a period encompassing six grim years, more than 17,000 men and women, from all walks of life had served in the factory to make a vital contribution to Britain's war effort. Their presence, in a variety of ways, changed the social and economic life of a part of the West Riding of Yorkshire and it, in turn, made an indelible impression on a substantial number of them. Their success was not achieved, however, without some dark days, and many obstacles which required patience and determination to overcome; nor was the odd 'rotten apple' absent from their ranks for, as Nigel Balchin wrote at the time," [10] ..... those who did the job were not gods or supermen. The sun did not stand still to give them a longer working day, nor did walls fall flat or erect themselves at the sound of a trumpet ..... To be told that what has occurred was a miracle leaves us not flattered but slightly indignant, like the old Scots engineer (who replied to such a suggestion on another occasion), 'Yon's no miracle. Yon's a proper piece of engineering.' The story of aircraft production in this country during the last few years is a story of Britain at its best and the British genius at its highest and most characteristic ....."

The workforce at Yeadon more than vindicated the siting of the factory there and the fact that, post-war, they were denied the opportunity to continue building aeroplanes, left many with a feeling of let-down. Throughout the war they had always been kept fully aware of their part in the general scheme of things but, as the conflict came to an end, the meretricious way in which information, as to their future, was divulged was less than adequate recompense for their labour.

Bernard Hepton commented, "..... I still think it a waste that such a place, geared solely to aircraft production, with the airfield attached, should become some sort of warehouse ..... Whenever I am back in West Yorkshire I take a run by there as a sort of evocation of ones first work experience; and a most enjoyable one it was. Had I not become immersed in the Theatre the aircraft industry would have been my career, because I was glad to be among aeroplanes - they must be beautiful to get up there, mustn't they? - and I am proud to have been a small cog in that amazing machine, and to have been connected with that great aircraft, the Lancaster ....."

The Coat of Arms of Yeadon contains a latin motto: Nosce Teipsum - 'Love and Loyalty', and there is evidence to suggest that such emotions affected many workers when their time came to leave the factory. Not unnaturally, a majority wished to resume a normal, peace-time, existence with their families; a substantial number of whom were domiciled outside the immediate area but, nevertheless, it was difficult to leave friends and workmates with whom one had spent, what would be for many, the most dramatic and exciting years of their lives. Mixed emotions certainly were conspicuous but, in

10 Quoted in 'The Aircraft Builders', HMSO 1947

the main, the pull of home and family was strongest.

> "... Goodbye dear Dale! You have been kind,
> Now I must go - I'll not complain;
> But Oh! How glad I'll be to find
> My feet on the road back home again."

These simple words of 'The Hawk', a well-known local poet of the period, most adequately, though inadvertently, summed up the situation.

On the expiry of his 'notice', Eric Dean was sent to work, firstly, with Arrow Aircraft, whose buildings adjoined the airfield at its south-west extremity, and thence to Dawson, Payne and Elliott: printing machinery manufacturers, in nearby Otley. From there, after a short while, he was despatched to Harrogate to join the Weights and Measures department of the Board of Trade .....

"Not long afterwards I was sent to visit a firm who were operating out of the old machine-shop at the northern end of the factory, refurbishing ex-Army lorries; then much in demand for civilian use. Naturally, I took a look around the old place, which still remained one entity from end to end, but when I came to what had been the Spray Shop (Dope House) there were piled thousands upon thousands of gas masks. Some were of the type which fitted completely over a baby and, all in all, there were so many that those at the bottom had been squashed completely flat. Of course, I also had to have a look at my old office which was a small, wooden, cabin divided in two to accommodate both A.I.D. and AVRO staff where, from the early days, we had gathered together some marvellous tools: micrometers, rules, levels, straight-edges, precision electrical instruments and so on; a veritable Aladdin's Cave of specialist, expensive equipment, which we longed to own but knew we would never be able to afford. We had kept them in a hefty box, secured by two, large locks. I found my desk and chair still there, as were some rather old Rolls-Royce engine drawings - not on the secret list - covered with dark grey dust, and the tool box still stood in its place; but the locks had gone and so had the contents!"

On 27th November, organised by the Ministry of Supply, a huge 'sale' took place at the factory to dispose of all surplus machine tools, automatic grinders, millers, drillers, presses, tool-room lathes, masses of general production equipment and a variety of war surplus items brought in from other factories - Rolls-Royce, Barnoldswick, being one.

It was announced beforehand that the equipment had been checked by AVRO engineers who confirmed it as being 'redundant to the firms requirements'. Prices were pre-set; these varying from £3-£4 for bench shears, via capstan lathes at £150-£250 up to milling machines at £600; giving an overall stock value of £500,000.

"Buyers staking first claim will get the machines," an announcement stated, and "..... rival competitors are expected to employ runners ....."!

The first potential buyer was the Manager of a Midlands engineering firm who arrived at 3.30a.m., and the hundreds of lots put together from a huge mass of war-surplus material made the sale a considerable attraction.

One bidder coveted several two-wheeled battery trolleys on offer and, much to his surprise, was able to purchase them at a very competitive price; no other potential buyer having noticed that the tyres on the trolleys were the same size as those used on several small cars, then emerging from years of wartime storage; and, with rubber being virtually like gold, he could not fail to make a great deal of money as a result of his perceptiveness. Little wonder he went away smiling.

Some lots received no bids, thus they were either 'left over' or sold at a knock-down price to anyone who cared to take them away. One individual found himself the owner of a pile of rather damp and dirty sheets which, he thought, might prove useful as cleaning material in his garage business. When he removed the grubby top sheet, however, there beneath he discovered forty plus, pre-war quality, bed sheets which, after minimal laundering, would be very much sought after. As to the origins of the sheets he would remain as mystified as those who looked upon the huge piles of plumbers washers, tied up in massive bundles, totalling in excess of 30,000 individual pieces of metal. AVRO Yeadon reduced to selling plumbers washers? How the mighty had fallen!

On 31st January, 1947, Randall Paine, who had arrived in the Autumn of 1940 as one of its first employees, finally left the factory, along with a handful of others who had been detailed to 'clean up and clear out'. Thus the last vestige of any connection with A.V. Roe & Co. Ltd., was severed.

Apart from the very limited commercial use of its northern extremity - perversely the first and, here again, the only area to be occupied - the vast factory echoed to the sighing of the wind, the creaking of its doors and the whisperings of its thousands of ghosts. There were no speeches; no fanfares; no

Peace

closing ceremony and, to this day, no tangible memorial exists to stand witness to its considerable achievements.

Shakespeare was both apt and prophetic when he wrote:

"When beggars die, there are no comets seen ....."

Photo 96a. Postwar advertising began in a subtle way almost as soon as the war was over. This ad appeared in the Wharfedale and Airedale Observer on 24th August 1945. copyright Dunlop.

Legacy

On 1st February, six months after the new Labour Government 'nationalised' the U.K. civil airlines into State ownership, British European Airways Corporation (B.E.A.C.) acquired the routes and many of the aircraft operated, previously, by a number of 'Independents'. Included among its acquisitions were 13 of the 14, 'Nineteen's' built at Yeadon for RAS; one of the originals: G-AGUE having, meantime, crashed at Liverpool (Speke) on 12th August 1946. On 11th June 1948 G-AGNI would ditch into the sea off Bradda Head, Isle of Man.

On 28th June 1948, the RAF, in conjunction with the U.S. Air Force and, later, a number of civil operators, began delivery of food and other essential commodities to the citizens of West Berlin: beleaguered by the Russians in an attempt to drive the Western Allies out of the city.

Included among the aircraft involved in the operation, which became known as the Berlin Airlift, were Yorks of No.47 Group, plus others owned by civil users and, from 1st July 1948 until August 1949 the type made 29,000 flights into Gatow carrying 230,000 tons (233.690 tonnes) of supplies.

The following Yeadon built examples are known to have taken part in the 'Airlift' and, where possible, their special tail numbers have been included: MW232[1] of No.99 Squadron '13'; MW267: KY-N of No.242 Squadron - '16': MW311: TB-C of No.59 Squadron; MW260: TB-K of No.59 Squadron - '19'; MW290: YY-Q of 241 OCU - '39' and MW198: OY-CW of No.511 Squadron.

Additionally, Skyways operated G-AHLV and G-AHFI which were built, originally, as 30 seat passenger aircraft to cover a twice weekly service to the Persian Gulf for the Anglo-Iranian Oil Company. These two Yorks were delivered from Yeadon in May and June, 1946, but G-AHFI crashed on 15th March, 1949, when involved in ferrying supplies to Berlin.

Elsewhere, aircraft built at the factory similarly continued on in service, as is confirmed by Wing Commander Alan B. Walker, R.A.F. (Ret'd):

"During the years 1948 to 1953 I flew 50 different maritime Lancasters ..... and I have marked on the separate list the 28 built at Yeadon ..... I did my first solo on type on RE211, when I was a Pilot Officer on No.13 Course at No.236 O.C.U. Kinloss on 14th October, 1948. I subsequently flew this aircraft on various occasions at S.M.R. (School of Maritime Reconnaissance) St. Mawgan. For example, on 1st May, 1953, I flew RE211 on a 'Casex' (anti-submarine exercise) off Portland with H.M.S. Hedingham Castle ..... The last time I flew RE211 was on 27th August, 1953, on OFE12 (Operational Flight Exercise) with a student crew for 6 hours and 15 minutes. At Kinloss RE211 was coded K7-M and at SMR it became H-B..... I first flew ASR3: RE159 (RL-L) of 37 Squadron on 17th March, 1949, at Luqa (see photo) and it was then camouflaged ..... it subsequently reappeared as an MR3 at SMR, St. Mawgan, where I last flew it on 7th July, 1953 ..... I also flew TX273 (the last Lancaster built at Yeadon) of which I took a snap when it was serving as 'U' Uncle of 38 Squadron at Luqa ..... Though I was not personally involved, it was one of the SMR Lancasters which took a very small part in the film 'The Cruel Sea' which was being filmed off Portland ..... The Lancaster had to play the part of a German FW200 Kondor, to which it bore no resem-

---

[1] MW232, built at Yeadon during January, 1946, currently resides with the Duxford Aviation Society (DAS) as G-ANTK, and is one of just two Yorks still extant: the other: G-AGNV, also a Yeadon built example, is on display at Cosford Aerospace Museum. MW232 began its service at Abingdon with No.242 Squadron in August, 1946, being transferred to No.511 Squadron at Lyneham in May, 1947, and thereafter, served with this Squadron throughout the Berlin Airlift. Flight refuelling operations followed when in the employ of Fairey Aviation but, on its cessation of operational service, MW232 was stored at No.12 MU, RAF Kirkbride. Sold to Dan-Air in July, 1954, the aircraft became G-ANTK and, thereafter, was used exclusively in freight operations which included flights to Australia, before being 'retired' to Lasham in May, 1964, where the York became a bunkhouse for the local Air Scouts! G-ANTK was, eventually, rescued by the Dan-Air Preservation Group which began its restoration but, unfortunately, this was found to be impracticable. On 23rd May, 1986, it was dismantled and removed by road to Duxford. Where it is hoped a rebuilding programme will be completed by 1998.

blance, so it had to fly around as a sinister dot on the horizon! In all I flew 1688 hours on Lancasters, of which 1546 hours were as captain."

Alan Boyd Walker

No.236 OCU Kinloss Sept. 1944 - Jan. 1949. 37 Sqn. Luqa Mar. 1949 - Jul. 1951. SOMR St. Mawgan Oct. 1951 - Dec. 1953.

AVRO 'LANCASTER' AIRCRAFT FLOWN 1948-53

ASR Mk.3 and MR (Formerly GR) 3.

SERIAL NUMBERS

PB 529	RF 322
PB 968	RF 325 Last 'Lancaster' flown 21.12.53
RE 159*	SW 284
RE 164*	SW 285
RE 165*	SW 286
RE 167*	SW 287
RE 173*	SW 325*
RE 181*	SW 327*
RE 185*	SW 334*
RE 187*	SW 336*
RE 200*	SW 338*
RE 205*	SW 344*
RE 211* 1st Solo on type 14.10.48 2360CU	
	SW 366*
RE 217*	SW 372*
RE 222*	SW 374*
RF 269	TX 265*
RF 271	TX 267*
RF 272	TX 268*
RF 287	TX 270*
RF 289	TX 271*
RF 291	TX 273*
RF 295	
RF 300	LINCOLN B2 Aldergrove
RF 303	RE300 25 July 1951
RF 306	SHACKLETON MR2 (Phase 3)
RF 308	WL 787 MOTU St. Mawgan
RF 318	WR 964 Aug - Sept 1968
RF 319	WR 966
RF 320	WL 739
	WG 533

* Built at Yeadon

After serving with a number of operational squadron's during the war Lancaster III's: LM639 and LM681 were involved with Flight Refuelling Limited, as G-AHJV and G-AHJU; the latter flying 438 sorties during the Berlin Airlift. ME540 was used by Boulton Paul and the Royal Aircraft Establishment (RAE) in gust-alleviation research; RE131 was fitted with a scaled-down version of the massive Bristol Brabazon's control system and RE137 was flown by Armstrong-Whitworth in research on its Python engine. Ultimately the aircraft was involved in research with the National Gas Turbine Establishment.

SW342 gave useful service to Flight Refuelling Ltd., prior to involvement with Armstrong-Siddeley on the development of its 'Mamba' turbo-prop and 'Adder' engines. Thus the influence of the factory went on into the jet age!

Additionally, eleven Yeadon built Lancaster MR.3's were operating with No.1 School of Maritime Reconnaissance (SMR) - the last unit to use the type - at St. Mawgan almost up to the day, 15th October, 1956, when the Lancaster was phased out of service. They were: (unit codes included where known): ME525/H-T, RE115/H-P, RE186/H-C, RE221/H-K, SW324/H-A, SW365/H-W, SW366/H-Z, SW367, SW370, and SW376; these being 'Struck off Charge' on 22nd May 1957. Earlier, on 18th October 1956, the same fate had awaited TX268.

Another of SMR's ex-Yeadon Lancaster's: MR.3 TX265 became the last of the type built at the factory to be lost while serving with the RAF when, on 22nd December 1953, it crashed on landing at St. Eval. MR.3: TX273, the last Lancaster to come from the production lines at Yeadon, was 'sold for scrap', ex-No.38 Squadron, on 6th September 1956.

Some thirty years later, David McNeill, who served with R.A.F. Coastal Command during the time the Lancaster was operational, wrote the following tribute:

"..... I have always felt sorry for anyone whose first flight was in a metal tube bound for the Costa Brava. Apart from the privilege (and that may sound pompous, but its true) of being occasionally and unofficially part of the crew of a flying legend, this was a real aircraft, built, flown and maintained by real people. It was no computer-controlled mystery of high technology wrapped and sealed in bland streamlining. It could be understood by ordinary human beings, like a huge old-fashioned car, and the frailty of the straining components which kept it from plunging headlong into the sea could be seen only too clearly. It was oil-stained and patched. The paintwork scuffed by clambering mechanics and the patterned surface of the wing spar was scratched and shiny. The paint was worn from the controls and the stuffing was coming out of the seats.

Legacy

There were pipes, wires and switches and huge scorch marks fanning out over the wings from the exhaust ports. It was a noble, beautiful, majestic, tatty old wreck and we shall never see anything like the AVRO Lancaster again ....."[2]

An evocation certain to turn many a dry eye damp, but it is only fair to say that such sentiments could, equally, be applied to the Handley Page Halifax which, similarly, soldiered on with Coastal Command into the 1950's.

* * *

During 1956, any M.A.P. bungalows still remaining intact, were used to house refugees from Egypt - here because of the Suez crisis - and what the hapless souls thought about them can readily be imagined!

In October 1961 it was announced that "..... the last 74 M.A.P. bungalows at Westfield, Yeadon, are to be demolished, being unfit for human habitation ....." There are those who would assert that such had been the case from the moment they were built! Thus the buildings disappeared; to exist only in the memory: unloved and unmourned.

At the end of 1963 seven Yeadon built Ansons, all C.19 series 2's, remained on the civil register: G-AGPF, originally converted from PH828, was operating with Skyways; G-AGWA with Meridian Airways Limited; G-AGWE with Derby Airways; G-AHIC, originally converted from Mk.XIX: TX241, was on strength at the College of Aeronautics at Cranfield and G-AHKX, the series 2 prototype, operated with Meridian Airmaps.

Other Ansons built at Yeadon remained in service with the R.A.F., not to mention innumerable others in military and civil use overseas. Mk.XIX: TX180 was used in the film 'Angels One Five', and Mk.XIX: TX218 appeared, briefly, in 'The Purple Plain'. G-AHKX subsequently changed ownership; ultimately operating with Kemps Aerial Surveys until 10th April, 1973 - 27 years of service! -when it was purchased for the Strathallen Collection. On 14th July, 1981, it was sold to British Aerospace, Woodford, for refurbishment, it is hoped, to flying status.

During May 1964: G-ANTK, the last York surviving on the civil register, was retired by Dan-Air to Lasham. Not a bad effort for an aircraft built, at Yeadon, eighteen years previously, as one of a type evolved from the Lancaster during a time of crisis, as a post-war stop gap!

On 28th June 1966, above Bovingdon, Hertfordshire, six Anson C.19's including: TX230, VL307, VL349, which were built at Yeadon, performed a farewell flypast to the type as it was phased out of service with the Royal Air Force. A little later, VL349, one of the last Ansons to leave the factory before it ceased production, made the flight officially acknowledged as being the last performed by a R.A.F. Anson. Thus ended more than thirty years of unbroken service; an occasion marked by the six Ansons, each in excess of twenty years old. 'Faithful Annie' indeed and, moreover, not a bad testimonial to those who built them!?

During 1969 the York and District Investment Company Limited purchased the factory for a figure reputed to be around £600,000 since when, under its auspices, the site has been progressively developed.

Currently, minus its wartime camouflage and adorned with a bright, modern, roof it is named 'Yeadon Airport Industrial Estate' and, having undergone considerable refurbishment, flourishes; being occupied by a number of companies involved in a variety of business activities as diverse as road transport, hi-tech engineering, and a bonded store for alcohol!

A section at the northern end of the building (where else!?) is being utilised by A.E. Turbine Components Ltd; a firm very much involved in the production of state of the art products for Rolls-Royce Aero Engines Division (and others), thus maintaining a close connection with former days.

Across the A658, Novia Plantation, now renamed Coney Park, and virtually devoid of the trees from which it took its name, houses Northern Helicopters (Leeds) Ltd. and H.M.S. Ceres,[3] a land based communications centre of the Royal Naval Reserve, in addition to being a storage depot for hundreds of cars, caravans and commercial vehicles which, ere long, will probably put paid to its already crumbling roads.

The former 'Bristol's', a little way to the west, remains extant and enlarged as a foundry; and, in

---

[2] Quoted in 'The Best Years of Their Lives' by Trevor Royle. publ. Michael Joseph (See Bibliography).
[3] The unit transferred elsewhere in September 1994, being replaced, at Coney Park, by No 2168 (Yeadon) Squadron A.T.C.

Legacy

Yeadon, the High Street and Town Hall have not been changed enough to be unrecognisable to the thousands who knew them, for a while, during the war years.

Of its 17,000 former employees who made AVRO Yeadon reverberate, Time, the great reaper, has taken its toll. Happily, however, many still remain and, among their ranks are those who, very largely, have made this book possible.

As to the 5,000 aircraft which they built all, but the merest handful, have succumbed to the scrapman's ministrations and, sadly, no Yeadon built Lancaster[4] or Lincoln survive: (see Appendices for details of all a/c built at the factory). Fortunately, York C1: G-ANTK resides at Duxford with its Aviation Society, undergoing a rebuild and York C1: G-AGNV can be viewed at the Aerospace Museum, Cosford, albeit in spurious markings: 'MW100', representing that of the York named 'Ascalon' which was used by Winston Churchill.

Additionally, nine 'Yeadon' Anson's are known to exist in the U.K.: seven as non-flying examples and two which, it is fervently hoped, will fly again: Mk.XIX's: TX 213, subsequently civilianised as C.19: G-AWRS, is based at the North East Aircraft Museum, Sunderland (Usworth); TX 214 is on display at the Aerospace Museum, Cosford; TX 226 is complete and displayed by the Imperial War Museum at Duxford; TX 228 awaits restoration at the City of Norwich Aviation Museum.

C.19 series 2: G-AGPG (originally Mk.XII: PH 828), which served as a demonstrator at Yeadon during 1945/46, can be viewed at the Brenzett Air Museum in Kent. C.19 series 2: VL 348, one of the last Anson's to be built at the factory and, ultimately, flown with the civil registration: G-AVVO, has undergone considerable refurbishment at Newark Air Museum, Winthorpe, where it can be seen by the public. Another C.19 series 2: G-AWSA, formerly MkXIX: VL 349, as which it flew the last official flight made by an Anson in RAF service, is preserved by the Norfolk and Suffolk Aviation Museum, Flixton.

The most exciting news, however, (briefly mentioned earlier) is that 'Nineteen' series 2: G-AHKX, first flown by AVRO's Ken Cook at Yeadon in November 1946, is in the process of being restored to flying condition by members of the Anson Restoration Group, at the British Aerospace factories at Woodford and Chadderton.

Another former Mk.XIX: TX 183, has undergone lengthy refurbishment 'somewhere in Scotland' since being purchased by Michael Fraser in 1982. This aircraft, which was completed in February 1946 and, thereafter, served with the RAF for twenty-two years, is expected to take to the air again very soon, and has been granted the civil registration: G-BSMF.

What a fitting tribute it will be to those who built these Ansons - and all the others - when 'Kilo X-Ray and 'Mike Foxtrot' eventually fly over the Pennines to visit their birthplace ? On that auspicious occasion, a whole Regiment (or Squadron) of wild horses will not keep this writer away !

In 1939, destiny willed that a chance remark, made by Captain Worrall to Roy Dobson, was partially instrumental in the siting of the factory at Yeadon. In 1942, J.B. Priestley made a visit there and, later he wrote of that period:

"We had a glimpse then of what life might be if men and woman freely dedicated themselves, not to their appetites and prejudices, their vanities and fears, but to some great communal task."

It was indeed a great communal task but, regrettably, it has become the habit, in some quarters, to disregard or even denigrate the achievements of those who, in a variety of ways, helped win the war. Yet, surely, this attitude is foolish for does not history repeatedly confirm that individual freedom - yes, even the freedom to voice disagreement with

---

[4] Yeadon built Lancaster GR.3 TX264 'BS-D(Dog)' of No.120 Squadron, Kinloss, crashed into Sail Mhor, Beinn Eighe, during the night of 13th/14th March 1951, killing all its crew. Part of the fuselage is still to be found in a gully on Coire Mhic Fhearchair which, at the time, became known to the Mountain Rescue Service as 'Fuselage Gully'. A badly bent propeller from the Lancaster is now displayed on a stone memorial outside the Mountain Rescue Team H.Q. at RAF Kinloss. There can be no other tangible reminder of the Lancasters built at Yeadon unless some additional item from the wreckage of the TX264 could be retrieved from its resting place. Perhaps the local landowner and the Ministry of Defence would voice no objection given that such a task was undertaken by a responsible group - and who better than the Kinloss Mountain Rescue Unit (if it should be willing) as part of one of its reguler exercises ? - and, thereafter, whatever was recovered was put on display by the most appropriate organisation: The Yorkshire Air Museum (not least because of its closeness to where TX264 was built) and due reference was made to the crew who died!

developments at ones local airport, if one so wishes, - is not an automatic provision?

Fifty years ago, the fragile bloom we call democracy was kept alive only through Churchill's promised 'Blood, Sweat and Tears'; yet, in his recently published poem: 'Faces Glimpsed and Never Seen Again', Philip A. Nicholson echoes the thoughts of many who lived through those terrible days:

'.....I mourned them then,
But now, surviving in a world
Indifferent to their hopes and dreams
I grieve more for the living.'

Flight Lieutenant H.F. Le Marchant, former navigator with No.s 57, 630 and 97 Squadrons voiced similar sentiments:

"....I will always feel honoured to have had the privilege of serving with such a wonderful team of people..... One looks for the same spirit these days in civilian life but, regrettably, it is not there...."[5].

To ignore such sacrifice and the need for it, is to risk the future yet again; for, just as there would have been NO protestors in a Nazi Britain, the same would apply now, or tomorrow, should mans baser instincts be allowed to prevail. It is, perhaps, no less than the duty of each succeeding generation to be ever mindful of the fact.

For the author, although not directly involved in its activities, memories of the factory, its multitudinous band of workers and the seemingly endless number of aeroplanes they built, will always remain. So, too, will the remembrance of the brave and often frightened young men who flew them; most poignantly recalled by one of their number who survived: Ron Smith, D.F.M.

'Here at close of day, I view with pride,
this sleeping English hamlet at the side
of running brook where trout uncaring play,
that chuckles clear and sweet upon its way
By village green where flowers brightly hem
a weathered stone, placed there for such as them
who laughed with me, and flew with me so well
through darkened skies until a blazing hell.
I would it be that they could find me here,
and know that what they gave in cold and fear
will live forever and forever dwell
about this blessed land I love so well.
And all of my tomorrows they denied
to keep the spring of freedom in my stride,
I will remember and, at times like these,
catch the fade of Merlins on the breeze. '

---

[5] (Quoted in 'The Hardest Victory': See Bibliography)

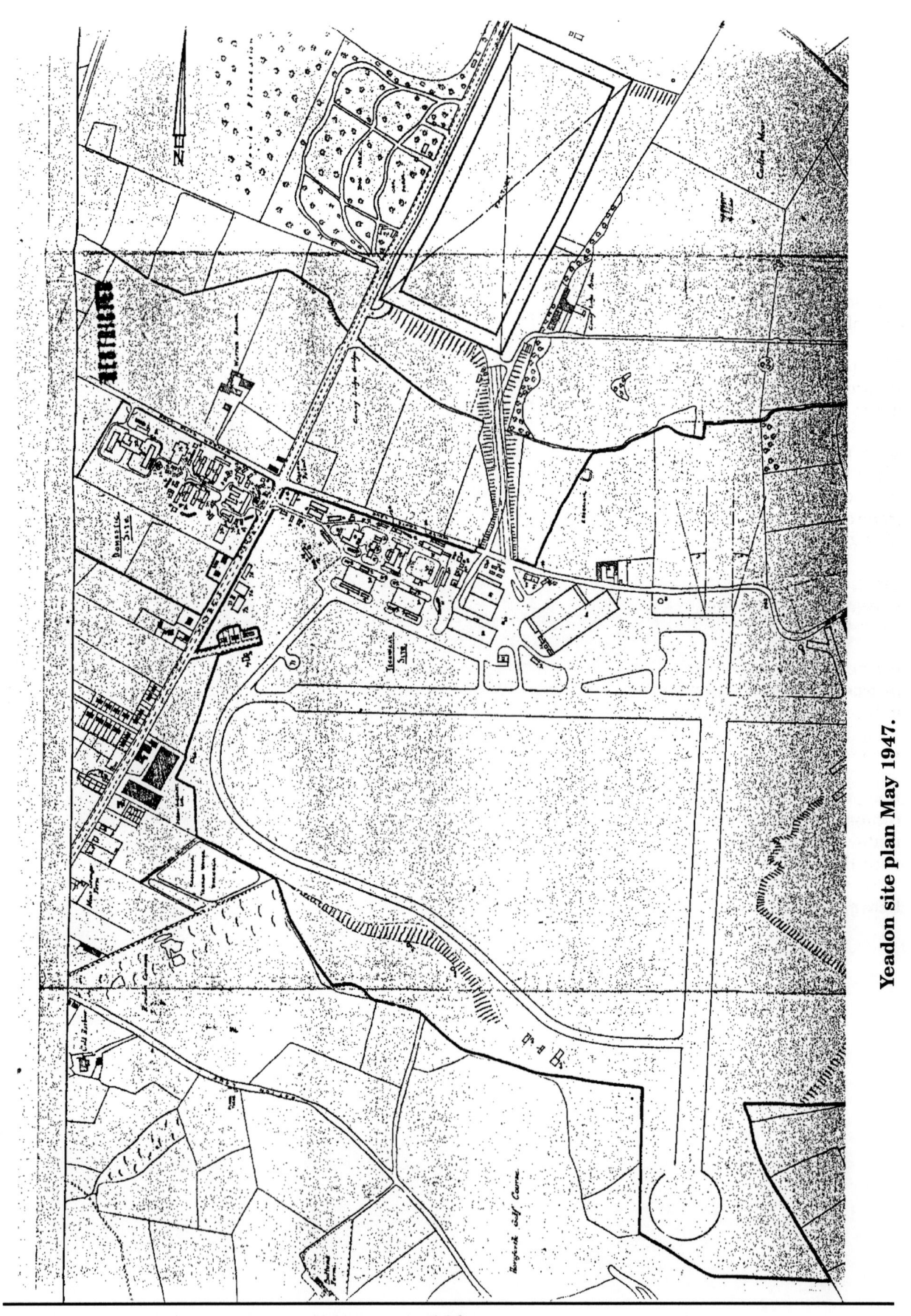

Legacy

Yeadon site plan May 1947.

Postscript

Clifford Smith was educated, firstly, as South View School, Yeadon, and then at Aireborough Grammar School.

When little more than 17 years of age he enlisted in the Royal Air Force Volunteer Reserve (RAFVR) and, subsequently, having first waited several weeks to be of the required age for 'call-up', he served ostensibly in the R.A.F., but still proudly RAFVR, until he met his death on 5th January, 1945, aged twenty-one.

After undergoing aircrew training, he began Operational service with Bomber Command in July, 1943, when he was posted as a Sergeant Navigator to No.77 Squadron at Elvington, near York. There he went on to complete a 'tour' of Ops., with Sgt. Cecil Manson (later Flt.Lt. D.F.C.) and his crew, taking part in some of the most daunting attacks carried out over Europe during the winter of 1943/44; including Berlin: 'The Big City', five times.

Later, after serving for a period, as an Instructor at No.20 OTU Lossiemouth, he returned to No.4 Group to begin a second 'tour'; this time with No.102 Squadron at Pocklington, having been promoted to Flying Officer and awarded the D.F.C. in the meantime.

His new crew, of whom five were Canadian, was commanded by Flg.Off. J.A. Bergman (RCAF), with whom he was flying on 5th January, 1945, when their aircraft, Halifax Mk.III: MZ796 'DY-M', was shot down 17 miles N.N.W. of Hanover, killing five of the seven on board. The captain and his bomb aimer, Flg.Off D.W. Dale (RCAF), survived to become POW's. They have since visited, and keep in regular contact with, the author.

Although Clifford saw action exclusively in several Marks of the Halifax, and this book is, primarily, concerned with a factory which built its rival, the Lancaster, in the event this is immaterial for, undoubtedly, he epitomized the kind of young man, all volunteers, who flew and died in a variety of aircraft with Bomber Command.

Courage and sacrifice was not the prerogative of those who flew in one particular type.

Appendix A (a)

This is one 'official' record from Yeadon to have survived the fire at Chadderton.

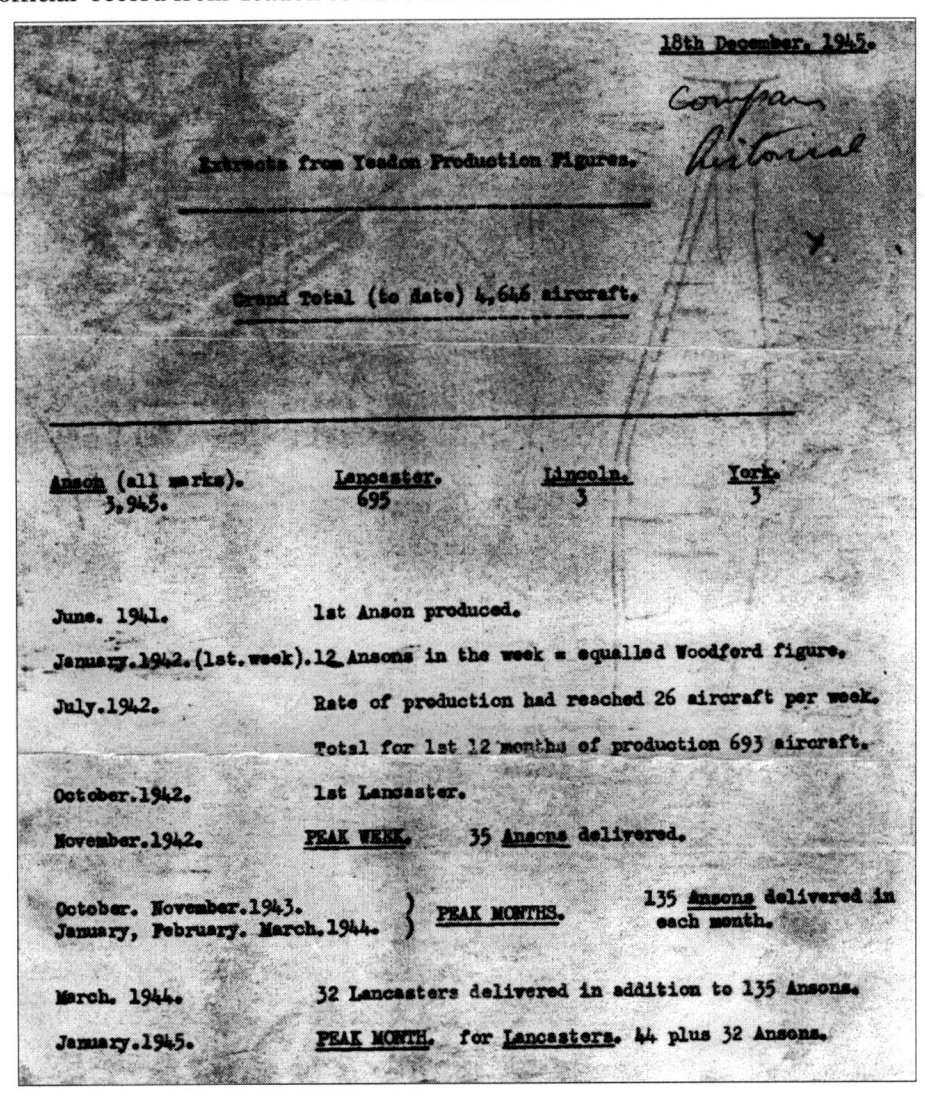

> 18th December, 1945.
>
> Extracts from Yeadon Production Figures.
>
> Grand Total (to date) 4,646 aircraft.
>
> | Anson (all marks). | Lancaster. | Lincoln. | York. |
> |---|---|---|---|
> | 3,945. | 695 | 3 | 3 |
>
> June. 1941.   1st Anson produced.
> January.1942.(1st.week). 12 Ansons in the week = equalled Woodford figure.
> July.1942.   Rate of production had reached 26 aircraft per week.
>   Total for 1st 12 months of production 693 aircraft.
> October.1942.   1st Lancaster.
> November.1942.   PEAK WEEK.   35 Ansons delivered.
> October. November.1943.)
> January, February. March.1944.) PEAK MONTHS.   135 Ansons delivered in each month.
> March. 1944.   32 Lancasters delivered in addition to 135 Ansons.
> January.1945.   PEAK MONTH. for Lancasters. 44 plus 32 Ansons.

The number of aircraft completed between V-J Day (15th August, and 31st December were as follows: ('completed' does not signify 'delivered').

```
Anson       76
Lancaster   12
Lincoln      2
York        27   Only 13 were delivered to the RAF and 3 to
           ---   civil operators by 31 Dec.)
Total      117
```

- 121 -

Appendix A (b)

The definitive verification of the identity of every aircraft built at a wartime factory is difficult; and more so in the case of a shadow factory such as Yeadon, which began production some time after the Manchester factories (with which it was associated) and closed with contracts, and aircraft, partially completed. To exacerbate matters still further, its written records were destroyed by fire at the Chadderton factory during 1959; thus the best summary the author can provide is one based on the research of several individuals who have made a comprehensive study of the subject - although not, necessarily, agreeing on every detail thereafter - and, for the following information, he is greatly indebted, directly or indirectly, to: J.J. Halley., F.K. Mason., D. Robertson., R.O. Sturtivant., Flight Lieutenant C.R. Sunderland R.A.F., (Ret'd) and G.A. Jenks of the AVRO Research Group.

Production at Yeadon

Type of Aircraft	Contract No.	Number Built	Serial Numbers Allocated	(Some No's were omitted; ostensibly to confuse the enemy!)
ANSON MK.I	61695/39	2763 (est.)	W2612-W2665	(Probably 50 of this batch)
	B/137211/40		DG689-DJ700	(Within this batch some a/c were built at Newton Heath).
			EF805-EG704	
			LS978-LV332	(23 diverted to Royal New Zealand Air Force)
			MG102-MH237	(one aircraft from this batch: MG159 was converted to become Mk.XIX prototype).
Mk.I	"	592)		
Mk.X	"	103)		
Mk.XI	"	90)	NK139-NL251	
Mk.XII	3077/C/20(a)	15)	PH528-	(First Mk.XI Ambulance: NK870. MkXII (Amb):NL153)
Mk.XII	"	248)	-PH866	(some Mk.XII's were converted
Mk.XIX	"	22)		to Mk.XIX's before completion).
C Mk.XIX	5037/CO.6(a)	100	TX154-TX257	
		1	VN889	(converted from PH860)
C Mk.XIX or C.19 (Not officially known as the latter outside the RAF; and, even then, not before June 1948)	"	60	(VL285-VL363)	Sources differ as to how many a/c were completed before factory ceased production.
AVRO 'Nineteen' (Civil)		52	G-AGLB-G-AHYO	Some of these were conversions from aircraft built earlier
	Total	**4000 approx**		

Plus spares for an additional 900 aircraft.

Appendix A (c)

Type of Aircraft	Contract No.	Number built	Serial Numbers Allocated
LANCASTER B.Mk.I	2010	10	LM301-LM310
B.Mk.III	"	340	LM311-LM756
B.Mk.I	"	44	ME328, 330, 350, 352, 371, 373, 374, 375, 376, 383, 384, 419, 420, 421, 431, 432, 433, 434, 435, 436, 437, 438, 439, 440, 445, 446, 447, 448, 449, 450, 451, 455, 456, 457, 458, 470, 475, 476, 477, 479, 480, 482, 490.
B.Mk.III	"	156	ME295-ME551
B.Mk.III	1807	87	RE115-RE226
B.Mk.III	"	47	SW319-SW377
B.Mk.III	"	11	TX263-TX273
Total		695	

There is some evidence to suggest that, in addition, R.5489 and R.5548 were completed at Yeadon, albeit that construction is credited to Manchester.

A number of aircraft with later serial numbers in the 'ME' series; half of the 'RE's and virtually all with 'SW' and 'TX' designations were converted to Mk.ASR.3 (Air-Sea Rescue) or GR.3 (General Reconnaissance) - later re-designated MR.3 (Maritime Reconnaissance), for postwar service with R.A.F. Coastal Command.

Two Lancaster Mk.I's: HK541 (built by Vickers at Castle Bromwich) and SW244 (built by MetroVick in Manchester), were fitted with 1200 gallon 'saddle' fuel-tanks for experimental long-rang tests in anticipation of possible operations in the Far East. The conversions were carried out at Yeadon utilising tanks built locally.

LANCASTRIAN (A conversion of the Lancaster having faired-over turrets and a capacity for 13 passengers).

A number were ordered as Lancaster IIIs but altered to Lancastrian C.IV's for the RAF and completed by July, 1946. They were not delivered to the RAF being transferred to Woodford, converted and delivered to civilian operators. The first six were given priority and converted at Yeadon:

```
TX274   C.IV   c/n 1279.   BSAAC, G-AGWG, STAR LIGHT,  5 Dec 1945.
TX275   C.IV   c/n 1280.   BSAAC, G-AGWH, STAR DUST,   9 Jan 1946.
TX276   C.IV   c/n 1281.   BSAAC, G-AGWI, STAR LAND,  24 Jan 1946.
TX280   C.IV   c/n 1282.   BSAAC, G-AGWJ, STAR GLOW,  28 Jan 1946.
TX281   C.IV   c/n 1283.   BSAAC, G-AGWK, STAR TRAIL, 15 Feb 1946.
TX282   C.IV   c/n 1284.   BSAAC, G-AGWL, STAR GUIDE, 13 Feb 1946.
```

Application for Cs of A for G-AGWG to G-AGWL made by Avro, 29 Nov 1945. All Cs of A issued to MAP.

BSAAC = British South American Airways Corporation.
c/n - constructor's number.

LINCOLN B.Mk.I 3858 2   SS713 - SS714 (One former employee in the finals at
        B.Mk.II   "   4   SS715 - SS718   Yeadon remains
                                               convinced that the factory built more.)
        Total   6

York: As to the quantity built at Yeadon, claims vary from 'the last 77' to a possible 138! The following, comprehensively detailed, list provides information on those aircraft considered most likely to have been involved with the factory; albeit that, in a few instances, this might have resulted in only partial construction.

Built for the RAF.

MW193 PCF 30 Oct 1945, No.511 Sqn.
MW195 LRF 30 Oct 1945, No.246 Sqn.
MW196 PCF 10 Nov 1945, No.511 Sqn.
MW198 PCF 6 Dec 1945, No.511 Sqn.
MW199 PCF 6 Dec 1945, No.511 Sqn.
MW201 PCF 1 Feb 1946, No.218 MU.
MW202 LRF 31 Oct 1945, No.246 Sqn.
MW203 LRF 10 Nov 1945, No.246Sqn.
MW205 LRF 28 Nov 1945, No.246 Sqn.
MW206 PCF 2 Jan 1946, No.511 Sqn.
MW208 PCF 10 Jan 1946, No.511 Sqn.
MW209 PCF 1 Feb 1946, No.218 MU.
MW210 LRF 27 Nov 1945, No.246 Sqn.
MW223 LRF 27 Nov 1945, No.22 MU.
      Cr. 2 Aug 1947, RAF Dishforth.
MW224 PCF 5 Feb 1946, No.218 MU.
MW225 LRF 27 Nov 1945, No.22 MU.
MW226 PCF 22 Feb 1946, No.511 Sqn.
MW227 PCF 14 Mar 1946, No.511 Sqn.
MW228 LRF 29 Nov 1945, No.22 MU.
MW230 PCF 14 Mar 1946, No.511 Sqn.
MW231 LRF 6 Dec 1945, No.22 MU.
MW232 LRF 7 Jan 1946, No.242 Sqn.
MW233 PCF 19 Mar 1946, No.511 Sqn.
MW234 LRF 26 Mar 1946, CRD.
MW235 LRF 2 Jan 1946, No.511 Sqn.
MW237 LRF 3 Jan 1946, No.242 Sqn.
MW238 LRF 26 Mar 1946, No.51 Sqn.
MW239 LRF 3 Jan 1946, No.246 Sqn.
MW240 LRF 1 Apr 1946, No.242 Sqn.
MW241 LRF 3 Jan 1946, No.242 Sqn.
MW243 LRF 2 Apr 1946, No.242 Sqn.
MW244 LRF 2 Apr 1946, No.242 Sqn.
MW245 LRF 29 Jan 1946, No.242 Sqn.
MW246 LRF 29 Jan 1946, No.242 Sqn.
MW247 LRF 9 Apr 1946, No.51 Sqn.
MW248 LRF 1 Feb 1946, No.218 MU.

MW249 LRF 29 Jan 1946, No.242 Sqn.
MW250 LRF 29 Jan 1946, No.242 Sqn.
MW251 LRF 1 Feb 1946, No.218 MU.
MW252 LRF 1 Feb 1946, No.218 MU.
MW253 LRF 22 Feb 1946, No.218 MU.
MW254 LRF 19 Feb 1946, No.51 Sqn.
MW255 LRF 11 Feb 1946, No.51 Sqn.
MW256 LRF 21 Feb 1946, No.51 Sqn.
MW257 LRF 21 Feb 1946, No.51 Sqn.
MW258 LRF 19 Feb 1946, No.51 Sqn.
MW259 LRF 27 Feb 1946, No.51 Sqn.
MW260 LRF 16 Apr 1946, No.59 Sqn.
MW261 LRF 7 Mar 1946, No.51 Sqn.
MW263 LRF 16 Apr 1946, No.51 Sqn.
MW264 LRF 7 Mar 1946, No.51 Sqn.
MW265 LRF 16 Apr 1946, No.511 Sqn.
MW266 LRF 19 Mar 1946, No.51 Sqn.
MW268 LRF 24 Apr 1946, MP.
MW269 LRF 24 Apr 1946, MP.
MW270 LRF 21 Mar 1946, No.242 Sqn.
MW271 LRF 19 Mar 1946, No.242 Sqn.
MW285 LRF 8 May 1946, No.1332 HCU.
MW287 LRF 14 Mar 1946, No.511 Sqn.
MW289 LRF 19 Mar 1946, No.1332 HCU.
MW290 LRF 19 Mar 1946, No.1332 HCU.
MW292 PCF 2 Apr 1946, No.242 Sqn.
MW295 PCF 16 Apr 1946, No.242 Sqn.
MW296 PCF 2 May 1946, CRD.
MW297 LRF 2 May 1946, No.1359 (VIP) Flt.
MW306 LRF 21 May 1946, No.22 MU.
MW307 LRF 31 May 1946, No.22 MU.
MW308 LRF 3 Jun 1946, No.22 MU.
MW309 LRF 17 Jun 1946, No.22 MU.
MW310 PCF 6 May 1946, CRD.
MW311 PCF 16 May 1946, No.22 MU.
MW312 PCF 5 Jul 1946, No.22 MU.
MW313 PCF 5 Jul 1946, RAE, Farnborough

Delivery dates are from Aircraft Record Cards of the Air Historical Branch, Ministry of Defence. These records are now available at the RAF Museum, Hendon. It is believed that a number of aircraft built at Yeadon were transferred to Woodford before delivery. For example, MW291 was delivered from Woodford, 1 May 1946, seven months after the jigs had been transferred at Yeadon. This lends credence to this belief but no confirmation has been found. The aircraft in this category are:

MW194	LRF	MW229	PCF	MW272	PCF	MW293	LRF	MW301	PCF
MW197	PCF	MW236	PCF	MW284	LRF	MW294	LRF	MW302	LRF
MW200	LRF	MW242	LRF	MW286	LRF	MW298	PCF	MW303	PCF
MW204	PCF	MW262	LRF	MW288	LRF	MW299	LRF	MW304	PCF
MW207	LRF	MW267	LRF	MW291	PCF	MW300	PCF	MW305	LRF

CRD = Controller of Research and Development, Defford.
HCU = Heavy Conversion Unit.
LRF = Long range freighter. (Contract No. 2429/C4A)
MP = Modification Pool, RAF Honington.
MU = Maintenance Unit.
PCF = Passenger-cum-freighter. (Contract No. 2429/C4A)
RAE = Royal Aircraft Establishment.
VIP = Very Important Person.

<u>YORK'S built at Yeadon for civil operators.</u>

c/n	Reg(civil) Mark	Mil. Serial	Operator, aircraft name and date of delivery
1213	G-AGNL	TS789	BOAC, MERSEY, 4 Jan 1946. C of A, 30 Jan 1946. Trooping: WW581.
1215	G-AGNM	TS790	BOAC, MURCHISON, 7 Nov 1945. C of A, 28 Dec 1945. Trooping: WW511; XA192.
1221	G-AGNT	TS796	BOAC, MANDALAY, 9 Oct 1945. C of A, 31 Oct 1945.
	ZS-ATU		SAA, Jun-Oct 1947. Trooping: WW514.
1222	G-AGNU	TS797	BOAC, MONTGOMERY, 7 Nov 1945. C of A, 14 Dec 1945.
	ZS-ATR		SAA, IMPALA, Jun 1946-Sep 1947.
	G-AGNU		BSAAC, STAR DAWN, Jul 1949.
1223	G-AGNV	TS798	BOAC, MORVILLE, 8 Nov 1945. C of A, 9 Dec 1946. Later MIDDLESEX Extant, "LV633".
1224	G-AGNW	TS799	BOAC, MORECAMBE, 19 Dec 1945. C of A, 24 Jan 1946. SAA, SABLE, Mar 1946-Sep 1947. BOAC, CARIBBEAN TRADER. Trooping: WW581.
1225	G-AGNX	TS800	BOAC, MORAY, 21 Dec 1945. C of A, 6 Feb 1946. Trooping: WW582.
1226	G-AGNY	TS801	BOAC, MELROSE, 3 Jan 1946. C of A, 23 Feb 1946. Trooping: WW510.
1227	G-AGNZ	TS802	BOAC, MONMOUTH, 4 Jan 1946. C of A, 7 Jun 1946.
	ZS-BRB		SAA, May-Jun 1947.
1228	G-AGOA	TS803	BOAC, MONTROSE, 9 Jan 1946. C of A, 28 Aug 1946. Trooping: WW542.
1229	G-AGOB	TS804	BOAC, MILFORD, 12 Jan 1946. C of A, 22 June 1946.

c/n	Reg(civil) Mark	Mil. Serial	Operator, aircraft name and date of delivery
1230	G-AGOC	TS805	BOAC, MALTA, 24 Jan 1946. C of A, 19 Apr 1946.
1231	G-AGOD EP-ADC	TS806	BOAC, MIDLOTHIAN, 13 Jan 1946. C of A, 2 Jul 1946.
1232	G-AGOE	TS807	BOAC, MEDWAY, 12 Feb 1946. C of A, 17 Jul 1946.
1233	G-AGOF ZS-ATT	TS808	BOAC, MacDUFF, 27 Feb 1946. C of A, 16 Sep 1946. SAA, Apr-Sep 1947.

Application for Cs of A for G-AGNL to G-AGOF was made by BOAC on 9 Feb 1945.

1236	G-AGSL	TS809	BOAC, MORLEY, 14 Mar 1946. C of A, 8 Oct 1946.
1237	G-AGSM	TS810	BOAC, MALVERN, 22 Feb 1946. C of A, 25 Oct 1946.
1238	G-AGSN	TS811	BOAC, MARLOW, 11 Mar 1946. C of A, 8 Nov 1946.
1239	G-AGSO	TS812	BOAC, MARSTON, 23 Mar 1946. C of A, 2 May 1946.
1240	G-AGSP	TS813	BOAC, MARLBOROUGH, 26 Mar 1946. C of A, 11 May 1946.

[1]Application for Cs of A for G-AGSL to G-AGSP was made by BOAC, 28 July 1945. Delivery dates for G-AGNL to G-AGSP are from BOAC records.

1300	G-AHEW		BSAAC, STAR LEADER, C of A, 27 May 1946.
1301	G-AHEX		BSACC, STAR VENTURE, C of A, 20 Jun 1946.
1302	G-AHEY		BSAAC, STAR QUEST, C of A, 9 Jul 1946.
1303	G-AHEZ		BSAAC, STAR SPEED, C of A, 24 Jul 1946.
1304	G-AHFA		BSAAC, STAR DALE, C of A, 18 Aug 1946.
1305	G-AHFB		BSAAC, STAR STREAM, C of A, 28 Aug 1946.
1306	G-AHFC		BSAAC, STAR DEW, C of A, 12 Sep 1946.
1307	G-AHFD		BSAAC, STAR MIST, C of A, 25 Sep 1946.
1308	G-AHFE		BSAAC, STAR VISTA, C of A, 30 Sep 1946.
1309	G-AHFF		BSAAC, STAR GLEAM, C of A, 23 Oct 1946.
1310	G-AHFG [2]		BSAAC, STAR HAZE, C of A, 28 Oct 1946.
1311	G-AHFH		BSAAC, STAR GLITTER, C of A, 4 Nov 1946.

Application for Cs of As for G-AHEW to G-AHEH above was made by Avro, 6 Apr 1946.

1316 G-AHFI   Skyways Ltd, SKYWAY. C of A, 13 May 1946.
Application for C of A for G-AHFI was made by Avro, 30 Mar 1946.

Yorks delivered to B.O.A.C. were of 18-seat capacity, 13 aircraft having facilities for 12 passengers as 'sleepers'. Those delivered to B.S.A.A.C., had seating for 21.

---

1   Also c/n 1271:G-AGPG, no further details known.
2   G-AHFG flew the first trans-Atlantic flight made from Manchester (Ringway): a trooping flight to Bermuda, for Skyways, diverted via the airport on 29th November 1952.

Civil Yorks (continued)

1340   G-AHLV   Skyways Ltd, SKY COURIER. C of A, 3 Jun 1946.
Application for C of A for G-AHLV was made by Avro, 22 May 1946.
1354   G-AHXN   FAMA.   C of A, 18 Jul 1946.
        LV-XGN   FAMA.
1355   G-AHXO   FAMA.   C of A, 12 Aug 1946.
        LV-XGO   FAMA.
1356   G-AHXP   FAMA.   C of A, 19 Aug 1946.
        LV-XGP.
Application for Cs of A for G-AHXN to G-AHXP was made by Avro, 4 Jul 1946.

1365   LV-XIG   FAMA.   C of A, 5 Dec 1946.
1366   LV-XIH   FAMA.   C of A, 12 Dec 1946.
Application for Cs of A for LV-XIG and LV-XIH was made by Avro, 24 Oct 1946. All Yorks delivered to FAMA were of 24 seat capacity.

BOAC   = British Overseas Airways Corporation.
BSAAC   = British South American Airways Corporation.
c/n   = constructor's number.
C of A   = Certificate of Airworthiness.
FAMA   = Flota Aerea Mercante Argentina.
Mil Serial = Military serial previously allocated.
Reg Mark   = Registration marking.
SAA   = South African Airways/Sud-Afrikaanse Lugdiens

Thus, it would appear, Yeadon was responsible for the production of 113 Yorks: 73 going to the RAF and 40 to civil operators. Just how many of the other 25, listed above as having been built for the RAF, were produced there must, regrettably, remain unconfirmed.

At the end of their service with the RAF the following 'Yeadon' Yorks were sold to a variety of civil operators; civil registrations being shown first:

G - AMUL	ex - MW308	G-ANUN/ANVO?	EX MW253	Registered in Canada
" - AMUV	" MW226	" ANXL	" MW196	CF HAS ex - MW290
" - AMVY	" MW292	" ANXM	" MW227	" HFP " MW233
" - ANGF	" MW254	" ANXN	" MW258	" HIP " MW287
" - ANGL	" MW231	" ANXA	" MW210	" HMU " MW203
" - ANSY	" MW193	" ACAN	" MW199	" HMY " MW237
" - ANTK	" MW232	" APCA	" MW295	

The other ex-RAF Yorks built at Yeadon were not certificated for civil use; ending their days being broken-up for spares.

The York remained in service with B.O.A.C. for thirteen years, therein accumulating 226,996 flying hours and 44 million miles, carrying 90,000 passengers.

Appendix B

On 7th September 1939, No.609 Squadron despatched its, by then, superseded Hawker Hinds to No.6 MU at Brize Norton. The aircraft were: K.5421, 5451, 5469, 5497, 5519, 5542, 6728, 6730, 6790, 6820, 6846, 6850, 7177, 7185 and 7188.

By the end of October 1939 the number of Spitfire's operating with No.609 Squadron (at Catterick) had increased to thirteen. All Mark I's, they were: L.1058, 1064, 1071, 1082, 1086, N.3024, P.9425, R.4173, 6631, 6706, 6906, 6979 and X.4587.

Aircraft of the Yorkshire Aeroplane Club, impressed into R.A.F. service on the outbreak of war:

Civil registration	Type	RAF Serial No. allocated
G-AAAA	dh 60G Gipsy Moth	X 5038
G-AAIA	" " " "	X 5037
*G-AAJW	" " " "	X 5040
*G-AALN	" " " "	X 5041
G-ABAL	" " " "	X 5118
G-ABCS	" " " "	X 5039
*G-ABJN	" " " "	AW 119
*G-ACJI	Short Scion	X 9375 (This aircraft was Scion prototype) (owned by Yorkshire Airways Ltd)
G-ACKS	dh 85 Leopard Moth	W 120 Crashed on take-off Netheravon, 13th August, 1942
G-ACSJ	" " " "	AW 117
G-AD1S	dh 87B Hornet Moth	W 9391
G-ADNE	" " " "	X 9325
G-AEZ1	dh 85A Leopard Moth	AW 122 To instructional air-frame 2982M, March 1942
G-AFDV	" " " "	W5783 Burned out at Ringway 19th March 1941.

* Aircraft which can be identified on photograph taken in 1937. See photograph no.7

Appendix C

Due to regular changes of personnel or, simply, carelessness the wartime diaries (or Operations Record Book's (ORB's) as they were officially known) of the various RAF units were often inaccurate or incomplete.

This was certainly evident insofar as No.20 EFTS was concerned for, almost unbelievably, no details of its fifty-plus DH. Tiger Moths were recorded, other than those aircraft involved in accidents. They were:

```
BB. 795, 800, 801, 803, 804, 805, 806, 808, 812, 814
 L. 6932, 6935
 N. 5446, 6484, 6540, 6812, 9180, 9430
 R. 4776, 5018
 T. 5382, 5809, 6177, 6596, 6612, 6789, 7051, 7052, 7054, 7087, 7236, 7414
 W. 7953
```

On 22nd September 1943, Tiger Moth N.6908 was ferried to 'Conversion Flight, Yeadon' by First Officer L.P.Murphy, accompanied by 'pilot's assistant' A.T.C. Cadet Sergeant Geoffrey A. Cooke, both of No. 6 Ferry Pool A.T.A., Ratcliffe.

Appendix D

The following are schedules of the programmes broadcast by the BBC live from the works canteen at Yeadon. The first, on August 7th, 1942, was an ENSA edition of its 'Break for Music' series, featuring the bands of Harry Kaye and Joe Loss.

The second, an edition of 'Workers Playtime' on 1st/2nd January, 1943. This was broadcast live to North America during the midnight dinner break, and starred George Myddleton and Bruce Merryl, Alex Munro, Parry Jones and Kenway and Young. The third was a 'Works Wonders', which gave prominence to amateur talent drawn from the factory; transmitted on the Home Service on 25th August, 1943.

'Workers Playtime' figured again, three months after the end of the war when, on 25th November, 1945, the programme was broadcast on the Home Service. By then, however, there was no longer a need for secrecy and the location of the factory was announced at the outset of the transmission; as indeed it was, similarly, in the Radio Times for that week.

The Houston and Stewart billed in this programme were husband and wife, Rene Houston and Donald Stewart: the latter never given the plaudits his rich singing talent deserved. (Any reader not familiar with his rendition of 'South American Way', with the Ambrose Band, should attempt to avail themselves of a copy!)

FORCES PROGRAMME FROM THE NORTH
Friday, August 7th, 1942

12.30 - 25   BREAK FOR MUSIC
             Harry Kaye and his Orchestra
             Sig. tune:- 'Let the People Sing'
             Woodchopper's Ball   (P. Maurice)
             Orch. & Vocal
             One Day when we were Young (Chappell)
             Get Your Loving from Me   (F.D. & H.)
             When Irish Eyes are Smiling (Feldman)
             Orchestra
             In the Mood   (P. Maurice)
             Orchestra & Vocal
             Sing Everybody Sing   (F.D. & H.)
             Joe Loss Introduces:-
             Anniversary Waltz   (F.D. & H.)
             Rose O'Day (Chappell)
             Deep in the Heart of Texas (Southern)
             Let's Have Another One   (P. Maurice)
             Sig. tune:- 'Let the People Sing'
             By the orchestra.

N/A Trans: 1st/2nd January 1943

23.30 "WORKERS PLAYTIME" - LIVE
(To be rec. OP. 261 SWN 12, Stand-by: DOK 1819)
HO George Myddleton)
HO Bruce Merryl Pianists
L Alex Munro
HO Parry Jones
HO Kenway & Young
George Myddleton & Bruce Merryl:
Autumn in London arr. Myddleton & Merryl   MS
Automne Chaminade arr. Myddleton & Merryl MS

Alex Munro
Thank you I'm alright   OC
Sleep Song B. Wood

B.S.T. Parry Jones:
Slumber Song   Schumann   B. & H.
The Church Bells of England   B. & H.

Kenway & Young
Mr. Pottle's New Year   R. Rutherford   MS

Community Singing
Jealousy   L.W.
You made me love you   Feldman
Pack up your troubles   F.D. & H.

R.F.U. "Calling all Workers" RA Band DECCA F 7638, less than 1'

HOME SERVICE PROGRAMME FROM THE NORTH
Wednesday, August 25, 1943

12.30 - 50 WORKS WONDERS: Please insert the following details:

Band:
Martial Moments   (Boosey & Hawkes)
Barbara Grainger:
Shine thro' my dreams   (Chappell)
Band:
For dancers only   (Macmelodies)
Tommy Freer:

- 136 -

For you alone	(L.G. & B.)
Comedian:	
Bless 'em all	(K.P.)
Harry Myers	
At the Balalaike	(K.P.)
Band:	
Memories of Lehar	(Chappell)

HOME SERVICE PROGRAMME: TUESDAY 20.11.1945

12.30 WORKERS' PLAYTIME (From A.V.Roe, Ltd., Harrogate Road, Yeadon, Nr. Leeds) (Variety Dept.)

With: Morton Frazer
Dawn Davis, Houston & Stewart
Bruce Merryl (pianoforte)
Introduced and produced by
Bryan Sears

MORTON FRAZER

Old Man Sunshine	Cinephonic
Too Soon	Southern
Lazy River	Southern
Bell Bottom Trousers	C. & C.
Smoke gets in your eyes	Chappell
Rose of Santa Lucia	Feldman
Coming Home	P. Maurice
Cheek to Cheek	Chappell

DAWN DAVIS

Remember Me	Cinephonic
I Could Never Tell	L. Wright
I Hope to die	C. & C.

HOUSTON AND STEWART

I'm Gonna get myself a merry little Xmas	
I'll be your sweetheart	Feldman

COMMUNITY SINGING

If I had my way	C. & C.

Appendix E

Earlier in the narrative, mention was made of Leslie Briggs' abhorrence of Air-Raid Shelters. The first indication of this phobia began on the night of 31st August/1st September, 1940, when, to avoid death or injury during an enemy raid on Bradford, he took refuge in a closely packed, smoke-filled, shelter on Sunbridge Road in the city.

During subsequent investigations into Luftwaffe activities in the area, the author has been the recipient of several pertinent documents, supplied by the Bundesarchiv in Freiburg. One is that headed GEHEIM! (secret), which is a copy of a briefing report, taken from the Operational Records of 6 Staffel, 11/Gruppe/Kampfgeschwader General Wever 4 (11/KG4) and is signed by its Commanding Officer, at the time, Major Doctor Wolff (see next page).

The document describes a planned attack on targets in Birmingham, Leeds and Hull by four of its aircraft - Heinkel HeIII's - on the night of 31st August/1st September, 1940 (the night Leslie Briggs escaped on early demise) and, among other details specified, is the time of take-off; estimated time of arrival over target; the course to be flown; bomb load to be carried, and the allocation of targets (ziel) which, apart from that for aircraft number 4, which was detailed to 'seek-out' industrial areas in the South of Hull, are denoted solely by a code number.

The really interesting fact, however, is that Bradford is **NOT** mentioned; nor was it in a similar report, issued three nights earlier, when 11/KG4 was also active in the area: then attacking targets in Leeds, Middlesbrough and Hartlepool - yet, on that occasion also, bombs fell within the greater Bradford area!

The author has not seen a reference to Bradford in any Luftwaffe briefing report for that period and, although this does not constitute conclusive proof, there seems a strong probability that, on these two occasions, at least, the city was attacked in error; the crews responsible - like so many others during the Second World War - mistaking their target: presuming Bradford to have been Leeds!

(For those unfamiliar with the area, it might be helpful to know that the boundaries of these two, large, conurbations adjoin.)

Briefing report of 6th Staffel II/KG 4, for the night of 30th August/1st September 1940: The night of the attack on Bradford. Source Bundesarchiv.

Geheim! 133

II./Kampfgeschwader General Wever 4 , den 31.8.1940.
Abt. Ia Nr. 1605/40 geh.

Einsatzbefehl für den 31.8./ 1.9.40.

1.) **Kampfauftrag für II./K.G.4:** Störungsangriffe mit 4 Flugzeugen auf Ziele im Raum Birmingham. Ausweichziele im Raum Leeds und Hull.

2.) **Beladung:** 1 Flugzeug 1 Flam 250 kg, 1 SC 500 kg, 12 SC 50 kg. 3 Flugzeuge 1 SC 500 kg, 16 SC 50 kg.

3.) **Betankung:** Zusatztank 400 ltr.

4.) **Flugweg:** Anflug: Eindhoven – Rotterdam – Ziel.
Rückflug: Ziel – Den Helder – Eindhoven.

5.) **Flughöhe:** freigestellt. Im Nachtjagdgebiet Amsterdam nicht über 500 m. Im Nachtjagdgebiet Lincoln nicht unter 4000 m.

6.) **Startzeiten:** 1.Flzg.(Oblt.Knauth)   Start: 22.55 Uhr   5J FP
 Angriffszeiten: Angriff: 01.40 Uhr.
   2.Flzg.(Oblt.Klotz)   Start: 23.05 Uhr   5J DP
                         Angriff: 01.50 Uhr
   3.Flzg.(Lt.Nützel)   Start: 23.15 Uhr   5J OP
                         Angriff: 02.00 Uhr
   4.Flzg.(Oblt.Andersch) Start: 23.25 Uhr 5J BP
                         Angriff: 02.10 Uhr.

7.) **Zielverteilung:** für alle Flugzeuge Ziel 1 : 737 und 7412
                                           Ziel 2 : 7025 und 8210
                                           Ziel 4 : Industrie Südrand Hull
   1. und 3.Flzg. :   Ziel 3 : 1029 und 2122
   2. und 4.Flzg. :   Ziel 3 : 10110 und 2121.

8.) **Abwehrlage:** Mit Ballonsperren (vor allem in der Humbermündung) mit Nachtjägern und mit Flak (gemäß mündl. Einweisung) ist zu rechnen.

9.) **Navigationshilfsmittel:** Knickebein II gerichtet auf Ziel 1.

10.) **Nachrichtenbefehl und Wetter:** siehe Anlage.

11.) **Startoffizier:** Oblt. Danzenberg dazu Lt.Morich und Lt.Ziegler.
   Koppeloffizier: Oblt. Giesbert.

Verteiler:
6. Staffel   4 x
Koppelöffizier 1 x
Abt. Ia   1 x
              6 x

Bibliography (and secondary reading)

Balchin, N., (for the Central Office of Information): 'The Aircraft Builders' - An Account of British Aircraft Production 1935-1945; HMSO 1947.
Beech, J., 'One WAAF's War' : D.J. Costello (Publishers) 1989.
Bekker, C., 'The Luftwaffe War Diaries: Macdonald & Co. 1966.
Bergel, H., 'Fly and Deliver': Airlife 1982.
Booth, J., 'The Day War Broke Out': Cambridge House Books 1984.
Bowyer, C., 'Tales From The Bombers': William Kimber 1985
Bowyer, C., 'For Valour' (The Air V.C.'s): Grub Street 1992.
Campbell, J., 'The Bombing of Nuremberg': Allison & Busby 1973
Cobham, A., '20,000 Miles in a Flying Boat': George Harrap 1930.
Cobham, A., (edited by Derrick, C.) 'A Time To Fly': Shepheard-Walwyn 1978 (re-print 1986).
Cooper, A., 'Bombers Over Berlin': William Kimber 1985.
Cooper, A., 'In Action With The Enemy': William Kimber 1988.
Curtis, L., 'The Forgotten Pilots': Nelson & Saunders 1987.
Deighton, L., 'Bomber': Jonathan Cape 1989.
Dixon, R., (edited by) 'Echoes In The Sky' - An Anthology of Aviation Verse' - Blandford Press 1982.
Fresson, E., 'Air Road To The Isles': David Rendell Ltd., 1967.
Garbett, M., & Goulding, B., 'Lancaster At War' Vols. 1-3; Ian Allan 1971-1984.
Gunston, 'Bill'., 'Rolls-Royce Aero Engines': Patrick Stephens 1989.
Hall, A & Taylor, E., 'Avro Anson: Marks I, III, IV and X': Altmark Publications 1972.
Halley, J., 'The Lancaster File': Air Britain (Historian's) 1985.
Hastings, M., 'Bomber Command': Michael Joseph 1979.
Holmes, H., 'A.V. Roe, The Man, The Company and Its Aircraft': Publicity Dept., British Aerospace Plc., 1991.
Jackson, A.J. 'British Civil Aircraft 1919-1972' Vols 1,2, & 3: Putnam, 1959, 1960 Revisions 1987 & 1988.
Jackson, A.J. 'Avro Aircraft since 1908. Putnam 1966. Revised and updated by R.T. Jackson, Putnam 1990.
Jackson, R., 'The Berlin Airlift': Patrick Stephens 1983.
Knight, D., 'Harvest of Messerschmitts': Frederick Wareing Ltd., 1981.
Lewis, P., 'A Peoples War': Thames Methuen 1986.
Lloyd, I., ' Rolls-Royce: The Merlin At War': Macmillan 1978.
Longmate, N., 'The Bombers (RAF Offensive Against Germany 1939-1945)'; Methuen 1983.
Lucas, Y., 'WAAF With Wings': GMS Enterprises 1992.
Margerison, R., 'Boys At War': Ross Publications 1987.
Mason, F., 'The Avro Lancaster': Aston Publications 1989.
Middlebrook, M., 'The Nuremberg Raid': Allen Lane 1973.
Middlebrook, M., 'The Peenemunde Raid': Allen Lane 1982.
Middlebrook, M., 'The Berlin Raids': Viking 1988.
(with Everitt, C.,) 'The Bomber Command War Diaries': Viking 1985.
Overy, R., 'The Air War 1939-1945: Papermac 1980.
Penrose, H., 'Architect of Wings': Airlife 1985.
Price, A., 'Instruments of Darkness: The History of Electronic Warfare: Panther.
Price, A., 'Luftwaffe Handbook 1939-1945 (Second Edition): Ian Allan 1986.
Price, A., 'Blitz On Britain': Ian Allan 1976.
Priestley, J., 'Daylight On Saturday': William Heineman 1943.
Ramsey, W., (edited by) 'The Blitz Then And Now' Vols. 1 & 2: After the Battle 1987 & 1988.
Richards, D. 'The Hardest Victory': Hodder & Stoughton 1994.
Roberts, R., 'The Halifax File': Air Britain (Historians) 1985.
Robertson, B., 'Lancaster: The Story Of A Famous Bomber': Harleyford Publications 1964.
Robinson, V, 'On Target': Verity Press 1991.
Royle T.. 'The Best Years of Their Lives': Michael Joseph 1986.

Saward, D., 'Bomber Harris - The Story of Marshal of The Royal Air Force, Sir Arthur Harris': Cassell 1984.
Shores, C., 'Fledgling Eagles': Grubb Street 1992.
Shute, N., 'Slide Rule': Heineman 1954.
Smith, R., 'Rear Gunner Pathfinders': Goodall Publications 1987.
Stroud, J., 'Railway Air Services': Ian Allan 1987.
Sturtivant, R., 'The Anson File': Air Britain (Historians) 1988.
Sunderland, G., 'A.V. Roe & Co. Ltd., Leeds and Bradford Aerodrome, Yeadon, Yorkshire': Privately circulated.
Sykes, T., 'The Yorkshire Aeroplane Club': Privately circulated.
Thorne, A., 'Lancaster At War 4: Pathfinder Squadron: Ian Allan 1990.
Wakefield, K., 'The First Pathfinders - The Operational History of Kampfgruppe 100 1939-1941; Crecy Books 1992.
Wood, D. & Dempster, D., 'The Narrow Margin': Tri-Service Press 1990.
Ziegler, F., 'Under The White Rose (The story of No.609 Squadron): McDonald 1971.

In addition, the 'Action Stations' series Vols. 1 to 10, published by Patrick Stephens Ltd., and compiled by C. Ashworth, M. Bowyer, B. Halpenny, B. Quarrie & D. Smith, have proved an invaluable source of background material; as, similarly, have various editions of 'Aeroplane Monthly' and 'Fly Past' Magazine.

Key to cover photographs.

Rear inside top, Photo 102.
The end of an era-not an aircraft or a worker to be seen! Note: the massive Flight Sheds/Finals behind the 'Civvy' hangar (similarly used as a Flight Shed) and, to the right, the 'Club House'/Flying Control building. Photographed from runway 10/28 during late summer 1946. copyright R Scatchard.

Rear inside bottom, Photo 17.
A rare photograph of the factory in its remarkable wartime camouflage; as viewed from the Fire watchers 'Spotting Tower' situated on top of the 'Civvy' hangar Flight Shed, on the airfield. Note: Hangar-type exit doors, roadway therefrom and, centre right, Coney House Farm: all three of which remain extant. credit R Scatchard.

Back cover. Photo 81.
Lancaster III:TX273, Anson XII.PH815 and York pictured with a group of workers between the Flight Sheds. 5th row back, behind the shoulder of man with a Trilby hat, centre, is Doreen Watson. To her right, Martha Bass and to her right, Nellie Dennison, all from the wire splicing department. photo via Mrs D. Varley (Nee Watson), credit R Scatchard.

Front inside top. Photo 101. credit C H Wood Ltd
Postwar view looking N/W. The camouflage has been removed showing the massive size of the factory, as similarly are the roads built for workers buses in Novia Plantation opposite. 'Hangar Door' exit and access road to the 'Finals' are easily identifiable, as is the 'Club House' beside the white fronted 'Civvy' hangar centre. The roof of Bristols can be seen to the West of the platation. Runways 01/19 & 10/28 show evidence of lengthening and repair work. To the West across the A658 is the RAF cantonment. The largest building there being the Airman's social hall. What was No. 609 Squadron's cantonment can be seen immediately to the rear of the two smaller hangars on the airfield perimeter.

Front inside bottom. Photo 6. credit C H Wood Ltd
1. Site of factory. 2. Coney House Farm. 3. The A658 Victoria Avenue, 4. Novia Plantation
5. Site of 'Bristols' is off picture top left, 6. Site of RAF cantonment, 7. Yeadon Dam, 8. Airport cafe and garage
9. Airport buildings, 10. No 609 Squadron cantonment, 11. Site of 'Finals/Flight Sheds, 12. leveling work for runway 01/19
13. William Murgatroyd's Mill, 14. The Fountain, 15. The Peacock, 16. Three trees & Plane Tree Hill
17. Site of 3.7" A.A. Gun battery, 18. Horsforth Golf course at bottom of picture below No. 18, 19. Approximate Spitfire crash site 1949.

Front Cover. Photo 80. credit F. Wright.
Works Manager, H W Harper(centre in dark suit) with a group of section managers and Snr Union Officials. 18th October 1945. Extreme left, ?Rymes, of the Assoc. of Eng and Shipbuilding Draughtsman; 3rd from left, R.P. Dodsworth, Chief Draughtsman Jig & Tool Drawing Office; 5th from left, Donald Winn; 7th from left, W Wright, Bradford Area Sec. of the Amalgamated Engineering Union. R.A.F. Officer:Group Captain B.D. Sellick DSO,DFC.